Interview with a Ghost

Also by Tom Sleigh

Bula Matari/Smasher of Rocks

Far Side of the Earth

Herakles (translation)

The Dreamhouse

The Chain

Waking

After One

Interview with a Ghost

• ESSAYS •

~

Tom Sleigh

Graywolf Press
Saint Paul, Minnesota

Publication of this volume is made possible in part by a grant provided by the Minnesota State Arts Board, through an appropriation by the Minnesota State Legislature; a grant from the Wells Fargo Foundation Minnesota; and a grant from the National Endowment for the Arts, which believes that a great nation deserves great art. Significant support has also been provided by the Bush Foundation; Target, with support from the Target Foundation; the McKnight Foundation; and other generous contributions from foundations, corporations, and individuals. To these organizations and individuals we offer our heartfelt thanks.

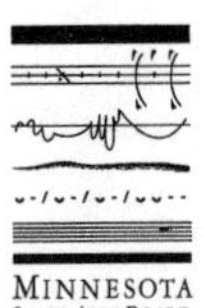

Supported by the Jerome Foundation in celebration of the Jerome Hill Centennial and in recognition of the valuable cultural contributions of artists to society

Published by Graywolf Press
2402 University Avenue, Suite 203
Saint Paul, Minnesota 55114

www.graywolfpress.org

Published in the United States of America

ISBN 1-55597-440-6

2 4 6 8 9 7 5 3 1
First Graywolf Printing, 2006

Library of Congress Control Number: 2005932356

Cover design: Kyle G. Hunter

Cover photograph: ©Dennis Wilson/CORBIS

Acknowledgments

I want to thank Fiona McCrae for her steadfast encouragement and critical eye, as well as Jeff Shotts for his careful and immensely helpful editorial suggestions, and Anne Czarniecki for her patient and rigorous care. Sven Birkerts, Askold Melnyczuk, Peter Campion, Alan Shapiro, Ellen Driscoll, Michael Collier, Robert Pinsky, David Ferry, Sarah Harwell, Josh Weiner, and Dan Chiasson were all extremely generous with their time and attention. Lynn Birkerts and Celia Lowenstein led me to Adam Phillips's essay on D. W. Winnicott, and Donna Masini also shared with me her knowledge of Winnicott. My thanks also to Theo Theoharis, Kim Cooper, Lloyd Schwartz and the other editors who commissioned these pieces. Lastly, I want to acknowledge my debt to Thom Gunn for his poems, essays, and friendship: this book is dedicated to his memory.

All translations of poetry are the author's, unless otherwise noted.

Grateful acknowledgment is made to the following for permission to reprint previously published material:

"To the One of Fictive Music" and "The American Sublime" from *The Collected Poems of Wallace Stevens* by Wallace Stevens, copyright 1954 by Wallace Stevens and renewed 1982 by Holly Stevens.

Used by permission of Alfred A. Knopf, a division of Random House, Inc.

"Home" and "Waking in the Blue" from *Collected Poems* by Robert Lowell. Copyright © 2003 by Harriet Lowell and Sheridan Lowell. Reprinted by permission of Farrar, Straus and Giroux, LLC.

"In the Park" by Tom Sleigh appeared in *The Chain,* Phoenix Poets Series, University of Chicago Press, Chicago, London, 1996. Used with permission of the author.

"Lamentation on Ur" by Tom Sleigh appeared in *Far Side of the Earth,* Houghton Mifflin Co., Boston, New York, 2003. Used with permission of the author.

Many of these pieces, or versions of them, appeared in the following publications:

"The Incurables" in *DoubleTake,* reprinted in *The Healing Circle: Narratives of Recovery,* Dutton, and *The Creative Nonfiction Reader,* Putnam.

"Education of the Poet," loosely based on "An Interview with Tom Sleigh," *Full Circle Journal,* Allegra Wong, ed.; and on *The Writing Life,* David Bradt, ed., *The Plum Review.*

"To the Star Demons" in *The Southwest Review,* reprinted in *Tolstoy's Dictaphone: Technology and the Muse,* Sven Birkerts, ed., Graywolf Press.

"Self as Self-Impersonation in American Poetry" in *Virginia Quarterly Review.*

"Too Much of the Air: Tomas Tranströmer" in *Boston Book Review.*

"Raleigh's Ride" in *Touchstones: American Poets on a Favorite Poem*, ed. Robert Pack/Jay Parini, eds., University Presses of New England.

"Frank Bidart's Voice" in *Boston Book Review*, reprinted in *Poets on Poetry Series: Frank Bidart*, Liam Rector, University of Michigan Press.

"In Rough Waters: Seamus Heaney's *Government of the Tongue*" in *Boston Review*.

"To Go Nowhere: Derek Walcott" in *Boston Book Review*.

"Visitations and Seductions: Thom Gunn" in *Boston Review*.

"Hers Truly: A Note on Elizabeth Bishop's Letters" in *Boston Phoenix Literary Supplement*.

"At the End of Our Good Day: Randall Jarrell" in *Partisan Review*.

Contents

~

Part III

Author's Note:

This book was written in the conviction that while art and life are separable, they aren't separate. In fact, the way private life, historical circumstance, and art converge is the story this book tells: the first section focuses on how our awareness of our bodies in sickness and health, pleasure and pain, and as a provoker of myth, historical reflection, and technological advance, shapes our understanding of not only how to write a poem, but what kind of poem might be worth writing. The second section speculates in a more direct way on how this understanding can be put into practice by suggesting new ways of thinking—and writing—about the self. That includes the question of what it means to say "I" in a poem, in all its psychological, historical, political, and aesthetic ramifications. The third section looks at poets who have found different ways to embody the ideal of poetry put forward in the second section, in which poetry doesn't so much take sides but is responsive to all sides at once, and in which finding ways to acknowledge the limits of subjective experience can become a source of formal innovation, as well as a way of expanding the emotional and intellectual range of contemporary poetry.

Interview with a Ghost (G)

~

I: What was your greatest failing?

G: You mean the failing that made me great? Or my worst deficiency?

I: Yes.

G: I believed in love, I never learned to sublimate, I never crocheted things or substituted God for my earthly desires or felt the need to jump to my feet when they played "The Star-Spangled Banner," even my poetry I used as a way to entice Eros, Freud tells us that those who live under the sign of Eros suffer suffer suffer though for me it was really more pleasure than suffer suffer suffer . . . I'm sorry, certain words stick in my throat, it's what happens in death, it's so hard to get your breath sometimes.

I: Do you think your poems will be read by posterity?

G: Posterity, a quaint concept here, we don't think about the future that way, it's too sequential, here everything is a bit like a circle, though that's not right either, more an ellipse, so that one minute it's noon, the next it's three in the afternoon, all rather disorienting. . . . But to answer your question in a way that your readers might appreciate, I was much too skeptical, or too hedonistic, to believe in "posterity," only people who have visions—and a lot of money—believe in the future, look at Shelley, all that "Triumph of

Life" business, then look at Keats, when Keats had a little money you know how he feels, two glasses down, well, why not me, why shouldn't I be counted among the great English poets, but at the end, coughing and coughing, cheated out of his inheritance, having pinched and scraped and barely got by, he ended up disillusioned, "Here lies one whose name was writ in water," though of course once he'd given up on posterity it came to him.

I: Can you tell us your views on autobiography as a mode for poetry?

G: I can't remember the details of what happened only an hour ago, here we really do take short views as Sydney Smith said we should, well, I'm not doing that badly, Sydney Smith, imagine, odd the things that stick, though many things are uncertain here, but as for autobiography, you may or may not believe in it: either way, in the best case it throws up possible ways of thinking yourself into a more truthful, if not a healthier, state of mind, and in the worst case, well, why elaborate, we all know the worst case.

I: Would you elaborate?

G: Just imagine living your life as if it were a factory that churned out poems, so many poems a year, so many publications a decade, so many honors and prizes to hang around your neck, well at least death is good for something, you don't have the impetus to lead your life in the hope of writing poems about it, though in comparison to the others here, my life seems more concrete for having been written down . . . of course the disadvantage is that my memories stick a little tighter, it makes me blush to think of the lies I told myself, lies about simple things are the worst, that I didn't like butter when really I loved it, only the calories made me anxious, now why didn't I write that down somewhere, fear of being loveless, so much time wasted in fear, well the expiation goes on forever, and my facelessness grows more absolute every moment . . . still, how odd to hoard the past in order to spend it in a poem.

I: Would you say that poets nowadays don't worry so much about the past?

G: Perhaps I brooded too much on how my past would look to me, five years, say, from my having written it down, but what poets do nowadays isn't exactly my concern.

I: I think you shortchange yourself.

G: Suckers, the living are often suckers, so easily taken in, praise, praise, always that hunger for praise, and there you are in the middle of it trying to make the life you laid down in your twenties and thirties stretch to cover your necessities in your sixties and seventies, just remember when Socrates uncovers his face as he's dying of the poison and he tells Crito that he owes a cock to Asclepius and asks that the debt be paid, well, Asclepius needs to be paid, he's sitting there waiting for his drachmas or whatever they used back then, not drachmas, maybe fish, fish was a rare commodity in those days, the Mediterranean isn't exactly teeming with fish, but look, poets today tend to be suckers, they buy into the present, what has the present done for any of us lately, but there they are shelling out what they don't have, they think they can buy off the past by making up the present in their own image, but why write if there's no past to look forward to?

I: You sound a little bitter.

G: No, no, that's my realism, how old are you, twenty-five?

I: I should warn you that my generation is sick of greybeard generalizations about us.

G: But there were ways in which I was younger than you at my death than you are now.

I: You mean my generation is worried about health insurance just in case one of us happens to go mad?

G: That wasn't what I was thinking, but yes, if you say so.

I: What do the dead think about, anyway?

G: For me, it's questions of realism, I mean what's more real than the body once you don't have one, when you're dead you think very hard about the body, especially since the face is so hard to envision, it keeps blurring and dissolving, those of us who think the hardest about the face have become my best friends here.

I: Why the face?

G: Facelessness is the rule here, and in contrast the face is where poetry happens.

I: Not the soul?

G: *(Laughter.)* You really must be twenty-five.

I: Actually, I'm twenty-nine.

G: Still too young to have had a gall bladder operation.

I: I wonder if you'd think better of me if I had a brain tumor?

G: Do you have a brain tumor?

I: Not that I know of.

G: I like the way you leave room for doubt.

I: Do you have any advice for younger writers?

G: I need to be going now.

I: Actually, I do have a brain tumor.

G: Then maybe we'll be seeing more of each other some day soon, won't we?

I: You know, if you were alive, I'd probably be in love with you. But in the end, I mean when I died or fell in love with somebody else, I'd have to abandon you.

G: Then it's a good thing for both of us that I'm already dead.

in memory of Thom Gunn

Part I

The Incurables

~

Fifteen years ago, in a place that now seems less likely than anything I could make up, I see myself sitting in a room in a Mexican clinic that treats patients on whom conventional medicine has given up. In other rooms there are other patients, some of them within days or weeks of their deaths. Perhaps to call it a "clinic" is too grand. The fact is, we have retreated to a converted motel—in better days, it served as a retreat for Hollywood stars like Gloria Swanson and Dorothy Lamour. At least that's the myth we trade among ourselves, compensating for the cracked ceilings and walls in our rooms, the chipped and dirty swimming pool, the haphazard palm trees, and the overgrown bougainvillea that clings to the faded whitewashed wall that surrounds the clinic grounds.

Removed from the world, we drink specially prepared juices each hour for fourteen hours, we eat vegetarian meals, we try to detoxify our bodies with frequent enemas. At the end of our first week, if the treatment is working, our immune systems will react with astonishing ferocity: our organs and tissues will begin dumping toxins into our bloodstreams, the cancer patients' tumors will start to dissolve. The result of all this purifying activity, in which the body supposedly gears up to heal itself, is high fever, nausea, acute pain in the joints as calcium deposits break down, foul odors, the sweats, sudden intense chills, even mild forms of mental disturbance and psychosis. The challenge is to stay ahead of the flood of poisons.

Only the fear of imminent death could make anyone stick to this regimen. Six, seven, or more enemas a day—the treatment seems lunatic fringe at best. But what can we do? Fasting, visualization, macrobiotics, laetrile, wheat grass juice—we've read the literature, we've given these alternatives a try. And still we're sick, our doctors still tell us there's nothing they can do. As our chances for getting well diminish, as pain or weakness turns us more and more inward, the only force turning us back toward the world is hope.

Having lived with a chronic blood disease for close to twenty years, I've become acquainted with the mercurial shiftings of hope. Hope is my ally when my health starts to decline, convincing me that I can raise myself up; but hope is equally my tormentor: in a good stretch of health, hope can lull me into thinking that my life is more or less normal—until the inevitable downswing, when hope seems merely self-delusion.

My illness is as rare as it is unpronounceable: "paroxysmal nocturnal hemoglobinuria"—which in simple English means "blood in your urine at night." The first time I noticed it was on a dank, hot, Baltimore spring morning a few months after I'd turned twenty-two. To keep my fear in check, I walked the floor of my apartment, halting now and then at the window to look down at a plane tree just beginning to leaf out above the Dumpster in the alley. I managed to convince myself that the blood lazily diffusing in the toilet water was a fluke of biochemistry—a verdict that the various doctors I consulted over the next three years tended to agree with. None of them came remotely close to making the right diagnosis—a fact I don't hold against them. There are so few cases that most doctors, including blood specialists, have never actually seen a walking, talking PNH patient.

The disease (*my* disease, I should say) has no known precipitating cause—but somehow a gene that should make a protective protein on the membrane wall of a red blood cell has gotten switched off. So when I get an infection or if I'm overtired, my oxygen-carrying red blood cells break down abnormally fast. In fact, if I contract a particularly fierce fever, my red cells begin to explode so quickly in my bloodstream that unless I get to a hospital, I can die—from loss of blood, from blood clots, from heart attack. And those are only the acute dangers: in the long term my disease can develop into leukemia, or my bone marrow can give out altogether—what the *Merck Manual* calls "aplastic anemia." But when my blood count is stable, I take an almost macho pride in my body's ability to adjust: a normal person reading this essay would probably faint in his chair and be in serious need of a transfusion if his red cell count were to plummet to the level that I now consider "healthy."

In these good periods, as if my illness were a demon lover, my muscles flex and bend: I try to appease my illness with feats of strength and endurance, to blind and nullify it by swimming and hiking and taking long walks.

But then, as always, comes the crash—I get a fever, my blood count starts to dive, hope neutralizes fear by fueling what I know is the excessive intensity of my fantasy life: as if to counter my lack of physical vitality, my daydreams grow wildly involuted. While the skeptic in me scoffs, I dream up obscure and mystical compensations for the knowledge that sooner, rather than later, my body will fail me.

The hope that my death mean something, mean something not just to my intimates but to the world at large, drives me in the most shameless and childish way to concoct extravagant, even grandiose, fantasies. The more elaborate the fantasy, the graver the circumstance: snowed in beneath hospital sheets, as I wave goodbye to my construction-worker roommate (whose blood count had inexplicably plunged to the level up to which I'm waiting to be transfused), the orderly slides me out of bed onto the green, plastic-pillowed trolley and wheels me off to X-ray. I'm to undergo a scan for blood clots in my lungs. While I breathe in the radioactive gas that will illuminate my lung tissue, I fight back my fear of death with a fantasy in which I embrace death: the plastic mask erasing my features, suddenly I'm hectoring and stoical, casually unconcerned by the approach of my impending execution. I spend my final hours convincing my closest friends that the soul is imperishable . . . then, without a tremor, drink off the fatal hemlock that my weeping jailer prepares for me. Unlikely or laughable as it seems, I'm reenacting Socrates' state-ordered suicide, my so-called crime to incite free thinking in the young. The fact that I'm terminally ill, and my death is less a sacrifice on the altar of free thought than it appears, is my closely guarded secret.

In *Phaedo,* the dialogue by Plato that recounts Socrates' death and his attempt to prove the immortality of the soul, I sense beneath his manner of disinterested, logical argument wild swings of hope and fear: hope that death will reveal ultimate truth, fear that all death means is that one's heart stops beating. How confident the philsopher seems in his talk of mind disencumbered of body, pure immortal mind! Yet beneath his deliberate cool as he elucidates the doctrine of the divine, eternal forms, showing how "Beauty and Goodness possess a most real and absolute existence," I sense in his willingness to take the poison something murkily self-destructive, almost suicidal. At the same time, his conviction that the soul is immortal is more than a little self-interested: as his proofs elaborately unravel into counter-proofs, he demonstrates not only the immortality of the Soul, but of his soul in particular. But these spookily contradictory motives aren't simply the product of an unacknowledged death wish or a manically hopeful need to reassure himself of his own indestructibilty—the philosopher seems equally intent on comforting his followers. Tenderly stroking the head of Phaedo, Socrates asks his young friend if he intends to cut his hair tomorrow as a sign of mourning. When the heartbroken Phaedo laconically replies, "Yes, Socrates, I suppose I will," the philosopher jokes that if his arguments fail, both of them will have to shave their heads today.

What I find most moving and troubling about this dialogue is the moment of Socrates' death, when he pits his own hopes for immortality against the implicitly skeptical method of his argument. Each time he establishes the Soul's indestructibility, he encourages his followers to contradict him, to poke holes in his conclusions until they are completely satisfied that the case has been proven. At last all doubts are vanquished, his followers accept his reasons, his approaching death and his eerily hopeful embrace of it are in precarious balance.

But now my fantasy takes over, the soul of Socrates inhabits my lungs, lips, teeth, tongue that have been arguing against the body as frail, corrupt—while the hemlock numbs my flesh, my friends feel my feet, ankles, knees, thighs to keep track of how far up my body the chill of the hemlock has progressed. My philosophic abstractions, my denigration of my own flesh are entirely forgotten before the mystery of my dying body. The elaborate dance of my intellect can't distract me or my friends from the sorrow and fascination of flesh passing away, flesh that means me, my hand stroking my friend's hair. My vision is blurring . . . to spare my friends the sight of my face, I've drawn a cloth over my head. But now a sacrifice that I've overlooked to Asclepius, the divine healer, keeps nagging at me: I uncover my face and fixing my eyes on Crito, the friend I trust most, I tell him, "Crito, we owe a cock to Asclepius. Make sure the debt is paid." When he assures me it will be done, I—

But here the fantasy comes full stop. I'm no longer Socrates; his soul has passed out of my flesh . . . my fantasy gives way to the fact that for almost twenty years, I've anticipated daily, whether consciously or not, the moment of my death. . . . The fact of my death, my *real* death, is a scalpel that cuts through tissues of ego and daydream: in another starker vision of the end, I see my body shiver a little while my lungs stop breathing. But my mind can't rest there, death is too reductive, it can't keep hope from spurring on my imagination: now Hermes appears and leads my soul flittering like a bat to the underworld. The soul of my dead father comes winging up to me, shrilling in a frequency I don't yet understand—except for the strange vibration of *hope*, the lone syllable in the language of the dead that is anything like the language of the lives of earth.

~

My father comes to me in a dream. His fur is white, his antlers branch above him, his muzzle is elongated, his nostrils quiveringly suspicious. His eyes see me but don't see me as he lowers his head to drink. The water drips from his jaws when he raises his head again, and now his eyes, which before were liquid, uncomprehending, wholly animal, stare back at me with human recognition. He seems to know me, but he himself—I can't tell what he's feeling or thinking. He takes a step toward me and as I put my hand out to touch his fur, his head jerks back, he looks at me warily—but then allows me to put my arm around his neck, bloodwarm, his fur more bristly than it looks. I feel joy to have him next to me, his fur, his muscled legs, the ridge of his long backbone—but the next moment he flattens into two dimensions, I realize that I'm looking at a mosaic. A voice that I can't locate says, "Stop, just stop it!" When I wake a moment later, I can tell that my health, which has been poor for the last few days, is better, magically better, and that the renewed strength I feel in my arms, and especially in my legs, has something to do with my dream.

~

In AD 174 Pausanias, the Greek travel writer, visited Epidaurus in southern Greece, the center of the cult of Asclepius. He tells us that Asclepius' father is Apollo, god of medicine, music, light, and prophecy while his mother, Coronis, is mortal. The polarity of an immortal father and mortal mother underscores the ups and downs of the god's fortunes. In one story of his birth, his mother leaves him to die on a mountain (ironically named Mount Nipple), while in another he is snatched by Hermes from his dead mother's womb just as the flames of her funeral pyre engulf her. Entrusted by Apollo to Chiron, the wise centaur, for his education, Asclepius brings the healing arts to such perfection that the gods of the underworld complain that they are being cheated of their dead—and so Zeus incinerates Asclepius with a thunderbolt. But the cult of Asclepius springs up all over Greece: Pausanias describes the god's many statues as being made of ivory and gold. The god is seated and a dog lies next to him. One hand grasps a staff, the other is held above the head of a serpent. As the god's birthplace, Epidaurus becomes one of the healing centers of the ancient world.

In Asclepius' wild oscillations of fortune—his exposure on the mountain, his rescue from his mother's funeral pyre, his ability to raise the dead, for which he himself is put to death—I perceive the force of human ingenuity struggling against the brute fact of death: Asclepius' brushes with death and his miraculous escapes seem an emblem of the human mind faced with its own mortality as it ricochets between hope and despair.

What in Epidaurus was called the Hieron, or sacred precinct, of Asclepius, finds its counterpart in the clinic dining room. This is the sacred space of our hope to get well. To an outsider, in our short-sleeved shirts and sandals we look as casual as tourists on a Mexican holiday. But the pallid woman who sits across from me, who seems to labor to bring her spoon up to her lips; the hoarsely breathing man next to me whose skin is more jaundiced than tan, concentrate on their food with fanatical intensity. In our sect of the sick, in which we secretly speculate on the ones among us who are too far gone to make it, our cardinal rule is to convince each other and ourselves that health can't be far away. As we sit eating at the battered wooden table, novitiates like myself glean knowledge from the old hands:

"Had your first fever?"

"No, it hasn't hit me yet."

"Mine lasted about four days—104 degrees, nausea, the works. The docs here are right about the peppermint tea. It washes out your stomach real good. And you should do double duty with the enemas. It really helps to knock the fever down."

I stare into an unseasoned soup of potatoes, onions, and leeks.

My ears fill with the hum of an industrial juicer reducing crates and crates of kale, celery, beet tops, apples, carrots to messy pulp squeezed by a hydraulic press into the elixirs we drink. All of us smell subtly of the Vaseline we grease our enema tubes with.

"Are you doing full-strength coffee enemas?"

"No, they told me to try tea for a while—just to go easy, at first."

To traditional practitioners of medicine, all this sounds crackpot—a hypermoralized quackery that stresses "cleansing," an almost ritualized regulation of eating habits and bodily evacuations that is reminiscent of certain practices of ancient mystery religions that stress the need for purification and rebirth: initiates into Mithraism were placed into a pit where the blood of a sacrificed bull streamed down on them from above, washing them clean of their sinful past lives; like Socrates' devotees, Pythagoras's followers believed in transmigration of souls, soul passing from body to body until it became so pure that it was released from the cycle of death and rebirth; Orphic cults prescribed ascetic practices to believers: no beans, no flesh, the wearing of certain kinds of clothes. Such ancient rites and disciplines seem oddball at best, akin in certain respects to the healing cult of the Virgin Mary at Lourdes. Mystical mummery, faith healing, it all sounds pretty dubious . . . but I wasn't going to discount the miracle that could cure me!

In the sacred groves of Asclepius stretched a long covered colonnade where patients consulting the god would sleep, see certain visions in dreams, and come forth cured the next morning. Did the dream of my father as a stag have a clinically measurable effect on the sudden improvement in my health? The temptation to link my dream with the therapeutic power of mental suggestion is hard to resist—especially when doctors can accurately describe the biochemical chain reactions that make me feel sick, but offer nothing concrete in the way of a cure . . . except for a potentially risky bone marrow transplant. High doses of radiation and chemotherapy to wipe out my bone marrow mean that I would have to live in hygienic isolation from infection. Temporarily without an immune system until the new marrow infused into me can take hold, I would be defenseless against the most innocuous of microbes.

When I contemplate undergoing a marrow transplant, I begin to allegorize the stages of marrow transplantation into a quasi-mystical passage from disease to health. First, the ritual ablution, in which my sinful marrow is destroyed: through an intravenous needle, Cytoxan swirls into my bloodstream, or I lie on the X-ray table absorbing megadoses of radiation. Then, in a germ-free plastic tent, I'm kept in isolation from the world's manifold pollution: utterly nauseous and wiped out in my high-tech chrysalis, I pass through the stages of my rebirth: my clean new marrow is IV'd into my veins and sucked up by the hollows of my bones; gradually, over a week or two of obsessive monitoring and blood tests, my new marrow cells proliferate and take hold . . . and if all goes well . . . if the graft is successful and my defective red blood cells don't return . . . if, during the month or so of my sojourn in this germicidal void, I've successfully avoided pneumonia and other life-threatening infections . . . then—at last!—my day of deliverance arrives: I take off my surgical mask, I leave my tent; through the hospital's automatic doors I step out into the microbe-infested air, I re-enter the world of temptation and risk.

A bone marrow transplant ought not to be mystified; it isn't an allegory of sin and salvation, of spiritual death and rebirth. But the relatively neutral phrase "bone marrow transplant"—nothing in the term hints at how extreme the treatment is. Of course, such neutrality buffers me from the knowledge that my doctors must deliberately bring me close to death as part of my cure: not quite as theatrical as being washed in bull's blood, but a whole lot riskier! Who can blame me for indulging in a little mythmaking? Even if I don't succumb to infection while my new marrrow is grafting, I'm still subject to the irony that to make me well is to make me ill: released from the hospital, in full possession of my new health, I'm haunted by my treatment's future consequences: just what are the long-term effects of high doses of radiation and chemotherapy?

~

I'm lying asleep on a doctor's examining table. My neck is crooked at a strange angle to the pillow, almost as if it were broken. I try to turn my head so that my neck is no longer twisted, but I'm so exhausted I can't even muster the strength to lift my head off the pillow. Now I hear a faint rustling sound and see water begin to seep around the edges of the table, advancing slowly the way the tide in a quiet bay advances. And then I realize that the room is suspended like a bubble of breath in the depths of the ocean. The water seeps in more quickly now, and I'm beginning to feel desperate: I can't keep the water out unless I get up from the table, but I'm so worn out I can't even lift my head.

~

In one case recorded at Epidaurus, a sleeping patient woke to find the spearhead embedded in his jaw miraculously extracted and placed into his hand. And there are other accounts where hysterical or similar afflictions were cured by the influence of imagination or sudden emotion. True or not, these stories were much like the stories we told each other over meals at the clinic. To an outsider, there isn't much spiritual uplift in these tales. In fact, in our relish to recount the history of our own bodily functions, we sound a little like the sinners in Dante's hell as they eagerly recount the history of their sins:

"My hands and feet began to sweat this afternoon in the weirdest way. But when they stopped, the headache I'd had all afternoon was gone."

"I was nauseous for a while this morning until I vomited up a lot of bile."

"My skin feels so greasy I have to keep taking showers. The doctors say I'm throwing off a lot of ketones."

"I did three extra enemas last night, and the pain in my kidneys isn't nearly so bad today."

"Every time I breathe, I smell this really strong whiff of motor oil. They say they have to paint the walls sometimes just to get the smell out of the rooms."

A bluff, relentlessly positive-thinking shoe salesman with lung cancer; a young English woman with cancer of the uterus, soft-spoken, determined to live for the sake of her new baby; a terribly frail, once beautiful, middle-aged schoolteacher, attended by her infinitely patient husband, her stomach cancer arrested, the tumor apparently neither shrinking nor spreading; the middle-stage multiple sclerosis patient, her legs tingling, numb, so that walking was becoming a struggle; we all listened with rapt, intense hope to each other's stories of toxins released and evacuated, of former patients restored to health resuming their lives, free of the ominous, chaotic fears that had driven us here, us, "the incurables"—or so we'd been labeled by conventional medicine that, for all its ingenuity, had reached its limit to help us. In an ironic swipe at the medical establishment that was naturally hostile to the clinic's methods, and with not-so-subtle hucksterism, the clinic used that label of "incurable" in its promotional literature, attempting a little mythmaking of its own: "Incurable" could be changed into its opposite; from cranks and outcasts obsessed with our own bodily excretions, we now became the elect, the superheroes of death and disease!

We had our stars of recovery, stars more luminous in our quietly desperate eyes than Gloria Swanson or Dorothy Lamour: the Alabama housewife with a brain tumor who was given a few weeks but now, completely recovered, had written a book about her cure; or the truck farmer with an almost certainly fatal, wildfire variety of melanoma, who was now so healthy that he allowed himself a drink and a cigar from time to time. An entire book chronicling the miraculous cures of the incurables was always ready at hand—we looked to it for encouragement, we convinced ourselves that our cases weren't nearly so dire, that all we need do was follow the regimen to be saved. And undoubtedly many were saved—the treatment did work, we met the survivors, talked with them, relived their medical histories from their abandonment by their regular doctors to their resurrection at the clinic. And of course many died—their condition was too advanced, for some physiological reason they couldn't tolerate the treatment, their immune systems were far too impaired by radiation, by chemotherapy, by sheer exhaustion.

After a few days at the clinic, as the doctors had promised, I began to have a "healing reaction." The day was hot, in the fields surrounding the clinic the weeds turned brown. Across the road from the clinic I was taking a walk in the tiny village where most of the nursing staff lived: a slab of concrete for a basketball court, small cinder-block houses painted pastel blues and with corrugated roofs, roosters and hens, dirt roads wandering up the hillside the village was built on. The eerie sense of normal life going on beyond the confines of the clinic made me realize just how extreme my state of mind was—hope that I would get well, that I could be as stolid in my health as the roosters and hens obliviously pecking at the dirt, had narrowed my attention to an obsessive concentration on my body's functioning. The sporadic drifting noise of conversation, of the sound of sweeping, of clothes being washed outdoors by hand on washboards and in tubs, of the backfire and drone of cars and small tractors, all these signs of daily domestic chores and routine labor argued against my own quiet monomania.

That my hope (and fear) could so limit my responses to the world showed me how sealed off I and my fellow sufferers were in our infinitely self-regarding battle with disease. The appalling self-involvement and secret egotism of the dying! Our tyrannical self-awareness tracked moment to moment the subtlest fluctuations in our breathing, body temperatures, and heart rates, while the day-to-day world we wanted so desperately to get back to, the world of easy sleep, of unregulated food and drink, of routine contact with one another—we automatically blocked out. Oblivious to life outside the clinic, all we could think on were the mortal chances of our own sorry, aching flesh. To break ourselves of the fear of death, to face it with the apparent confidence of a Socrates!

At Epidaurus, the temple of Asclepius was filled with votive offerings—marble eyes, ears, legs, hands, feet, all the parts of the body that the god had healed left behind in simulacra as a remembrance of the god's grace: the wounded arm exchanged for the well arm, the blind eye left behind for the sighted one. Long lists of cases inscribed in stone slabs record the method of consulting the god as well as the manner of his cures. The god's way of treating wounds (dressings and cautery) and broken bones (various kinds of splints) must have seemed to the patients more common sense than miracle. But the cures that depended on supernatural intervention—the miraculous mending overnight of a broken vase, for example—tease my imagination most. Why shouldn't I wake up some morning with all my cracks seamlessly mended? But my skepticism returns; I shrug off such hopes. My oscillations between belief and doubt mirror exactly what the god's patients must have felt: it seems that in later times the efficacy of the old faith healing fell into disrepute, and the priests substituted for it elaborate prescriptions concerning diet, baths, and regimen: in many particulars quite similar to the treatment I was following in Mexico.

But here in the village, removed from the clinic, in the hot sunshine, I was outside of my obsession, my body seemed for a moment like any other body. Someone looking at me wouldn't have known from my appearance that I was sick. Why didn't I behave like Socrates in the face of my own death? To buy a rooster from a villager, slit its throat, and offer it up to Asclepius was no more eccentric than enemas, "healing reactions," and the company of the other incurables. Hope? Was this alien state of mind part of the punishing operations of hope? Malignant hope that kept me frantically pursuing health? Would it be a form of suicide to refuse to compromise with mortality? To abandon hope, to inure myself to physical suffering and eventual death . . . if only I could keep my head clear of my body's special pleading, "Do this and this, you'll recover, you'll get well."

Perhaps I was addled by the heat, and certainly I was in the first throes of the "healing" fever that the doctors at the clinic had predicted. But at that moment, in a village whose name I can't even remember, I felt free of the clinic. The houses' pitted cinder blocks and mortar scalloped between the courses; the wooden fences around dirt yards; the scrounged camper shells ingeniously propped on cement foundation walls and used as toolsheds and bedrooms; these imparted a sense of almost supernatural order and normalcy, of an unimpeachable certainty of well-being.

This state of well-being was impersonal: it had nothing to do with me or the relative state of my health; a diamond absolute, it held sway no matter what kind of doctor or medicine I put my trust in, no matter who got well or who died, no matter what hope promised or failed to deliver. If the clinic in its extremity mirrored the sacred groves of Asclepius—last refuge of the sick and dying—then the village that afternoon was like workaday Epidaurus, seat of unself-conscious well-being, normalcy, and order. Yet how foreign those words sound in the ears of "the incurable," inspiring both awe and despair. Though I could sense that power as operative in others' lives, I myself had never felt so far from health, even at the very moment when the sunshine and heat seemed most resplendent with health-giving qualities.

Now, when I think of Asclepius' power, I see kings as well as peasants, each praying to be healed, lying down for the night on the cold marble. I see the god in his benevolence appearing to the sleepers, filling this head and that with its own special, miraculous dream. Even Alexander the Great's father, Philip of Macedon, visited Asclepius' sacred groves and left his breasplate and spear on the god's altar. But then I imagine the sick and dying whose dreams weren't colored by the god—wouldn't the god's decision to heal some but not others also make him a figure of dread? But small matter if the god favored Philip, or chose instead to cure the poorest bondsman in his kingdom: both visits would be punctiliously added to the other inscriptions, more evidence of the god's influence and power.

~

Shortly afterward my fever spikes, and my stay at the clinic comes to an abrupt end. My nausea and chills, my red blood cells breaking down so quickly that my urine turns black—it's quite clear to everyone that unless I get to a hospital immediately, a real hospital, I might die.

While my mother drives me toward the border and a hospital in California, I focus on the emergency as if it's someone else's body, someone else's life at stake. My mind is weirdly cool and distant, my body aches, aches and shivers, fever blurs my vision: I feel afloat in a plunging elevator, only the elevator is my body descending farther and farther from that untroubled, expanding light that is my own awareness watching, detached, invulnerably serene, unmoved by the tense voices talking far below . . . my voice, my mother's voice discussing what to say to the doctors, deciding *No,* we can't tell them about the clinic; that *Yes,* the body in trouble may need a blood transfusion.

The farther my body falls, the more attuned grows my perception of how weak my arms and legs feel, how light my pulse—my breathing, too, is beginning to plunge, my body and breath separating so completely that body seems infinitely heavy, stone-stupid, elemental. . . . Now we've reached the emergency room, the neon keeps twisting and writhing, wrenching itself away from the fixture, then starkly dissolving into the shadows. In the bed next to mine someone is moaning about his headache, a headache so terrible that his moans create a disturbance like a heat wave, pulsating, a force field of blank pain.

From far outside my body I feel my heart speed up, beating so quickly that the darkness the neon dissolves into rises into my eyes and flows over and around me, reaching even to the place where now I'm nothing but hovering Being above my own voice crying, "I can't breathe, I don't believe I can breathe." A hand grips mine—the headache, the moans, they belong to this hand. Tears come to my eyes when I realize that no matter how fierce the pain the headache and moans spring from, the hand that belongs to this pain has come to comfort me, to calm me so that I can breathe until the nurse gets there with oxygen.

My body is still free-falling, my heart flutters so quickly and faintly it seems about to stop. I sense panic trying to pierce the spreading blackness that holds me until I hear inside my head a voice so authoritative, so utterly self-convinced and godlike that it might as well be Socrates arguing over the soul, or Asclepius come to me in a dream: "Wonder Bread helps build strong bodies 12 ways, Wonder Bread helps build strong bodies 12 ways, Wonder Bread . . ." The oxygen mask fits over my face, through my strengthening breath my brain and body begin to fuse back together; now my heart starts to slow, the slogan from the old TV commercial that has surfaced from my childhood, and which I used to chant to myself whenever I was worried or afraid, inscribes itself on pure untextured mind—which again feels the impress of my identity . . . and with that comes fear, naked, raw fear . . .

That I knew this could happen, that fever almost always results in my red blood cells' obliteration, drives home that I am ill, chronically ill, that my disease can kill me, has almost killed me. My desire to get well, my hope to return to the unconscious ease of assumed health, now seems wildly absurd. I can't stifle the voice needling in on every side, *How can you lead your life if life means that you must be ill?*

~

More than a decade later, I'm sitting at my mother's dining-room table, still one of the incurables. I'm about to play a role that I've played many times—the survivor, "the old-timer" of death, the *philosophe* of disease. I always feel a little fraudulent—but my feelings aren't the point: my mother has invited over her neighbor's seventeen-year-old son who has lymphoma. He's tall, with an athlete's torso and legs—but his muscle tone is beginning to slacken in his chest and abs, the result of his illness's onslaught, of radiation and chemotherapy.

"I'm out of school for a while," he says, "but hey, that's OK—", and gives an ironic smile. I recognize the style of humor: slightly deadpan, rueful, making much of negatives, already he's realized that the world can't easily tolerate more direct displays of emotion.

"I'll bet it really hurts to have to miss school, huh?"

"Oh yeah, I wake up weeping every morning!"

We trade jokes back and forth, each of us instinctively understanding the fear that drives our joking, but also enjoying our shared sense of being different from other people; of being members of a club that in theory everyone belongs to, but that only some of us, and only at certain moments of our lives, are truly enrolled in.

"It's not going so bad—my hair fell out in patches so I just shaved my head. I like wearing a cap anyway, so what's the difference?"

"Hey, my hair just falls out on its own!"

Around and around we go, slipping in bits of our medical histories. The more I learn about his condition, the more despairing I feel about his chances; one reason why he's asked to meet me is to let me know, a stranger uninvested in his life, what no one else near him can bear to hear: that the odds aren't good, that in a year or two he may well be dead. But it's not only despair we feel underneath the joking—our laughter is genuine: I sense in him an intense pride in carrying himself bravely, in his refusal to say too much, in his stoical restraint.

I've played this scene before in more fraught circumstances. I'll meet with the friend of a friend of a friend who's scared, vulnerable, valiantly keeping in check anxiety and dread. We talk about alternative treatments, both of us knowing that if the doctors pronounce you terminal, a miracle is required . . . and miracles, our glances agree, are in short supply. . . . After these conversations I always feel drained, I wonder why I put myself in these situations: Am I a kind of death junkie, getting off on intense emotion? Does it reassure me to see someone sicker than myself?

This kind of self-accusation becomes its own dodge: how much easier for me to cocoon myself away from such people, to keep myself insulated from their pain and dread. My motives for meeting them may be less than altruistic, but wouldn't it be worse to refuse to meet this young man, so dignified in his fear, so intently matter-of-fact about the prospect of his own death? Yet in my role as elder statesman how dislocated I feel, the incurable still secretly lusting after a cure, my acceptance of my fate a not so subtle ruse to trick myself into thinking that my condition is as routine as the sunrise. The constant threat of mortality has shaped me the way wind shapes a tree, bending the trunk in the direction that it habitually blows. Or I sometimes think of myself as moving in a different gravitational field, the heaviness and clumsiness of my movements contrived to look almost normal. It's only when I meet up with someone like this young man that I understand the extent of my own psychic accommodation to this field's warping force. Akilter from the sudden, strange intimacy we share, I realize I'm a little afraid of him—no, not him, but of everything he's suffered and may still suffer. Does he feel the same about me, as if fear and despair were infectious? Yet what greater consolation can we offer than the physical reassurance of our failing, but still bravely persisting bodies?

I suppose the point is to overcome what is negative in these feelings, to recognize in our jokes our shared sense of a common fate, even in our veiled, perhaps mutual fear, a genuine bond. But aren't these things also sources of estrangement—from ourselves, from other people, from the world?

Now we finish talking, we say good-bye. The tension I've felt the whole time we've been together tightens inside me, I feel helpless to protect him or myself, inadequate to the enormity of the trial that each of us one day will face. I consider what may be his fate—and realize, almost with a kind of envy, that he could soon know more than me about what it means to be "incurable . . ." As I watch him walk away, unexpectedly he turns and calls out to me, "Good luck!" For a moment I'm a little ashamed: Shouldn't I be the one wishing him luck, I, the old-timer, "the incurable"? What have I given him, after all? Is it simply the fact that I'm still alive, striving to lead a relatively normal life, which makes me seem special in his eyes and so spurred him to seek me out? As if by pretending to be healthy in the eyes of the sick, I might slip out from under the watchful gaze of my own fate and actually cross back over the border between disease and health? Yet I, too, wanted to meet him, to share this intimacy of our estrangement from the world of free and easy flesh. How young he is, how vital his body seems despite the alien pallor beneath his tan—my hand moments ago held his, and I can still feel his skin's warmth fading from my skin.

~

The voice you dream is mine—bend down to me, come listen: I'm one of Asclepius' yellow snakes, the one his hand reaches out to; or else I'm his dog stretched dozing under his chair. In snake language, in dog language, he whispers why you people suffer, why you, among all these others, are fated to get well, and why you, with the same illness, already belong to the gods of the underworld. His voice in my head inhabits the marble of his statue, the stone so cool against me reassuring in its chill. You patients who leave me offerings, I barely notice you, I'm so intent on the delicious cool that rises and flows through me . . . As I lie here, my belly listens to the marble, I hear it whispering to me in the voice of the god. At night when you're asleep and my tongue licks into your ear, you too may learn what the god knows. Bend down to me, come listen, in the god's own words, to the reason for your life and death, the reason for your suffering and pain, the reason why the god will or will not heal you.

Education of the Poet

~

He goes to a literary conference, and on the evening that he's to speak, he discovers to his dismay that the conference organizers have decided to make his talk the occasion of a fund-raiser for a literary magazine. He knows he should talk off the cuff, make jokes, be jolly . . . but ad-libbing repulses him and, more to the point, scares him: his prepared remarks may be too formal for the event, but hey, it's all he's got—and so with a sense of doomed finality, he steels himself to let things unfold as they will. It's a catered affair, and as he's standing there, two other people at the conference discuss the cheeses. He likes cheese, but his cheese connoisseurship is pretty sketchy. That yellow stuff must be cheddar—but it turns out to be Edam. He can see his relatives, farmers and schoolteachers homesteading in Texas and the western Kansas prairie, looking askance at those cheeses. And that's when it dawns on him that his education as a poet is the education of an autodidact. He feels not only a little foolish, but inadequate to those cheeses, their aura of pedigree and chummy privilege . . . but since he hasn't eaten all day, he shrugs off his unease and cuts himself a slice, puts it on a cracker, and eats. It's delicious, oozing and gooey and shimmering and vaguely lascivious. He thinks of the tiny town where all his people are from, the buffet at the VFW hall, the boiled beef and the whipped potatoes and the translucent, jiggling, green Jell-O, yes, and the marshmallows, the small ones he ate by the handful when he was a kid. Now he overhears what you might call highbrow guy-talk, guys arguing about the nature of the Sublime, whether or not the Sublime can exist, well why can't it, Sublime Schmublime what you're really experiencing is nostalgia, no I'm not, all right paranoia, no, it's awe, you think it's awe but really it's just paranoia, the image of a cliff about to fall on a boat, you can't tell me that's not paranoid, and he smiles and says, Hey, this cheese tastes great, sublime even, and he cuts them each a slice to shut them up. And as he munches, he feels how homemade he is, and wouldn't it be better if he'd had a more formal education, especially since he's been asked to lecture on his education as a poet, but he tries to quell his doubts by rehearsing his talk in his head, and when they ask him to speak, he starts speaking:

"I want to pick up on some of the themes laid down yesterday and the day before by X and Y. Both of them spoke about the education of the poet. X, who grew up in the '60s and '70s, focussed, in part, on how her interest in experiences that combined both metaphysical terror and awe—what certain philosophers called the Sublime, and which Timothy Leary linked to LSD in his 1967 lecture, "Turn On, Tune In, Drop Out"—had led her to poets as various as Edna St. Vincent Millay and Leslie Scalapino.

Y, who grew up during World War II, spoke of various paradigms of a poet's education—the court education of a poet in classical China, the Renaissance ideal of the courtier in Elizabethan England, the "high tea," high culture, WASP snobbishness of the Ivies and Oxford University, and then he talked about how his own working-class background both helped and hindered his development.

So what I want to do is to talk a bit about my own education by first talking about my own prehistory to language, what you might call the preliterate influences. Allen Grossman says that most poets at the beginning of their vocation are trying to learn to speak the language of one of their parents. By this, he means that poetry is almost always an attempt to forge a way of speaking that both reflects one's connection with an origin, but also signals an inevitable estrangement from it. My mother's voice was fluent and extravagant, words came naturally to her and were a pleasure of the first order. My father, on the other hand, was laconic and sweetly quiet, using words for their utility, their ability to arrange life, and not for their volatility and ability to derange life. From this intersection, I'd like to hazard that as a poet I consciously tried to learn my mother's language by my interest in densely wrought rhetoric, and at the same time wanted to delimit language and honor my father's quiet through my fascination with trying to master traditional formal conventions like rhyme and meter. I spent much of my twenties learning to write by slavishly imitating almost all of Robert Browning's various rhyme schemes and meters (I must be the only person in the world who did an imitation of Browning's *The Ring and the Book*), from blank-verse dramatic monologues to rhyme royal to crazy monorhymes that would give Poe's "Bells bells bells" a run for its money. I even took a read at an obscure translation of Euripides' *Herakles,* in which Browning tries to recreate Greek syntax in English. The result is fascinating and utterly unreadable, which gave me heart many years later to set out to do my own translation.

At about this same time, I was also taking on board the laterally propulsive syntax of Wallace Stevens, in which the sentence plays out in subordinating clause after clause elaborating and qualifying in a seemingly endless stream of association. One of my favorite poems from this time is Stevens's "To the One of Fictive Music":

> Sister and mother and diviner love,
> And of the sisterhood of the living dead
> Most near, most clear, and of the clearest bloom,
> And of the fragrant mothers the most dear
> And queen, and of diviner love the day
> And flame and summer and sweet fire, no thread

Of cloudy silver sprinkles in your gown
Its venom of renown, and on your head
No crown is simpler than the simple hair.

Now, of the music summoned by the birth
That separates us from the wind and sea,
Yet leaves us in them, until earth becomes
By being so much of the things we are,
Gross effigy and simulacrum, none
Gives motion to perfection more serene
Than yours, out of our imperfections wrought,
Most rare, or ever of more kindred air
In the laborious weaving that you wear.

For so retentive of themselves are men
That music is intensest which proclaims
The near, the clear, and vaunts the clearest bloom,
And of all vigils musing the obscure,
That apprehends the most which sees and names,
As in your name, an image that is sure,
Among the arrant spices of the sun,
O bough and bush and scented vine, in whom
We give ourselves our likest issuance.

Yet not too like, yet not so like to be
Too near, too clear, saving a little to endow
Our feigning with the strange unlike, whence springs
The difference that heavenly pity brings.
For this, musician, in your girdle fixed
Bear other perfumes. On your pale head wear
A band entwining, set with fatal stones.
Unreal, give back to us what once you gave:
The imagination that we spurned and crave.

The balance between the near, the clear, which I take to be my father's voice, and the injunction that the poem should not be too near, too clear, which seems the province of my mother's voice, perhaps explains why when I read this poem I feel their voices intertwined and so sponsoring my own voice. And yet the ending of the poem sounds a note of estrangement when it speaks of the unreal: I have always loved the unreal, and my adolescence as a drug user bears this out to the point where I consider my drug days as one of my major influences. That my drug use was a form of experience that estranged me from the speech of my parents and initiated me into a new community of speech, what you might call the secret lingo of doper slang, bears out Grossman's claim that our development as poets is not only finding a point of origin, but also finding yourself moving beyond it willy-nilly.

But let me continue for a moment with some of the preliterate influences and move into the first moments when I actually encountered poetry. I suppose my first source of poetry was the shared babble that my twin brother and I spoke when we were babies just learning to talk. We didn't speak English for a good year and a half—which caused my parents considerable worry. What, were we idiot savants (or just plain idiots), locked into our own microcosm of twinness? And then my mother—who has been known to tell "a stretcher," as Huck Finn would say—recounts that one morning she came into our bedroom, and overheard us in Beckett-like colloquy, speaking the first English words she remembers us saying—not mama or dada—but my brother Tim, shaking the bars of his crib, calling, Dean Martin! while I called back, Jerry Lewis!

Martin's and Lewis's voices were so much a part of my ear because my parents ran a drive-in movie theater in a small east Texas town, out in piney woods country, and you could always count on Martin and Lewis to bring in a crowd. My mother ran the snack bar, my father the projector, and when they couldn't afford a babysitter, I went to the movies, probably from the time I was two years old. About dusk, just as I was getting sleepy, my twin brother and I would be helped up in the window-well of our old green Plymouth. He slept on one side, and I slept on the other, while my older brother curled down below on the car seat. Of course there was a speaker in the car. I would hear the actors' voices begin to talk as I was on the edge of sleep, and then I'd be out; but the voices would continue on as a kind of background to my dreams. I always fell asleep just as the movies began at dusk, and the voices coming through the car speakers were like the voices in my dreams, the two intermingling to make a kind of poetry: especially since I thought the voices in dreams were the voices of dead people come to tell you things that you were forbidden to hear during the day.

Long after we sold the theater and I'd forgotten the circumstances of falling asleep in the Plymouth, I found that when I shut my eyes and started to drift, I'd hear voices and music. I didn't know what caused this until I mentioned it to my father many years ago—and I suddenly realized that all this had imprinted on my nervous system and that I was duplicating my experience, as a very young child, of hearing first the movie music swell in the car and then of listening to the actors' voices entering my dreams.

This was my first experience of being transported to another realm by language. As I said earlier, my father is a taciturn man, my mother a talented talker. During the day, I lived between these two poles of language that had all the dirt and beauty of domestic dailiness about them. But almost every night at the drive-in, I experienced an extraordinarily heightened sense of language coming from this other source—literally, a disembodied speaker. It was the eruption of the dreamlike into the moment between sleeping and waking, in which the day world got suddenly transported into that space which is strangely sacred and wholly unpredictable. The riskiness of it is one of the most intense and beautiful parts of being alive. That's one of the things that poetry activates in people, that quickening of psychic experience.

Some years later, just as I was learning to read, I was riding in the car with my parents and, as I looked up at a movie marquee, what I read was *The Last Battlelion.* In the zoo in Utah, the state where we now lived, there was an animal called a liger, a cross between a lion and a tiger. The animal's name was Shasta. I was struck by these strange displacements of language that, in a crazy way, all fit together; I imagined Shasta engaged in heroic acts, the standard kind of fantasy kids have about dying on the floor after their parents have maybe yelled at them—the beautiful corpse fantasy. When I asked if we could go see *The Last Battlelion* they laughed at me—of course the title of the movie was *The Last Battalion*—but it was a profound moment for me. I saw the double nature of language. Their laughter made me aware that language was an adult property, that it had the power to not only name the world, but to organize it. This was shocking because it put me up against my own ignorance and lack of power. But now, as a writer, I still insist on the imaginative privilege of reading "battalion" as "battlelion" because doing so projects me into another realm of imagination that exists side by side with the nuts-and-bolts world, and puts them into an interesting tension.

I think my first experience of a poem proper occurred when I was out visiting my grandfather in Kansas. He was a dry land wheat farmer, orphaned at eleven, and largely self-taught. I remember his bald, high-domed forehead gleaming while he recited "The Face on the Barroom Floor." He performed it with verve and clearly enjoyed playing up the melodrama. He then launched into what he called "the bear dance," which meant he shuffled in circles in the middle of the living room—his own kind of performance poetry, accompanied by the whirring racket of locusts outside in the windbrake junipers, and my mother tinkling out a little show tune on the upright piano. I know this sounds vaguely "folkloric"—the rude, good-hearted prairie sodbusters doing their thing of a Saturday night. But he was thoroughly enjoying himself, as was my mother, and they both were aware of the figures they cut: you could almost see them winking at themselves in the mirror, as if to say, *Oh yes, we know how absurd we look—but why shouldn't we look absurd!*

I think of the bear dance and it reminds me of one of my favorite paintings—a group of bears up on their hind legs dancing in the forest, but still perfectly like bears, nothing sentimental or anthropomorphized in their depiction: they have the same kind of elegance and artifice and creaturely strangeness as you see in Watteau. And they look far more at home in their dancing than Gilles does in his Pierrot clown whites. Poetry has always seemed a little like that—animal grace in clown whites.

And then I remember my mother reading aloud to me from Thoreau's *Walden* about the ant war. I was completely astonished by ants being talked about in that way—satiric and precise and more horrifying than any first-person account of the carnage of human war. But equally vivid for me is the strange intimacy my mother felt for the book—a dimension of her character that moved her outside the category of "Mom" and into the category of "Weirdo." How I longed to understand her pleasure in the words, and how baffled I felt by her privacy inside them. What added to the strangeness was my mother's lineup of wigs on her dresser: three expressionless Styrofoam heads looking down at us while she read, as if she had more personalities under each of the separate 'dos' than I'd ever imagined.

I owe so much to my mother: she was a high school English teacher, and a kind of one-woman Renaissance in a spectacularly conservative, Mormon, mountain town. She taught *Lord Jim,* which created a scandal one spring semester—*Lord Jim,* for God's sake! Could it have been that Jim acts like a coward, and explorations of cowardice weren't good for us tender-minded, James Bond/gonad-obssesed little blighters? Or was it that Jim was a skeptic, an incomprehensible person to others and himself, that made him such a threat? Not likely. Anyway, *Lord Jim!* was a battle . . . and then we moved to San Diego.

As I said, the poetry there was the drug lingo I picked up: dude, spade vein, hero (for heroin), lids, keys, dope, weed, Acapulco Gold, Panama Red, Thai sticks, stoned, high, wasted, rush; and then an arcane doper/surfer vocabularly that described various gradations of cool and uncool: "bitchin'" girl, "bitchin'" guy, which meant you were hip; a "woody," meaning someone who was clod-hopper stupid and jejune; and "hard," which signified egregious uptight mindless aggression. But perhaps the most profound moment of poetry in my surfer days was subverbal: I once spent a night high on LSD on a beach in San Diego pretending to be a seal among a pack of seals. They stank, had awful dog breath, and were nicked and cut, with welts here and there on their mottled gray and black skin. While I was stoned, I remember thinking that I loved these seals as I love my brothers and my family: for all their creaturely, bodily, three-dimensional fragility and potential for harm. And sometimes in the city I get a sense of human bodies as being distinctly animal, and I feel a great sense of joy in that, though of course I could just be tapping into my "inner" Whitman, getting a little Whit-manic . . .

And then I remember coming across a bookstore in La Jolla called The Unicorn and picking up a book of poetry—blither by someone named Prather—sensitive notations about falling leaves—that I couldn't fathom. I realize now that he was a middle-aged man writing about middle age as if it were interesting: even then I suspected the writing of sentimentality, but the tone was new to me—serious, intimate, introspective—qualities that I found alien even as they attracted me.

But my first real experience of poetry was going to *Othello* with my mother. We read the play together before we went, and I remember loving and hating Othello: hating him for bragging about himself after he killed Desdemona, and loving him for his torment and sense of high purpose: in other words, Othello was as much an adolescent as I was.

Later in my twenties, I went to Mexico to do anthropology. I was employed at La Casa de Na Balom, the house of the jaguar, situated at the edge of San Cristobal de las Casas. My employer was the Swiss photographer and anthropologist, Gertrude Blom. She was a legend throughout Chiapas, a sort of Old World grand dame who played hostess to every anthropologist in southern Mexico. Na Balom was one part hotel, one part research library, and one part colonial kitsch: the rooms were all theme rooms, each theme based on a highland Chiapas village: you could sleep one night in the Zinacantan room, decorated by their intricately embroidered blouses; the next night in the San Andreas room, deep blue textiles; the third night in the Chamulan room, heavy wool tunics, and so forth. I suppose you could say that living at Na Balom helped me to recognize and understand my own romance with experience. To prove something, I must prove it on my own pulses, as Keats once said. My time at Na Balom showed me how to do that—the adventure in my head that was Mexico often had little to do with what I was actually experiencing. But as the months passed, I learned how to short-circuit my clichéd ideas of myself as an adventurer and began to open myself to the work of fathoming what was around me and how different it was from anything I knew. Stock responses are boring in life and in art. And so Mexico opened me as a person, and later as a writer, to the sheer strangeness of things and to the demands that that strangeness puts on an artist to be faithful to it.

At Na Balom this lesson was brought home to me one night in a truly bizarre manner. As part of my duties, Trudy asked me to show two of our guests how to use their knives and forks, and other intricacies of the modern world. These turned out to be Lacandon Indians, the tribe most like the ancient Maya in customs and language. They'd been flown in from the jungle in a rickety four-seater, and Trudy had arranged for them to have medical checkups. Don Jose was suffering from intestinal worms (so was I, and so were most of us who were present that night) while Cayum Yuk Mosh was being tested for TB. They were both dressed in bark gowns that reached to their knees, their thick black hair halfway down their backs, and they had a shy, but humorous way about them that showed how strange they found life outside of the rain forest—which was where they'd lived their whole lives, at least till this evening.

They kept staring at Trudy, as did we all: she was seated at the head of an immensely long, hand-hewn mahogany table. Her chair resembled a throne, high-backed and outsized. To complete the image of aristocratic eccentricity, two giant Russian wolfhounds sat at attention on either side of her chair. From time to time, she would throw them scraps over her shoulder, an ironical gleam in her eye, as if to say, *you-know-that-I-know-that-you-know-how-out-of-bounds-this-is-but-get-over-it.* And as I got to know Trudy, I did get over it. She was an original photographer, an immensely generous and kind person. And even if she was always borrowing back my salary a few days after she'd given it to me, I knew she'd pay me back . . . only to borrow it back again—our own private version of certain World Bank transactions. She was also extremely vain: and that night at dinner she was dressed in a fantastical green brocade gown and had just told one of the more glamorous guests, in her most deadpan, outrageously frank way, a woman who piled her hair in a messy Brigitte Bardotish beehive, that she looked like a bird's nest—"But I mean that as a compliment," said Trudy, "for you see, my dear, I like birds' nests." You get the kind of place it was.

As I said, Trudy had asked me to take care of our Lacandon guests: she had taken up the cause of the Lacandon against the timber companies: she took rich businessmen down to the jungle to show them how the Lacandones lived, a practice that helped ensure their survival, but doomed their cultural "purity," their "authenticity," qualities they cared about, but devoid of all self-consciousness. I packed the gear and the provisions for the expeditions, as they were called, and had bad conscience about it, but not enough to say anything to Trudy. The fact was, without the money she got from these rich gringos, the Lacandones would have been wiped out by disease, the timber companies' greed, the Mexican government's complete indifference to their plight, and their own inbreeding: there were less than a hundred of them left alive in the Usumacinta River valley between Chiapas and Guatemala.

Since they used knives all the time, at supper we got through the knife part just fine. But I have no idea what they thought I was doing by making a show of how to hold a fork: no one could have looked more ridiculous, and more like a nineteenth-century cartoon of an imperialist, than me waving my fork under the noses of these baffled, but friendly men, as I tried to discreetly teach them the fine art of spearing fried squash blossoms. I kept thinking that they must have seen those businessmen use forks during their jungle getaways, and so all I'd need to do was to brandish the fork in a slightly exaggerated way to get them to understand. And eventually they did use their forks, gripping them like knives, which was good enough for all of us: my sense of my own absurdity made me feel as if all my clothes had been suddenly stripped off and I was sitting there, butt naked. But that was nothing to the moment when they made it clear to me that they wanted to use the bathroom. And so I led them to the toilet in the library: I pointed to the toilet, pulled the chain (it was an overhead tank), held up the scraps of newspaper we used for toilet paper, and began to back out of the room. I have never felt more ridiculous than at that moment: I see Cayum staring at me in a puzzled manner, his long black hair catching the light from the exposed bulb dangling down from a black cord, his eyes crossing a little bit from the glare. Don Jose had simply turned his back to me, his eyes looking up, as if he were peering at something off in the distance. At that point, I was overwhelmed by the cultural difference between us, the absolute foolery and folly of thinking these men required my assistance, and most immediately, by the problem of what to do: short of demonstrating myself how to use a flush toilet, I couldn't imagine how to possibly convey the point of all these pipes and chains and cracked porcelain. So I beckoned them to follow me, and led them to a far part of the garden bordering on a ravine that, I confess, I sometimes used if the toilet was occupied and the worms in my gut were kicking up more than the usual ruckus.

I left them there to find their own way back, and when they returned to the library, we sat in amiable silence until Cayum, whom I later got to know quite well, pointed out a bow and a set of arrows mounted on the wall. This bow and these arrows were exactly the kind that he used in hunting in the rain forest. He took them down, put them in my hands, and we both had a moment of mutual recognition: there was more than a hint of irony in his gesture, but it was friendly irony that later developed into one of the emotional signatures of our friendship. Cayum had turned the tables on me, in a way that I was all too grateful for. Sometimes the strangeness of the local does win out over the imperatives of the global: my metropolitan way of conceiving Cayum's experience was completely inadequate to what had transpired between us that evening. And so if poetry is also an art that helps to ratify and preserve the strangeness of individual moments, my experience with Cayum was one of my main lessons in that—though I'm the first to admit that after months of worms, I was delighted on my return to the United States to be able to take for granted the rituals of sanitation and communality represented by a centralized water and sewer system.

But while I was in Chiapas, the strangeness of what I was experiencing opened me to more nuanced and truthful ways of feeling. And I'd say that that access to feeling, and the fact that I was speaking Spanish all the time, made me feel even more homesick for the sound of English than I already was. That's when I began to write—little sketches of what I'd seen or done, or short portraits of some of the expatriates or anthropologists that I'd met. One night in the library, the poet Charles Bell, who had a house in San Cristobal de las Casas, read aloud Tennyson's "Marianna." I loved the repetition of the refrain, "I am aweary, aweary," partly for its musical languor and sensuality, and partly because it reflected my own feelings at the end of the working day at Na Balom that generally started at dawn, when I'd escort Trudy down to the garden to gather vegetables while keeping the wolfhounds in check as they lunged on their leashes at the packs of skinny strays that constantly roamed the mud-rutted streets. And then there was library work, mainly archival, sorting through the thousands of photographs Trudy had taken and that would eventually be on permanent display at the National Museum of Anthropology in Mexico City. And then the strangeness of dealing with the guests, so that sometimes Na Balom felt more like Fawlty Towers: imagine Basil Fawlty leading a tour to a village festival where one of his charges, dressed in mountain-climbing gear, lederhosen, and carrying an ice axe, ends up stuck in a tree, having climbed it in pursuit of an orchid. I also remember helping to bandage the paws of a baby monkey that an anthrolopogist, Robert Bruce, had brought back from the jungle. While I held the monkey's neck from behind so that it couldn't move its head and bite Robert, he talked about the *Popol Vuh*, the Maya sacred book, discussing the glyphs in a combination of colloquial and technical speech that now seems to me an almost ideal idiom for poetry. And then I remember reading Allen Ginsberg in a bookstore on a getaway to Cuernavaca: his was one of the few books in English, and as I said, I was extremely lonely for the sound of English and how it put me in touch with my old English-speaking self. The hand-waving extrovert I'd become as a Spanish speaker sorted rather badly with the introvert who wanted to retreat from all this strangeness and hide in books. Ginsberg's English, though, was so bizarrely inventive that it afforded a bridge between my English self and my Spanish self. I remember feeling momentarily at ease in both selves during the time I stood in that bookstore, trying to make out "Howl." Doing the kind of work I was doing in such an isolated place meant spending a tremendous amount of social energy trying to be like the people you're with, and I suppose that's where I really began to develop "negative capability."

When I got back from Mexico, I was suddenly gripped by the idea of writing about my mother's life—an idea that didn't go very far because I chose a style completely inappropriate to it. I was interested in doing something mandarin like Virginia Woolf, which was totally foreign to my experience and to my mother's experience. The woman grew up on a Kansas dirt farm, she was the first person in her county to go to college, and I was trying to write piss elegant sentences, full of lavish rhetorical flourish.

But that's when I began to sit down and write every day for three or four or five hours. I've done that for years now. Of course I don't write a poem every day. I'm not a Methodist about it. I love the quiet and the solitude of being available to whatever impulse may go past me, and in a way it's become a deep psychic need. I don't think it necessarily has much to do with the quality of what I write, but having the time to think through your life is invaluable. And it's given me a large amount of unpressured time to read. Edging out along the branch, waiting for it to break off—that's the kind of concentration it takes to write well over a long period of time. Inspiration is knowing what branch you're on and how far out you are on it. Then you need some sense of continuity, some sense of consolation in the process of writing, and I find that in the contemplation, the sitting and quietly thinking.

A sense of being out of place while trying to find a place for myself in language has probably been the main stimulus and source of my writing life since my anthropology days. And so you could say that feeling alienated from my surroundings has been one of my major educative experiences. My exposure to the city, an Eastern seaboard city, dense, difficult to navigate, nothing at all like the freeway fluidity and blur of the West Coast, has been a major part of that curriculum. I think my sense of language has been deeply affected by the multiple layers of sensation that overwhelm you as you walk the streets of cities like Brooklyn and Boston. There's a particular corner in Cambridge that serves as a model for how language can approximate that layering. On the side of a brick building located near MIT, as you approach it from a side street, you read in twenty foot high white letters

STORAGE WAREHOUSE
FIRE PROOF

But if you approach this same building from a different side street, which joins Massachusetts Avenue at a more oblique angle, the sight lines are such that the first three letters of "STORAGE" are cut off by the building's side and the "F" in fire is also deleted: so what you see is

RAGE WAREHOUSE
IRE PROOF

What's wonderful about this transformation, in addition to the nineteenth-century flavor and wit of "ire," is that the redness of the brick also becomes part of the visual pun, as if the brick itself were red hot from containing all the rage inside. Perhaps the perimeter of the warehouse is guarded by "battlelions," rather than junkyard dogs. But I think much of what I've written about the city, both in its obliquity and slightly hallucinatory intensity, reflects that complex layering of experience.

Speaking of hallucinations, I remember visiting my brothers in Boston when I was in my middle twenties and being astonished at the run-down glamour around Beacon Street and the Charles Street Jail. My older brother worked in a sandwich shop called The Yellow Submarine, and in those days it was a clearing house for all sorts of drugs. My brothers and I dropped acid on the night of the Perseids and stayed up all night walking along the river, then sitting on the roof of their apartment building on Hemenway Street and watching the meteors fall until dawn. Wordsworth's sonnet about the view from Westminster Bridge captures that night:

"[. . .] silent, bare/Ships, towers, domes, theaters, and temples lie/Open unto the fields, and to the sky; [. . .]/The river glideth at his own sweet will . . ." Of course, LSD made the whole thing more raucous and raunchy, but the reflection of the MIT dome in the Charles made the sweetness of that moment part of the "sweet will" that drugs and poetry could on occasion grant you.

Of course the city has less benign aspects. For many years in Cambridge, I lived across the street from public housing on Sherman Street in North Cambridge. And now, in Brooklyn, I live across the street from the Gowanus Houses, one of the larger public housing complexes in New York. Both of these neighborhoods have gone through cycles of slump and gentrification. The income disparity in my neighborhood in Brooklyn is huge and seems to be getting worse, partly because of the Clinton welfare bill and Bush's Reagan-like policies. So poverty on the street is common, though it doesn't feel right to call it poverty, either. I guess I want to take people one at a time—and to call someone "poor" without taking the time or having the opportunity to know what their life feels like to them, seems presumptuous.

The limit of what you can and can't know about other people becomes more and more a preoccupation as I get older. It seems like the basis of an ethical understanding for how language can make the world more present, but without presuming to know more than you really do: I remember a man named Bill who used to spread out a blanket and put on it all kinds of odds and ends: children's clothes, rings and necklaces, old doorknobs, waterlogged magazines, even a plush teddy bear with one eye hanging from a thread, so that the bear had this hilariously evil, leering look on its face. Bill called his square of the sidewalk his "boutique." I don't know if he meant this ironically or said it with pride or if it was just slang. He was out on the sidewalk fairly regularly for most of a year and had a glad, welcoming air about him generally, though there were days when he'd look right through you. And then he disappeared. Now, I can't walk over that square of sidewalk without thinking of Bill sitting in the sun with his head uncovered or huddled under a tent of plastic if it was raining, the corners of the plastic weighed down by old books. I'd like to think that if Bill's presence is still there for me, that it must be there for others too. I want to imagine that every person who has ever walked on that particular square of sidewalk leaves an invisible trace of themselves until that bit of sidewalk is scribbled over with millions of such traces, including Bill and his boutique: I want my poems to be saturated with the presence of people and things in just that way. But I also want to be wary of saying too much, of betraying those traces by making them too tidy or reducing them to abstractions like "homeless" or "poor."

When I first came to Boston, I lived on a shoe string, partly because I was suffering from ill health and had no health insurance. For two years, I really didn't know how I would make ends meet from one month to the next and got by partially by receiving fuel assistance. And then after that, there were periods up into my late thirties when I've been extremely hard up, mainly because of medical expenses. And this taught me how lucky I am to be a poet because all you really need is paper and a pencil. But it also taught me the sort of scared, harried, helpless dread you feel when you have to choose buying food over getting a haircut, or worrying about whether you can pay your rent and utilities or buy a book. Obviously, this has nothing to do with real poverty, but it does color your way of thinking about the city: you look at certain neighborhoods as talismanic of class, of your own class aspirations—and that kind of looking tends to make you focus on details, which is good discipline for writing poems: is the house run-down or kept up? Are the porches in good shape? What would it be like to live in that bedroom under that tree on this street?

And by the same token, I tend to take the city one person at a time, like Bill and his boutique, which seems to me a very useful exercise for a poet—I look at faces and bodies with a lot of concentration, and I tend to associate faces and bodies with the way the brickwork looks behind them, with the kind of windows I see those faces looking out of. Human bodies and the material body of the city link up in the way I look at the street, and I suppose that in my poems this can give the city a feeling of the phantasmal, though the phantasmal in my case is more often due to the effect of trying to be hyperreal. Of course, I can see the city as a kind of phantasmagoria of architecture, though I can't sustain that state of mind for very long. In Boston, it's easier to experience the architecture in that way because of the centrality of the river and the way it reflects the city skyline. But in New York, where the scale is so much larger, and the buildings dwarf you, the architecture is fairly resistant to abstraction—at least for me. I suppose that's because the grid of New York is already representative of an abstraction in its pervasive geometry of rectangle, square, circle. For some reason, those ideal shapes insist on themselves, and tend not to lead me beyond them into some other realm. And that also seems to me like a worthwhile way of thinking about poems: traditionally, poetry is supposed to transport you beyond the world, but I think virtual reality and simulacra are so ubiquitous that perhaps it's more of a challenge, and transporting in ways that are based in our fledgling understanding of ecology, to stay grounded and look at things at eye level.

This resistance to abstraction is made all the stronger by the fact that New York is really a series of quite distinct neighborhoods, and so in that way the scale of the city is more intimate than Boston, simply because Boston feels like a series of towns that grew togther. But you get to know a neighborhood—as opposed to a town—street by street, block by block. During the crack years in New York, which are over, for now at least, the gangs and crack cowboys made me much more wary and alert to my surroundings. Nothing like fear to engrave a scene in your mind: I once saw two guys with knives, standing on First Avenue and Sixth Street in the middle of the afternoon, robbing one person after another as they walked by. You feel vulnerable, seeing something like that, and you become hyperaware of who is walking behind you, how much light there is, what you would do if you're attacked. Then street smarts, having a sense of realistic danger, knowing where people hang out and when, become important: and so you focus on your square of the sidewalk, your angle to the corner, the speed of the footsteps behind you. And so when writing about the city, I tend to start with the literal, do something of a linguistic space walk, then return to the literal: though the space walk is always dependent on the street. Right now, my neighborhood in Brooklyn feels safe—but I'm alert, and that alertness keeps me focussed on details, careful observation of who is standing next to what building when. And that habit of attention carries over into my work.

Perhaps part of what I'm talking about in my experience of the city is how fear keeps you focussed on the streets that can be both sources of pleasure and danger. But fear of what the world might do to you is simply another manifestation of my prime instructor, one we all share, though some learn their lessons earlier than others: the fear of mortality. In my case, I've had a blood disease since I was twenty-five. The mean survival rate is ten years after diagnosis, so I've been lucky. But I'm conscious of the fact, and have been for many years, of the kind of pressure that might come if you were convinced that today was your last day: now what are you going to say. Of course, the standard response is that you sit down and play a game of chess or go outside and pick tomatoes; that there's something banal about thinking you'd do anything different from what you'd do ordinarily. But for me it's an interesting paradox, sitting comfortably at the desk, not suffering in the least, while at the same time feeling the mental pressure of that last day hovering just out of sight. I think this is why I love Proust: he spends 2,000 pages complaining that he can't write the great work, yet all the while you're turning the pages that belie his complaint and, in fact, comprise the great work. And then in the final volume of *Remembrance of Things Past,* after having found literature a poor reason to write anything, he discovers a reason to write: to try to reveal to the people around him, whom he's known intimately, the truth about their lives—even though it's a truth that they are likely not to want to read. I don't think he means unsavory revelations, though there are plenty: rather the texture of those lives, the essence of them. And in poetry this can be done in a very un-Proustian, un-autobiographical fashion, the indirection of Stevens, for example, in "To the One of Fictive Music," in which you can read a heavily disguised allegory about the nature of Stevens's marriage while at the same time focussing on the poem as an exploration of the muse as interior paramour. I would also say that the experience of illness and of periods of invalidism create a sense of alienation from the world of the healthy; and often alienation can be an index of originality. Elizabeth Bishop speaks of how greatly prized originality is in a poet's work, but that nobody ever talks about the depth of alienation that is part of that originality.

And of course alienation is a product of particular experiences: it just doesn't happen to you, as if the universe itself were an alienation machine. When I first got ill though, it was hard not to think that the universe had it in for me. And my state of mind probably wasn't helped by the fact that I'd been immersing myself in Dante: during my first extended stay in a hospital cancer ward, I couldn't help but associate the seventh floor—the top floor, as it turned out—with the architecture of Hell, since that was where the cancer patients were assigned. I had a sense of joining the company of the elect, a kind of inverse Inferno in which the sicker you are the higher up you are. Naturally, the psychic pressure that builds during an experience like that carries back into your work. In writing a poem, there are infinite numbers of details to choose from: and I imagine that some of the poems I've written represent, in a way that is as oblique as Stevens and certainly open to fictional impulses, a momentary balancing of that psychic pressure against the weight of less extreme experience, something domestic, say, that seems to have nothing to do with anticipating your own death. In other words, it's an important part of artistic conscience to try to counter alienation with formal intelligence and decorum so that alienation doesn't overdetermine the scope and range of what you're capable of responding to in your poems.

Thom Gunn is a poet whose work embodies this dynamic between alienation and ordinary experience. In *The Man with Night Sweats,* you never feel a generic response to the lives and deaths of the men he writes about. AIDS is an important aspect of the poem, but doesn't limit the poem or make special claims on our sympathies simply because of the subject matter: *Oh no, here comes another AIDS poem.* Everybody has an individual death, and there's a justice and clarity about the terms of each death, so that each of the elegies captures something essential about the person. The thing I'm impressed by most is how the forms Gunn uses, often rhymed couplets or quatrains, establish a distance from the subject, yet permit extraordinary self-revelation. When you're dealing with material that's so emotionally charged, a form that makes rigorous demands on you is a way of chastening the desire to be operatic. And I don't mean simply traditional forms. Robert Duncan's great poem about the microbes in his body that will eventually kill him, "In Blood's Domaine," uses the page to create a highly organized field that is nonetheless open to improvisatory elements. And if illness has taught me anything, it's how improvisatory, makeshift, and homemade the world can feel, particularly if you yourself are experiencing fluctuations in health, the good and bad days that force you, as an invalid, to keep adjusting and re-adjusting your expectations about survival, how much time you have left before you finally die.

But this constant need to adjust and re-adjust means that your nature is forced to stay open to new possibilities: and this openness has carried over into my choices about the kind of poetry I most want to write. To return to Thom Gunn's example, he once said in an interview that you should lay as broad a foundation as you can, which for him meant reading and falling in love with writing radically different from his own, as is evidenced by his affection for Robert Duncan, Allen Ginsberg, and Mina Loy. He said it would be a shame to be writing the same kind of poem at fifty as you were writing at twenty or twenty-five. Perhaps in the spirit of this, I've always felt to the side of the schools that were prevalent. I was interested in a sort of highly wrought, formal poem when Deep Image was the period style. Then when New Formalism came along, I was far too interested in the sort of highly cadenced free verse of Basil Bunting to fit with that program. I want to be the kind of writer who can draw on Ginsberg and Merrill, Duncan and Gunn, Mina Loy and Elinor Wylie, Robert Lowell and John Ashbery. Or my grandmother, for that matter, who was the least literary of people, but a good storyteller. One of her more outrageous tales had to do with a bunch of rattlesnakes that crept into a milk tank and got so hot they filled the tank up with snake sweat and drowned.

The literary landscape is littered with various "isms": I can even imagine the critic who would label my grandmother's story as being in the vanguard of "herpetologicalism." But if I'm to be honest, the debate as to whether poetry should be referential or nonreferential, whether to be a Constructivist or an Expressivist, while an interesting one, isn't very helpful when I sit down to write. I believe with Randall Jarrell that poets are rather helpless, that their subjects and orientations toward language choose them: will has never seemed a substitute for imagination, and without imagination you have nothing. And maybe because this shows in me a kind of skepticism about too conscious a sense of knowing what I'm doing, it surprises me when poets and critics like to set up one poet against another, and talk about these poets with immense sophistication and authority, but singularly lacking in the self-suspicion that there may be more things in heaven and earth than their philosophy allows for. Underneath these pronouncements lies the anxiety of not knowing if what you are doing is of value. All of us want to feel that the future will be hospitable to what we make, and all of us fear that it won't be.

Best not to know too much all about it. I've often suspected that most of us have had all the "big" ideas we're going to have by the time we're in our twenties, and that our lives are spent working out those ideas with ever greater complexity. Again, I choose not to look too closely at those ideas, and when someone tells me what they think they are, I thank them, and promptly try to forget everything they said.

The end of his talk feels jarringly abrupt. The applause is what it is, and as he nods in recognition of the crowd, he backs away, and almost bumps into a pedestal on which some Day of the Dead skeletons are playing cards and whooping it up in a cantina. He reflects that the talk was too personal, and certainly inappropriate to the occasion. But after this many years at the game, such doubts are so reflexive that he shrugs them off as the usual hangover of self-loathing after having made himself the object of public display. The illusion is that he has revealed himself, but he feels more opaque to himself than ever. Well, what of it? Wasn't that the consequence of his final statement? "Know thyself" has always seemed a bit of a cheat. Which self and at what moment and in what way? And now a friend of his is telling a story about how he can't sleep at night, until he went to a sleep lab, where they wired him up and monitored him all night long. When they woke him up, he said that he'd had a very good night, at least for him. When the technician looked dubious, he kept repeating that really, he'd slept as soundly as he ever has. And then the technician said, "Did you know that in the 6 hours we monitored you, you woke up 130 times?"

Syringe Dreams: On "In the Park"

~

I have syringe dreams. The most vivid one is of a syringe sparkling in the middle of a Formica tabletop that extends into infinity in every direction. The dream is utterly silent, still—except for the invisible force field that pulsates around the syringe: a long plunger and narrow ampule; a hair-thin steel spike; a nearly invisible sharp point. The syringe seems sentient, and radiates an almost paranoiac intensity.

I remember the needle—I was ten years old—that first brought me knowledge of morphine. I was in the hospital for a minor operation on one of my sinus cavities. Already I was well acquainted with syringes: as an asthmatic child, from the time I was six years old I received shots twice a week from Dr. Ball. My mother tells me that I hid under a chair and wept from fear the first few times I had those shots. To this day I clearly remember the half-stifled panic I always felt on the mornings I had to face Dr. Ball—a tolerant, bemused man who never lost his patience with me, his bald head burnished by the neon.

But the needle that brings me morphine feels different from Dr. Ball's syringe. There is infinitely more ceremony around this particular injection. Unlike my routine of asthma shots, in which I ride my bike to and from the doctor's office, I'm in a hospital bed attended by, not only a doctor, but his nurse. The doctor himself loftily directs the nurse as she rolls up the sleeve of my hospital johnny and guides the needle into my vein (spade vein, I'll later learn to call it). My mother stands beside me, holding my other hand, and I feel important in a strangely fraudulent way—similar to the way I feel now when I try to work up the solemnity to pray. The colorless liquid is injected into my bloodstream. I can feel the morphine spreading, with a delicious warmth, up my arm until it hits me in the back of the brain. Then I'm adrift, calm, subsumed into the drug's high.

Five years later, for complex personal reasons, I find myself seeking out needles and the sensations they can bring. To say that I've learned from needles is an understatement. Needles travel across all lines and barriers, social, ethical, metaphysical. In pursuit of what needles bring, you can end up scrounging in friends' medicine cabinets, or trying to steal and fence near worthless junk. I have also seen needles make people so generous with drugs and money that they dole it out as freely and hilariously as if they were Lords of Misrule. Some of what I've learned about myself from needles has made me ruefully unhappy; but needles have also revealed to me qualities that I most value in myself and others: an openness to experience, a considered attraction to risk.

When I first began to write "In the Park," I wrote it from the outside: I'd seen a young man on a bench in Tompkins Square Park in New York City's lower east side (at that time nicknamed "Needle Park") who was high on heroin and into a heavy nod: Mohawk haircut dyed red and green, body piercings (nose and ears), heavy black Army surplus boots, camouflage cutoffs, and a black T-shirt that featured some band's world tour. The bench he was seated on seemed weirdly insubstantial, as if it were a cloud that kept shifting as he shifted the position of his body. He was trying to sit upright—that's how it looked to me—but his body was so rubbery he kept sliding sideways down the back of the bench until he would list at a forty-five-degree angle, bobbing a little, almost like a boat about to sink. I pitied him; then felt paternal concern; then recoiled on myself when I admitted that both these feelings were affectation. In fact, they disguised disgust, and my disgust disguised fear. So I went to the opposite extreme and tried to identify with him: Wasn't he like me at his age, curious, eager for adventure and risk?

Then I tried to clear my mind of all these associations and see him as objectively as I could. What I saw was a fourteen- or fifteen-year-old boy with a half-leering, absorbed look of joy on his face, his lips breaking into little goofy grins of pleasure, his eyes rolling up into their sockets like someone about to have a fit. There was nothing remotely threatening about him—he was, if anything, the most vulnerable person in the park at that moment, certainly incapable of protecting himself from muggers or the police.

As I said before, I tried to write "In the Park" from the outside, focussing on this boy as the catalyst for all the language I would need to render the experience of watching him. The poem stuck in physical description—accurate enough—but not very charged emotionally. Then I decided to make the whole thing rhyme—terza rima, because it's hard, and because I had the inkling that there was something of the Divine Comedy in the experience: hell=scoring; purgatory=shooting up; heaven=the high. A pilgrim (myself) meets an exemplar (the boy) of certain spiritual and ethical qualities. Lastly, the park itself seemed the geographical equivalent of Dante's dark wood.

I don't want to be too schematic here. These associations were largely in the back of my mind. What I most concentrated on was the story the poem told. It wasn't until I brought my own experience of needles to bear by writing myself as a teenage drug user into the poem while writing the boy out, that the poem found its shape. And yet I didn't eliminate the boy entirely. He persists in vestiges of the physical description concerned with how I envision myself when high. Once I got the story, I dispensed with some of the rhymes, or buried them in the middle of lines, in order to get rid of padding and to make the diction more colloquial. Yet I kept the tercets as an homage to the scaffolding of the terza rima. In all, working at it on and off, the poem took me almost two years to finish.

It's now been more than twenty years since I last did heroin. Hero, horse, smack, the slang sounds pretty dated now. Intravenous drugs were never a specialty of mine—I did them as part of my general curiosity about drugs. I have friends who went much more deeply into them, to the point of serious addiction. Two of those friends died, one ended in jail. It's a sad fact that I've lost track of all the people I did drugs with in my teens. Perhaps I needed to for my own self-preservation; or perhaps the unique affection that we bore one another (and which I still feel) was so entangled with the drugs that once I tapered off my drug use and more or less stopped, our attachments to one another were necessarily weakened.

When I wrote "In the Park," I felt in contact again with the spirit of my drug buddies. Though the poem is perhaps more minatory than celebratory, the process of writing it allowed me, however slightly, to recover part of the inner richness of our affection. That's why I think of the poem, whatever else it may be, as a love poem.

Eddie, Jack, Wild Bill, myself at fifteen—it's tempting to think that any one of us could have been sitting alongside that boy I saw in Tompkins Square Park. It makes me ashamed to admit that I was repelled by him, that I initially tried to distance myself from him by blanketing him in pity and concern, and then romanticized him by making him my alter ego. What did I know of him except his physical appearance? And of course it's impossible to know if Eddie, Jack, Wild Bill, and Tom the Bomb would have had anything in common with that teenager except for heroin.

Time isn't as malleable as the imagination, and empathy, too, has its limits. With the gulf of thirty years between us, perhaps it's sentimental to imagine me and my pals sharing that bench with him. The meaning of drugs and drug use are different for De Quincey, the high Romantic opium eater, for Tom Sleigh, the hippie experimenter, and for that punked-out boy. Only if I'd risked speaking to him, of opening myself to his world, could I have entered, at least partially, into what he was truly thinking and feeling. But in his condition, nodding out on the bench, what at that moment could he have told me?

In the Park

Tourniquet tight, spade vein rising, I must have done it
Three or four times before I realized it was me easing the needle
Into my vein. My friends crouched, waiting for their turn,

Our eyes fixed on the plunger slowly pressing down.
It was as close as I'd ever felt to anyone, those moments
We huddled in the bushes: The earth's acid stinks

Rose corrosive in our nostrils, our craving
To see how hard how fast the high would hit
Making us smile into each other's eyes and ask,

Hey, dude, are you getting killed?
—And then we'd throw back our heads to laugh and laugh,
Oblivious to the cops or the passersby who glance

Then glance away, swerving to avoid
That glowing knot of energy . . .
Why didn't I O.D. or end in rags

Or do time like my dealer friends?
By summer's end, stoned on my bench as smashed glass
Gleams at my feet, the way my head lolls back or pitches

Forward to nod and nod, my loosened limbs
That shiver and twitch while my flesh drifts like fog,
Are irrelevancies: All I see are their eyes

Parleying with risk, dense with desire . . . our shared euphoria
As that fuse of warmth in each one's veins
Explodes pleasantly pulsing in the brain,

Lifting and dissolving us, embraced by the drug's
Slow downward drag, our shoulders shrugging in a drowse . . .
How old was I, fifteen, sixteen? Like a ghost

Wrapped in mist I'd drift home late, and wait for the lights
To go out. Then I'd glide past my parents' door,
The furniture swirling round me in the dark,

And lie down in bed in the silence piling
Stone on stone . . . How high that wall had grown
Since I'd turned thirteen: The adult world (and wasn't I

Part of it, swinging a pick for a construction crew?)
Returned my stone-eyed, stonefaced stare:
How different from the park where

We slapped each other's hands and gauged to
The least grain the hit we'd share, blood brothers, soldiers
Of sensation. I'd hear bright whirling voices

Talking me to sleep, the park like an oasis
Glimmering through the dark . . . and then bannering faces
Like opposing flags arguing and arguing till dawn . . .

I'd wake leaden-eyed: Whose voices had I heard?
That wall so high it seemed impossible to scale,
We'd mumble "Good morning," "good-bye . . ." Almost the last time

That I shot up my father caught me tying off
In the bathroom. I was so far gone I hadn't noticed
His routine searching of my clothes, my mother's frown

Egging him on. The shower I left running
Beat down dully as we wrestled for my fix, me groping
At his hand as he flushed it away, his frightened grin

Imploring me to stop. We peered at each other
Through the steam before our gazes numbly dropped,
Mist drifting round us in soft slow motion:

I'd made myself over, no part of me theirs,
But belonging to Jack, Eddie, Wild Bill—the risks
We incurred now flurrying up inside to scare me:

Trembling like my father, our eyes welling with shock,
I saw myself stripped of my rebel's bravado,
My needle a prop, yet so perilously real

That what happens next seems almost laughable:
"This is hard drugs," shouts my father. "You shouldn't
Steal stuff from my pockets," I shout back.

And then a shamefaced, fidgeting silence
Which he breaks by touching me gently on the shoulder,
Touching me, I realize now, as if I were still

His child, and his touch could fix what is unfixable . . .
Fists clenched, cursing at the waste,
I muscled past him and ran to the park:

Where could I cop, how much hero did I need
To buy to sell to make back what I'd lost?
. . . That self I was which only in adventure

Could feel itself tested and so taste joy
(And wasn't it part sexual, that hunger to get high,
Nerve after nerve roused to pleasure?) haunts my eyes

When I see some boy trashed on a bench like mine:
That jargon's edginess, "trashed" "killed" . . .
What happened to Jack, Eddie, Wild Bill? Or the glamor

Of my works tarnishing in the rot of crumbled leaves?
And that boy I was, if I could see him now . . .
—He looks so young, as if he were my son

Sitting in the park, his face floating
In the neon dark as he scratches lazily
With a wobbly forefinger his stubbled cheek

And temple. Now the blood-webbed whites of his eyes
Roll up, his lips sag open, the syllables dragging across
His tongue dragging in my ears: *Dude, want to get killed?*

SPACEY ROOMS: A Note on Translating "Lamentation on Ur"

~

My interest in translating began when I worked as an anthropological assistant for Gertrude Blom in San Cristobal de las Casas, the capital of Chiapas, the southernmost state of Mexico. I was asked to translate field notes and museum text into English, and I also led tours in Spanish and English through a makeshift museum that displayed knee-length tunics made of bark, wooden bows that somewhat resembled the English long bow, arrows tipped with green and blue and red parrot feathers, cups and bowls fashioned out of mahogany or clay, and other domestic flotsam and jetsam of the Lacandones—a group of isolated Mayan Indians most like the ancient Maya in customs and language, who live in the rain forest in the Usumacinta river valley between Chiapas and Guatemala.

These disparate objects, wrenched out of their uses from the hands of their makers, had a sort of melancholy about them. Beautiful as objects, but without the rain forest and the Lacandones to give them a sense of purpose or belonging, they were like the objects in Elizabeth Bishop's poem about Robinson Crusoe come home to England, Crusoe still haunted by the island where he was marooned. A knife that on the island of Crusoe's exile "reeked of meaning, like a crucifix," devolved into "uninteresting lumber" once the island and its attendant spiritual and material difficulties, its soul-making strangenesses, were left behind.

This sense of alienation from a world that once was home, for better and worse, and is now a source of estrangement, seems to be part of the reason I'm drawn to translation. If we think of ourselves as language islands in an archipelago that is all the languages of the world, and of the sea surrounding us as the universal drive toward language—what certain linguists call "deep structure"—then translation is the attempt to experience that structure through the alienating medium, the at first incomprehensible strangeness, of another tongue. And since I've done translations from Greek, Latin, and ancient Sumerian via a French translation, I'm sometimes persuaded that what we're also doing as translators is trying to write the Ur language that bound us all together before the tower of Babel collapsed—the moment before each of us became our own island, when language was seamless, originary.

Another way to put it is to simply talk about translators' temperaments: if you're the kind of translator who tends to see unity in multitude, then you belive that translation is an exploration of the genius of that originary language. You would agree with Walter Benjamin that bad translation is an attempt to convey "information"—Benjamin's scorn for the thought that translation is to render transparent one language via another. As he said, "No poem is meant for its reader." Instead, once you've recorded the surface content, what you're left with is the untranslatable element—the essence in the original which the translation's language points to as a supreme language; a supreme language, of course, that the translation points to as a possibility, and not a realizable fact. If this is your orientation, then you will paradoxically want your translation's language to be as deeply affected by the original as possible, as a way of getting closer to that Ur-language. You may adopt the literalness of approach, say, of Hölderlin in trying to embody Sophocles in German by making German come up with syntactic equivalents for Greek syntax.

Or it could be that you have the kind of temperament that believes the originary language has been shattered beyond repair, and so translation is an exploration of the genius of the translator's language and not the original's. To say it more precisely, translation becomes the process of taking the genius of the original and putting parallel to it the genius of the translator's language—parallel because the two are always separate and never equivalent; parallel, because they admit that there can be no definitive intersection between the original and the translation—in other words, the original and the translation are inextricable from their local, historical contexts and should remain that way.

In that case, you will say with Ezra Pound that his translation of "Homage to Sextus Propertius"—note that Pound says "Homage," as if to indicate that Propertius is more a persona for Pound to play with than an ancient poet to reproduce—is more faithful to his Latin original than Edward Fitzgerald's "Rubáiyát of Omar Khayyám." Of course, this doesn't mean that Pound's translation is faithful, if by faithful you mean an interlinear word-by-word equivalent. In fact, Pound's Propertius is wildly different than Propertius in the original. Propertius is a rather solemn, desperate, on-the-edge loverboy, while Pound's Propertius is an inadvertent comedian, cheerfully promiscuous in his heterogenous mixture of deliberate anachronisms, skewed syntax, and clashing dictions. Lines in which "devirginated young ladies" are "doing homage to my palaver" even though "My cellar does not date from Numa Pompilius, /Nor bristle with wine jars,/Nor is it equipped with a frigidaire patent" is the kind of fractured, parodic English that seems to want to out-British the British in pretentious, imperial ponderousness, but keeps tripping over its own tongue: it's as if the author didn't know English well enough to distinguish between written officialese and everyday slang. The result reminds me of the Greek *pension* owner trawling for guests who once gave me his card just after I'd gotten off a Greek ferry at 2 a.m. Leaping out of a jeep, he pressed his card into my hand. I read his name in bold letters—**IACOVOS**—and centered underneath his name the encouraging announcement: SPACEY ROOMS. I immediately swung my duffel bag into the back of his jeep, certain this was my kind of place.

And so if you imagine a British classicist as being an intellectual wannabe to the "glory that was Greece and Rome," one who would abhor the howler of mistaking SPACEY for SPACIOUS; and if you're an upstart American like Pound who wants to satirize that wannabe's imperial pretentions; then what better way to do it than to write in an English that mocks the expertise of the wannabe, that points out to the wannabe that he will never wear a toga, that far from being an imperial Roman he is only an English don. And a colonized English don at that, still bowing and scraping to his long dead Roman overlords. Nothing is more infuriating to a thoroughly colonized soul than the spectacle of another colonial (a colonial times three in Pound's case—an American striving to make his way in England by translating an Imperial-era Roman poet) who has only made it partway there—which may be why English classicists of Pound's time reviled his "Homage." And so Pound's Propertius writes a bizarre, comic, and at times wonderfully eloquent English that is a send-up of the classicist's professional expertise and pride, his fetish for "accuracy." And since in Pound's hands the content of the poem is a relentless mock of British imperialism via ancient Rome, the idiom Pound deploys is a fiercely funny indictment of the imperialist's attempt to spread not only his power, but his culture as well. Ironically enough, when Julius Caesar crossed the Thames in 54 BCE, his accounts of his invasions of barbarian nations were fated to serve as inspiration to Victorian-era public school boys who would later be posted all over the world in the British Empire's service. And so Pound's mockery of the *pax Britannica* via his mockery of the *pax Romana* shows how translation can be a political gesture, and how the idiom itself can be a form of "up yours."

Pound's strategy of writing English as if it were a foreign language finds a strange counterpart in the story a friend recently told me. Charlotte Black Elk, the great-granddaughter of Black Elk, the Lakota whose oral testimony makes up the text of *Black Elk Speaks,* has been translating John Neihardt's English translation back into Lakota and then back into English. This is because there is no truly adequate written notation for Lakota, since historically it exists primarily as an oral language. And so Black Elk's words exist only in Neihardt's English translation—which in any case is the translation of a translation of a translation. Black Elk's son, Ben, translated Black Elk's words orally into English, while Neihardt's daughter took notes. And from his daughter's notes, Neihardt produced *Black Elk Speaks.* Neither Neihardt or his daughter spoke Lakota, so perhaps a more accurate title would have been *Black Elk Through His Son Ben's Oral Translation Speaks to John Neihardt's Daughter Who Takes Notes and Then Gives Her Notes to Her Father Who Writes Black Elk's Words Down in the Way That He Thinks a Lakota Like Black Elk Ought to Speak.* However, since Black Elk's great-granddaughter is fluent in both Lakota and English, she compares Neihardt's English translation to her own knowledge of Lakota speech and renders back into written English what she feels is a more accurate version of what her great-grandfather might actually have said. Here, the relation between the written and the spoken takes on a political dimension that is as anti-colonial in nature as Pound's mauling of Propertius. But whereas Pound's departure point is to send up Propertius by writing a wildly unliteral "homage," Black Elk's great-granddaughter is committed to the opposite goal: accurate transmission of Black Elk's spoken words.

Faithful or promiscuous, the translator is always translating into a cultural context that is different than the context of the original, as Pound's "Propertius" and Black Elk's great-granddaughter's version of Black Elk's words makes clear. I've touched on the possibilities for subtle political action that a canny understanding of that context can make possible. But there are also attendant dangers in playing fast and loose with context. This is profoundly the case with Pound's translation of Chinese poems called "Cathay"—though it would be more accurate, as anyone who has read Hugh Kenner's chapter on "Cathay" in *The Pound Era* will agree, to call this sequence of poems the invention of Chinese poetry in English. Who could have imagined that a trot which renders the Chinese characters in the first stanza of "Lament of the Frontier Guard," by Rihaku (Li T'ai Po), as:

North barbarian (regions around) gate much wind sand

Serene lonely finally, till now end old

tree fall autumn grass yellow

ascend high lookout barbarous prisoner (enemies' force)

desolate castle sky, vacant large desert

Frontier village not left wall

would come out sounding like this:

> By the North gate, the wind blows full of sand,
> Lonely from the beginning of time until now!
> Trees fall, the grass goes yellow with autumn.
> I climb the towers and towers
> to watch out the barbarous land:
> Desolate castle, the sky, the wide desert.
> There is no wall left to this village.

As a sequence, the poems depict intimate scenes of domestic life contrasted with an ill-defined, but omnipresent threat of war: an atmosphere quite similar to our own terrorist-obsessed moment. What is interesting about these poems is how Pound's depiction of warfare makes it difficult to tell which side is which: the viewpoint is always the underdog's, never the victor's. In fact, the poems were published as a not-so-oblique commentary on World War I militarism, in which Pound's sympathies lie with the common soldier who is stumbling through mud, gas, and barbwire before being machine-gunned or sniped or blown to bits by grenade or stickbomb, or by badly aimed barrages of both friendly and enemy shell fire.

That's one way of looking at the context that surrounded the publication of "Cathay." Another way of looking at "Cathay" is suggested by the archaism of a title like "Cathay": Chinoiserie, or exoticism. Just what Pound's translations have to do with their ancient classical Chinese originals is an interesting problem for a much savvier linguist than I will ever be. But the danger I'm pointing to is of a kind of consumerist eclecticism, in which all literary traditions are easily available to us through the medium of translation.

This eclecticism presumes that effects in one language are always available in another: if you want to write like the Peruvian poet, César Vallejo, in English, just start with a dash of surrealist description, add an account of being beaten by a rope, stir in some metaphysical questioning, *et voilà:* a Deep Image poem of the 1970s. Of course, a good poem could be written by following this recipe, but what I'm getting at is the relation between a poem written in one tradition and exported into another. Should the translator strive to make the original look a little weird out of its own cultural context? That would be Benjamin's position. But Pound's beautiful rendering of "Cathay" makes his particular idiom for this sequence ring so deep in the inner ear that it's become a kind of a norm, almost a convention, for how all Chinese poetry ought to sound in English.

In other words, Pound's "Cathay" translations tend to supplant the original, at least in a monoglot culture like our own. This sequence of ancient Chinese poems that Pound translated have become the naturalized sound of Chinese poetry in English. Black Elk's spirit would recognize the irony here of having your translator supplant you as the "original." Perhaps the most paradoxical case of "the original" as authentic and authoritative is the Japanese poet who writes poems in the voice of a survivor who suffered through the atomic bomb dropped on Hiroshima. These poems, when they were published in the *American Poetry Review* in 1996, had a distinctly Poundian cast to their idiom, as if the poet were rewriting "Cathay" in a World War II context, though the poems were supposed to have been written in Japanese. Here are three lines from Araki Yasusada's notebooks:

iris moon sheaths
scubadivers chrysanthemums also
deer inlets dream . . .

Of course, the fragmented phrases resemble Pound's trot before Pound rendered them into English syntax. Was this a Japanese poet whose English reading had included Pound's "Cathay," and thus influenced how he wrote in Japanese? Of course, it turns out that the poems were written in English by an American, identity unknown, though the smart money is on a poet in the Midwest born after World War II. In other words, the poems were English originals passed off as translations, the idiom echoing Pound's idiom in "Cathay," since that's how all things originating from the Far East ought to sound. The poems were later denounced by the *American Poetry Review's* editors and declared a hoax—though it should surprise no one that the poems had their defenders: If *APR* published them, why shouldn't they be valued as poems in their own right? Why get hung up on questions of "authenticity" and "authorship" if the poems passed editorial muster? This incident illustrates, in spades, the linguistic and cultural complexities of what we do when we set out to translate.

When I look at my own translations, I find parallels to certain problems and opportunities in Pound's procedures in translating "Homage to Sextus Propertius" and "Cathay." Back in 1990, less than a year before the first Gulf War, I was in Paris at the Louvre, looking at the Mesopotamian antiquities, Assyrian and Sumerian: immense doorposts and ornamented gates several thousand years old. I poked among the vitrines and came across a cuneiform tablet transliterated into French. It was about the destruction of the ancient city of Ur, a city I knew nothing about, and which I'd always assumed was simply legendary. I was drawn to it for purely personal reasons, copied the French onto the back of an envelope, and had the vague idea of doing something with it in English. When I got back home, the envelope sat on my desk, lying dormant, while I was immersed in reading Horace's *Odes.* And then one day I picked up the envelope and began to do a translation of a Sumerian original in a French translation via a stanza cribbed from Horace's ancient Latin. I did my version of it in a heightened, but still colloquial English, and called it "Lamentation on Ur," hoping that the nineteenth-century formality of "lamentation" would give it the feeling of "antiquity." And then a few months later the first Gulf War broke out, and I discovered that Ur actually exists. In the former regime of Saddam Hussein, it lies next to an Iraqi airbase in southern Iraq near the Kuwaiti border. On the site is the remains of an ancient ziggurat, which was lightly bombed by an American bomber, perhaps because its terraced pyramidal shape looks like part of the adjoining airbase. Or perhaps because the Iraqi army placed on the ziggurat an old Russian MIG fighter jet, *sans* engine, in order to lure American bombs. Or perhaps because the "smart bomb" simply went astray. In any case, a translated poem that I'd carried over from one culture that flourished several thousand years ago, into the New World Order that was starting to consolidate in 1990, and which I'd undertaken without any particular political agenda in mind, but only because the poem seemed to speak of war and destruction and loss as being a generalized, inescapable condition, this translation had suddenly become a political poem—not at all my intent, but the result of events that overtook all of us and to which we now have to measure up to in more ways than translating and writing poems. But it ought to be acknowledged that the energies latent in this ancient text shows how translation can be a form of poetic making that both renews our sense of the destruction of Ur, even as the dead medium of the poem's original, cuneiform, suggests how tenacious and stalwart a force poetry can be in the face of Ur's loss. This clay tablet, in all its fragility, is a token of poetry's power to endure.

But that endurance isn't a static holding out, but a dynamic capacity to re-tool: the many removes that the poem went through—Sumerian to French to Latin to my English—seems to me emblematic of how translation as a process is a kind of triple-threat machine: it's at once an alienation machine because of the way the original language is subjected to the spell of radically different languages and cultural assumptions; a time machine, in that it transports us backwards to the destruction of Ur and forward to what may be a string of many "Gulf Wars"; and lastly, a projection machine, in that it shadows forth an image from one language, even a dead language, and gives that image a spectral life in our own troubled moment:

Lamentation on Ur

2000 B.C.

Like molten bronze and iron shed blood
    pools. Our country's dead
melt into the earth
    as grease melts in the sun, men whose
helmets now lie scattered, men annihilated

by the double-bladed axe. Heavy, beyond
    help, they lie still as a gazelle
exhausted in a trap,
    muzzle in the dust. In home
after home, empty doorways frame the absence

of mothers and fathers who vanished
    in the flames remorselessly
spreading claiming even
    frightened children who lay quiet
in their mother's arms, now borne into

oblivion, like swimmers swept out to sea
    by the surging current.
May the great barred gate
    of blackest night again swing shut
on silent hinges. Destroyed in its turn,

may this disaster too be torn out of mind.

To the Star Demons

~

Two images from my childhood: a vast white screen stretches horizon to horizon, and on it, a dinosaur fights with a caveman. The second is of a rocket ship, a plaque of heat and flame rippling out across the launchpad as the rocket lifts off in slow motion, and crawls up the sky until the first-stage booster flares out, separates and falls away, and the second-stage engine begins to fire. When I think of these two images, the caveman fighting with the dinosaur, and the Minuteman rocket taking off, by some ethereal chemistry they merge one into the other: the caveman and dinosaur fade into the rocket motor's white fire, and the white fire blanks out into the whiteness of a piece of paper—the piece of paper that I'm writing on. Hollywood's images of the diceyness of prehistoric life, and newsreel footage of rocket ships climbing the sky, are pure poetry for me.

Never mind that it's only Victor Mature showing off his pecs, which, by today's standards, could use some buffing up—and so what if it's Raquel Welch glamming around like a prehistoric Eve? That T rex looks like he means business, even if he is made of papier-mâché. And that other, more workaday image of a first-generation rocket booster that will become the Intercontinental Ballistic Missile (ICBM) that in turn will usher in the Cold War of nuclear detente—well, as a kind of dark joke, I see this as my family legacy, the underside, in fact, of that Hollywood poetry that first made me aware of the power of images. I still can't resist the sight of a rocket taking off, even though I know that the same technology can be used to power an ICBM.

The drive-in movie theater my family ran all during my childhood came to an end with the advent of television—at which point my father got a job on the ground floor of the space program. Although they were radically different ways to make a living, for me they seem continuous. My father's work eventually resulted in a kind of spectacle: the spectacle created by a movie projector that he ran from the projection booth; and the spectacle of the collective brain power, made manifest in a rocket booster, of the guys who worked in my father's "space jockey" division. What remained invisible to me as a child were the processes of abstract, technological thinking that made such spectacles possible.

But it seems important to me now to think about those processes as it relates to poetry. Technological thinking and poetic thinking—at least in the way that I understand them—have always seemed a little at odds. Technological thought has tended to result in a world that grows ever more virtual, a trend that is irreversible. While for me, one of the most important purposes of poetry is to preserve the texture of the world, to make language fight against its own abstract nature and become something as concrete and tangible as the paper it's written on. Also, poetic thinking is primarily concerned with the congruence between the thought and the form the thought takes, while the processes of technological thinking are often divorced from the consequences of the machines that are created. It's troubling to me that as a boy I never considered the results of my father's work in the space program. The teamwork and lack of ego that my father and his fellow engineers put into the development of rocket fuel and rocket motors eerily contrast with the end result of nuclear missiles hidden in bunkers and silos all over the world. So I'd like to explore some of those boyhood associations, and try to link them to the ways that I now feel poetry and the abstractions of technological thought may or may not intersect.

It's no exaggeration to say that the writing of poetry underpins my mental life. I mean that in the most literal way possible: I wake up with the by now unconscious assumption that poetry is going to happen someway, somehow, even if it's the kind that doesn't get written down: a quick perception, a sudden phrase, the registering of some detail. Perhaps some peculiarity in my hardwiring makes this almost inevitable, but the kind of poetry I've been able to write is full of texture: description, for me, is a kind of revelation, and Ezra Pound's idea of the "luminous particular" holds great appeal for me. I suppose that may be why I'm fairly suspicious of large-scale generalization, and why I sometimes find it hard to connect the sweeping claims made for and against computers, say, with the actual plastic box, lit screen, and invisible circuitry. Or perhaps this disconnect springs from my childhood sensitivity to the sheer physicality of things. "No ideas but in things," said William Carlos Williams. And that could have been the motto of my childhood. And yet Williams also says that the "imagination uses the phraseology of science." And when I think about my father's two jobs, I can see how vexed and contradictory my relationship to technology is. But before I speak of that relationship, I'd like to look at two instances of my first awareness of technology.

My first encounter happened when I was four or five years old. My feet pushed the treadles of a tricycle that lurched across our muddy yard, my sense of power over the gears and wheels, the silver handlebars and rubber grips, dovetailing in the thought, I'm a Texan. My pleasure in mastering this machine made me feel my body as an extension of the tricycle's steel. I was also dimly aware of feeling superior to the cat pouncing at the tricycle's wheels. Maybe it was a caveman's way of thinking, but my tricycle seemed like adequate compensation for my lack of fur and claws. And my naivete in thinking that size equalled superiority underscored the connections between my happiness, Texas as a metaphor for power, and my own physical sense of mastery whenever I turned the tricycle's handle bars. In a way, I had become a kind of abstraction to myself:

the tricycle and I became one thing, the machine subtly engrafted onto my sense of self. In my new, faintly sinister incarnation, I was flesh to the waist, all steel below.

The second important enounter with technology happened after we sold the drive-in theater, left Texas, and moved to a town high in the Rocky Mountains: I was fascinated by sprinklers—"rainbirds," as they were called, because the sprinkler heads had the look of a bird's head and beak. The spray they sent flying across the park's grass caught the sun and occasionally refracted into rainbows. The water would slice across a bronze statue dappled in bird lime. It stood next to a dilapidated tennis court, the concrete slab cracked from thaw and freeze and the occasional earthquake. The mechanical ratcheting of the sprinklers felt a little creepy. As opposed to my tricycle, the "thinginess" of them wasn't amenable to a child's fantasy life. And since I didn't know other kids, they made pretty lame playmates. I remember shouting at the rainbirds, calling them all kinds of insulting names, and once I kicked a sprinkler, which turned on me and soaked my T-shirt with a blast of spray. I tried to imagine what a rainbird would feel on being kicked, but even then I knew it was just make-believe. The sprinkler was so alien, so man-made—inert. I couldn't make my fantasies stick to the slick, wet steel. Of course, it was loneliness that kept me from connecting with my new environment. That, and the strangeness of a world stripped of private association, the kind I had in Texas and that would develop over time, until I felt that this new town was again home. But for the moment I experienced that special kind of inner poverty that Wallace Stevens called "a plain sense of things."

As for the park statue, I thought that maybe if you walked by it late at night it would come alive, but during the day, whenever I imagined it coming down off its plinth and talking, I was a little spooked. I used to ask it questions, about what I can't now remember. Of course, it never answered back, not even in make-believe. The statue was supposed to be a Mormon Prophet, Brigham Young. The seagull shit on its head—the shit of Utah's state bird—made it comically tormented: the bird lime had streaked into a long, comic-book tearstain under one eye. And it seemed as if the dour, visionary gaze was staring up into the neighbor girl's bedroom window. At any rate, it held aloof from me. And the more it resisted me, the more like a thing it became, until I more or less ignored it completely.

Now, when I think of this paradoxical seesawing between the statue's material presence and the prophet-cum-Peeping Tom it was supposed to represent, I'm puzzled: how alien the statue was in comparison to the giant images projected on the drive-in screen. Passing before the eye at twenty-four frames per second, these celluloid phantoms were far more real to me than the several tons of bronze up there on a concrete plinth. As I said, I suppose this had something to do with the familiarity of Texas. But it must also have been because the movie actors' voices came out of the speaker's grille. As I lay listening to them in the window-well of the old green Plymouth, not really watching the movie, I'd drift a little bit on the current of those voices before falling asleep. Far from being chimeras or indifferent like the statue, they seemed as concrete to me as the hand puppets I used to play with, talking for them, following improvised scripts as if I myself were an actor. I ventriloquized those puppets' voices in much the same way that the speaker seemed to: when I looked at the speaker, it was like a steel head, or a head in a helmet with the visor down. All the different voices of the actors on screen had been temporarily stored inside that head set up on a pole, so that the entire parking lot was full of these knight heads that could talk in men's, women's, and children's voices, and could also sound like cars, trains, wars, dinosaurs, anything you could imagine. The odd thing is, since my parents were off running the theater, these voices were like substitutes for consoling parental presences. I don't ever remember being frightened by any of the noises or dialogues or movie music that came out of those heads.

The statue's metal presence, on the other hand, had a weird, ramrod stiffness to it that reminded me of my mother telling me not to slouch around, but to stand up straight. So maybe my alienation from the statue was in part a reaction to my mother's admonition, and in part a heightened awareness of the living quality of human flesh that the walking, talking film images seemed more in possession of than the statue. Plus, the leap of abstraction between the images on screen and the way real people talk and act wasn't nearly so difficult as making the connection between the statue and a real person. The statue's bronze physicality was hard to animate. It seemed like its own thing, almost like another race of human being. I suppose you could say that the draping folds of its overcoat, its tarnished bronze finger weighed more heavily in my imagination than the fact that it was supposed to represent a Mormon prophet.

That I still think of the statue as a sort of alien being, details of anatomy and not an integrated body, indicates my failure to imbue the statue with either my own private meanings or to see its culturally determined ones. But to speak of the statue's meaning in this way assumes that the meaning of all artifacts must be rooted in human subjectivity and possess aesthetic or social utility. You could make the case that the statue existed in its own right, its quiddity expressed by the angling plane of the nose, the brow's perpendicular. Cleared of what Wallace Stevens called "our stubborn man-locked set," the statue takes its place with the drive-in's cash register, the glass cases of the snack bar, the movie projector and the speakers, the cars, the component parts of all these, along with all the other products of our technological civilization, to create with their human makers a vast field of interrelated, irreducible existences.

As I said earlier, my relationship to technology is vexed. And my affinity for poetry to make the world concrete perhaps accounts, in part, for why this field, in its very vastness, so troubles me. A phenomenologist like Heidegger, who seems infinitely at home with this field and the abstraction necessary to envision it, refers to it as "the Being of beings." Perhaps my early exposure to the movies has conditioned me to think of the world as a theater of individual fates and dramas. An abstraction such as "Being," which bears no trace of what Yeats called "the fury and mire of human veins," can result in ethical indifference to how best cope with that fury. Human passion as the starting point of philosophical inquiry couldn't be further from Heidegger's commitment to discovering a transpersonal basis for existence.

Would Heidegger have embraced National Socialism as readily as he did if he had not so arrogantly disdained philosophical works "written by men fishing in the troubled waters of 'values' and 'totalities'"? Surely a clearer sense of values and totalities would have made Heidegger ponder this affiliation more carefully. And I would say that his commitment to certain kinds of philosophical abstraction is not unrelated to a technocratic way of thinking that produces results, but takes no responsibility for the way those results are used. Think of the chemists at Tesch and Stabenow, a division of I. G. Farben, who developed the fumes of Zyklon B as a pesticide, and then supplied nineteen tons of it in 1942–43 to Auschwitz-Birkenau alone.

While I find it frightening that certain kinds of abstract thinking can gloss over the most horrific forms of suffering, I can see how a particular cast of mind would experience such tail-chasing formulations as "the Being of beings" or "the presence of what is present" as a form of liberation from our relentlessly utilitarian, technocratic web. But philosophers and poets play on different keyboards, though some of the notes may resonate the same. In my case "the presence of what is present" in our technological world finds itself mirrored most clearly in a poet's literalizing imagination.

Paradoxically enough, W. H. Auden transforms the traditional Eden—the original technology-free environment—into a local paradise made absolutely "present" by the poet's inclusion of industrial age machines numinous because of their association with

Auden's childhood: overshot waterwheels, beam engines, saddle-tank locomotives. On the same emotional axis, but at its polar extreme, lies Robert Lowell's evocation of infernal America: "yellow dinosaur steamshovels" gouging "their underworld garage"; "a commercial photograph" that "shows Hiroshima boiling// over a Mosler Safe, the 'Rock of Ages'"; "giant finned cars" whose "savage servility/ slides by on grease" evoke a fierce, no less concrete, negative of Auden's nostalgia for a less complex phase of technological development. What keeps both poets from easy platitudes—parsonic ones in Auden's case, fire-breathing ones in Lowell's—is their need to give a face to fleshless abstractions such as "Paradise" or "the evils of Capitalism." In their poems at least, both seem reluctant to imagine larger meanings entirely separate from personal associations. They are wary of mouthing post factum generalizations, what Saul Bellow once called "crisis chatter."

In his *Autobiography* Yeats disdains this kind of punditry, calling it "a machine, one can leave it to itself; unhelped it will force those present to exhaust the subject, the fool is as likely as the sage to speak the appropriate answer to any statement, and if an answer is forgotten somebody will go home miserable. You throw your money on the table and receive so much change . . ." Yeats sees a kind of automatism driving accepted social and intellectual forms, cant underwritten by the mechanical operations of logic. Yeats's attitude suggests why Heidegger was so deeply concerned to discriminate between technological utility and technology's essence, which he characterized as the ability to create, to plan and organize freely: the kind of logic that reduces a forest to so many board feet, or that views a horse as horsepower only, is incapable of wandering out of its own deep-worn ruts. Between the "presentness" of a horse or a forest, and the obvious uses to which they can be put, stretches an almost unbridgeable conceptual gulf. This failure to discriminate between "being" and "being used" not only debases technology's essence—it also devalues my tricycle, the drive-in movie screen, the rainbirds and the statue of the Mormon prophet, each an irreducible instance of the "presence of what is present." But since I'm partly a literalist, my mind tends to blank out before such a phrase. For me at least, it lacks the emotional and sensual immediacy, the "real world" concreteness of Auden's paradise or Lowell's hell.

My ambivalence toward certain forms of metaphysical abstraction (mere defensiveness against abstractions I can't grasp?—in Heidegger's terms "to grasp" an idea is to have an *a priori* assumption, not at all the same activity as thinking) drives me, as it drove Lowell and Auden, to give a unique face to the "beings in Being"—a counter-impulse to ham-handed Being automatically kneading myriad human actions and contemplations into one abstract, metaphysical lump. Perhaps my aversion to this kind of discourse also has as much to do with the portentous self-importance of its style, its neologisms and quasi-tautological, hieratic circling that at times seem dangerously close to kitsch: the U.S. Army recruiting jingle—"BE all that you can BE!"—possesses a certain Heideggerian flair.

But my main objection is how easily such language can divorce itself from horrific social realities, glossing over the effects of the atomic bomb, say, by calling it, as Heidegger did, "the grossest of all gross confirmations of the long-since-accomplished annihilation of the thing . . ."—a formulation that emphasizes the importance of its own terminology over the human beings incinerated by the bomb. Yet I also feel the need to resist the myth about the bomb as technological depravity, comparable to Auschwitz, perverse as Dr. Mengele's experiments; not because its effects aren't horrific, but because such a myth erases the individual workers who produced it—and I do mean workers, not the head scientists or military chiefs of staff. High in Alamagordo, among the hundreds of other classified workers who hadn't an inkling of what they were helping to create, was Mona Rowe, destined to become my great-aunt; so the development of the atomic bomb is for me as much a part of my family lore as one of the pivotal events in human history.

When Mona, a confirmed smoker who died of lung cancer, her last days spent one breath puffing on a cigarette, the next inhaling oxygen from the merciful *techne* of an oxygen mask, was in her twenties she served on the Manhattan Project—but only as a clerk filing parts of some unknown mechanism about which "Oppy" (so she called him) knew the whys and wherefores. She was taken by military intelligence to the top secret mountain fastness at Los Alamos so that not even her family knew her whereabouts. There she met a man in the storage warehouse, had an affair, became pregnant—and supposedly gave up the child for adoption (since no one else in my family has ever mentioned this cousin, I sometimes wonder if the child wasn't aborted—but this is the story as I recall hearing it). If it seems anticlimatic to focus on my aunt's story rather than the development of the bomb, consider how difficult the whole predicament must have been: Given the times, did she feel impelled in this fishbowl of classified information to keep her own predicament top secret? But because she lived in barracks, after a time it must have been impossible to keep her pregnancy to herself—how soon after she began to show did her fellow workers start to gossip?

And from a point of view less personal and more public, if the security officers noticed at all, how did they view this lapse from the straight and narrow? An indication of "loose morals"? A security risk? Or perhaps the war effort took such precedence in everybody's mind that no one paid much attention to this young woman's private troubles. In that case, given the strictness of her upbringing in a small farming town isolated in the Kansas prairie, she must have had some long nights in reaching her decision not to marry and give up the child.

But whatever the scenario, in thinking about my aunt's troubles I share with Lowell and Auden a sense of history that is public as well as private: provided you can find convincing links between the two (not as easy as it sounds), one doesn't have to be subservient to the other. The historic importance of the atomic bomb doesn't obliterate the personal importance of my aunt's dilemma, at least not for a poet. I see the atomic bomb and her private concerns in emblematic relation to the larger concerns of the Manhattan Project. This is the corollary to my attachment to a way of poetic thinking that makes the world concrete. The divorce between the conceiving of the atomic bomb, and its actual effects, illustrates the difference between what I've been calling poetic thought and this tendency of technological thought. By the same token, the kind of history that can tell my aunt's story and not lose sight of it in the billowing mushroom cloud, is a history that values not only the big picture, but the events of a single life. Again, I think of that perspective as a poetic one because of its focus on the texture and singularity of each person's experience. And in keeping with that singularity, my aunt's version of watching a bomb blast differs from the conventional wisdom. That the Manhattan Project was a sobering, but ultimately positive scientific accomplishment isn't at all what her story reveals.

Given protective goggles (or was it simply pieces of tinted glass?), she and her fellow workers gathered in a bunker and watched the blast rise up . . . she said that some fell to their knees, some prayed, some wept, some got quiet, some lost control and grew hysterical, shouting and crying and carrying on. One thing was common to all of them: everybody was scared to death, and everybody wanted to get out of that bunker and flee as far from the blast as they could. Not surprisingly, when I asked her how she reacted, she turned out to be one of the quiet ones. She told the story in the most matter-of-fact way, like someone telling you about the events leading up to a parking ticket, smoking all the while, alternating one drag on her cigarette, one on her oxygen mask. And though she herself never told me about her personal troubles—I pieced that part of the story together from snippets her sisters let drop from time to time after Mona died—it's as if I can hear underneath the prayers and the crying and her matter-of-fact description of the explosion, my aunt's voice grown young again as she tells her beau that marriage is not for her, at least not with him.

And so in my imagination this long-lost cousin and the development of the bomb are both located on a sliding scale that reaches from the personal to the historical. Up the scale in the direction of the historical, where I locate the national war effort and the destruction of Hiroshima—an event I can only distantly comprehend—I feel an inchoate guilt. What fraction of the bomb's destructive power can I attribute directly to Mona? At the same time, moving back down the scale in the direction of the personal, I try to imagine the father of her child: What sort of man was he and what happened to their relationship after the child was either aborted or placed for adoption? Were they able to remain friends? And what was the fate of my prospective cousin?

I've often wondered if that early affair was a factor in her remaining single all her life. Rakish, sly, she was frank about sex in a way that I found refreshing, if a little embarrassing for a teenager. Certainly in later life she was no ascetic: her carnal knowledge; her fierce addiction to cigarettes; the mushroom cloud she helped create, now so overexposed it too has become kitsch; her independence of mind—all these associations establish a range of impressions, from the personal to the historical, against which I can measure her character and at the same time bring the world into sharper focus. In a vein similar to my aunt's small-scale/large-scale relationship to history, the atomic blast that at ground zero melded sand into glass also inspired one survivor thirty years later to wish that she'd picked up her scissors knocked by the shockwave onto the schoolroom floor: "Why didn't I stretch my hands out to take them? Those scissors sent by a friend in Hawaii. They were sharp, shiny and would never rust." In this survivor's imagination her scissors become both an emblem of hopeful connection to the world beyond the blast and of spiritual endurance on the edge of despair: How far away that world-of-friends-in-Hawaii-who-send-you-scissors must have seemed when the shockwave hit! Thirty years later the historical significance of the bomb is irradiated by the memory of her lost scissors' seemingly indestructible shine.

This sliding scale of significance from the personal to the historical not only includes this woman and her scissors, and the image of my aunt, coproducer of the atomic bomb, sucking oxygen from her mask, then sucking on her beloved, mass-marketed, mass-produced cigarettes. It also includes the image of my father: first in his retirement, hooked up to a dialysis machine, his blood voyaging beyond his body through plastic tubes; then during his working life, which as I said, after he sold the drive-in theater, was spent analyzing the best way to fuel rocket motors. A solid propellant man, he took us more than once to watch booster tests. I remember rising before dawn, hungover sleepy, then feeling a little grouchy in the backseat, Jill our family dog slack-tongued and panting, my mother asking my brothers and me to stop hitting each other. At the trial site we sat in the car surrounded by other families in their cars, our eyes focussed on a large hole ringed by dirty snow about a hundred yards away.

I remember being afraid that if the trial went badly my dad, gentle, quiet, impassive, would have to work longer hours than he already worked and that his calming influence on our home life would be lost. At ignition, the car began to tremble, the motor roared as loudly as the T rex that used to stalk across the drive-in theater screen, the wall of heat rising from the bottom of the pit rippling the air as high as the tallest trees back by the road, the packed snow shimmering and melting, the lip of the hole incinerated to mush. It lasted less than a minute and when the burn ended, my father walked back to our car from where he'd been standing with the other engineers: he was faintly smiling, exhilarated by the camaraderie and shared sense of success, his quiet sweetness in weird contrast to the ferocity of the motor: "Pancakes," he smiled, "let's all go out for pancakes."

As a kid, I didn't think too consciously about the juxtaposition of pancakes and the technological achievement of an ICBM.

It was just what Dad did. Of course I knew about the Russians, and Communism, and how Khrushchev beat his shoe on a desk, something that President Kennedy would never do. And I remember being terrified during the Cuban missile crisis that our town would be one of the ones that the Reds would target because my dad helped make missiles. But even so, the threat of nuclear war, though real, was difficult to truly comprehend: the bomb shelters that some of my neighbors built were as much forts to play in as they were last-ditch attempts to survive a nuclear war. In the happiness of the moment, the domestic pleasure of blueberry pancakes smothered in syrup completely overshadowed the Cold War arms race that enabled my father to pay the check. And if my father had qualms about his work, he kept them to himself: he was never well paid, being a technical man and not an executive, and keeping us clothed and fed, let alone splurging at a pancake house, was struggle enough for him: the daily grind of supporting us wasn't exactly conducive to moral reflection, and besides, he was in no position to afford his scruples. Plus he genuinely liked his work at the plant. The other technical men in his division respected and liked him; and since my father had few friends outside of work, the plant doubled as the hub of his social life.

Still, I was dimly aware of the paradoxical nature of my father helping to make weapons of mass destruction, while at home he was gentle and unassuming. But I was very much my father's son: I remember taking tremendous pleasure in a toy rocket powered by pressure from the garden hose, and in a replica of a nuclear Shark submarine fueled by baking soda that prowled through the soapy depths of the bathtub or navigated around submerged pots and pans in the kitchen sink. In my Eden such toys would be as essential as Auden's industrial-age machines.

When I think of the Cold War era, for me its contradictions, personal, familial, and historical, form into a kind of collage. President Kennedy's and President Johnson's faces are placed cheek to cheek with Nikita Khrushchev's and Leonid Brezhnev's faces.

Imagining them this way, they possess a kind of iconic power that supersedes their historical dimension. But their faces also have a touch of the supernatural, even the demonic. Beyond even the miracle-working powers of saints and martyrs, they remind me of the star demons of gnostic lore, celestial beings in the service of the demiurge whose power could create but also destroy worlds. But the collage wouldn't be complete for me unless the personal and familial didn't also appear alongside the historical. In fact, the private and public face of the world seem almost like one face, so that it's hard to tell which is figure and which is ground: I see alongside the American Presidents' and Soviet Premiers' faces my own face reflected in my father's face, my aunt's face reflected in her lost child's face, and all these faces bannering out like flags across a rising mushroom cloud.

~

On February 17, 1600, Giordano Bruno, the mystic philosopher, having spent eight years in prison by order of the Inquisition, was publicly burned at the stake as a heretic in the Campo dei Fiori in Rome. Seven years later, Johannes Kepler, the astronomer and a fellow Copernican, wrote to a friend that the "unfortunate Bruno, who was roasted on coals in Rome . . . believed that the stars are inhabited." This is consistent with Bruno's belief that we live in an animistic universe operated by magic: the world possesses a sensitive and rational soul, the stars are angel-like demons, their number infinite in accordance with the infinite nature of the All. The popular notion that Bruno preferred to die rather than renounce Copernicus's assertion that the earth revolves around the sun, and so broke with medieval Aristotelianism and helped to usher in our modern technological world, ignores the fact that Bruno supported Copernicus's theory, not on scientific grounds, but because the astronomer's diagrams were really magic symbols whose gnostic meanings the ignorant Copernicus had failed to understand. Far from being a scientific enthusiast, Bruno thought of himself as a Messiah magus whose mission was to reform Christianity by returning it to its gnostic roots.

In Giovanni Mocenigo's testimony to the Inquisition, he accused Bruno of founding a new religious sect, "the Giordanisti," dedicated to his mystical teachings. The ecstatic nature of his doctrine was based on the use of magical talismans, images and diagrams to draw down the celestial influences from the planets and stars, themselves divine beings, and imprint these on the memory so as to acquire universal knowledge and supernatural power. (The mind as super computer? And yet the computer feeds on invisible electric impulses, not images—as a poet, I'm deeply attracted to Bruno's absolute faith in images: Does it come as any surprise that Bruno was a poet as well as a mystic?) So Egyptian hieroglyphs, which Bruno interpreted as sacred images taken from the natural world, had latent in them the language of the gods. He also invented images of his own; this one, for example, was supposed to draw into the mind the beneficent powers of the divine Sol: "Apollo with a bow and without a quiver, laughing." Contemplation of these images would transform the practitioner into a magus attuned to the monad of the cosmos, his earthly self transcended and reformed to a divine being.

This synthesis of natural magic, celestial effluvia, and spiritual reform seems wholly alien to modern scientific thought. And there's evidence that Bruno lived in a state of mental excitation and euphoria bordering on insanity. But the power to channel divine influences that Bruno ascribed to his images and diagrams strikes me as deeply connected to my interest in poetry as a means to make the world concrete. Through images, poetry also attempts to quicken our mental life, to bring into our minds a picture of the cosmos, which in Greek simply means "order." And so poetry brings us a certain order of things, most likely temporary, but nonetheless real. Bruno's faith in images to deliver up ultimate realities is akin to my faith in poetry to deliver up a version of the world that is full of luminous particulars. And it's interesting to note that up until the Enlightenment, the processes of scientific thought and of poetic thought were more similar than they are now. Science was also a form of cosmological exploration. Bruno's understanding of Copernicus is an obvious case in point. But when science in the late 1700s became more and more a utilitarian pursuit, such that science became the instrument of technological development, then the gulf between what I've been calling technological thought and poetic thought begins to widen.

But before this gulf opened up, technology and magic, just as poetry and magic, went more or less hand in glove. This is particularly evident in certain kinds of medical technology as it's evolved since the Enlightenment. Franz Mesmer's MD thesis, published in 1767, claimed that celestial gravity, through a weightless, ineffable fluid called ether, exerted influences on the human body that accounted for various diseases. He later developed this theory into his infamous notion of "animal" magnetism, a quasi-mystical force charging the nervous system that Mesmer, dressed as a magus, would therapeutically adjust by passing his hands up and down the patient's length, but without touching the person's body.

It's a short step from Bruno's belief in celestial influences operating on the mind for spiritual benefit or harm—there was "good" magic as well as "bad"—to Mesmer's conviction that such forces operated on the human body, also for good or ill. Although Bruno's notion of a living, animistic universe had been replaced in Mesmer's day by a mechanistic one, some of Bruno's mystical cosmology persists in Mesmer's methods: when treating patients, he would wear a robe embroidered with Rosicrucian alchemical symbols, a practice clearly related to Bruno's use of magical images (some scholars suggest that the Rosicrucians may have been an offshoot of Bruno's mystical sect, "the Giordanisti"). In our less flamboyant day, the white lab coat has equally potent meanings, though perhaps more for the patient than the doctor. And the notion that Mesmer's hands could sense pathology inside the body bears partial resemblance to the X ray. The difference is that science ascribes the X ray's power to see into the patient's body to impersonal natural laws, while Mesmer's power over his patients was due to the magnetic force of personality.

Or so it seems from the scientific, that is to say, the technological point of view. But what of the patient's point of view, his wrist encircled by a plastic bracelet with his name, date of birth, and hospital ID number printed on it, his clothes exchanged for a washed-to-rags johnny open at the back for easy access to the doctors' and nurses' hands, his faith in his own body displaced by his hope (and fear) of the IV dripping into his veins, the needle jabbed through his skin an unceremonious initiation into the society of the sick?

During my father's last illness, I remember watching him receive a blood transfusion, the slow drip of the blood thinned by saline sliding through the tube seeming every bit as charged with "animal" magnetism ("animal" derived from *anima,* the soul) as Mesmer could wish. The physiological difference that two units of blood made in my father was astounding: his mind ceased to hover in its spaced-out lassitude and drift, he seemed literally to be pulled back down into his body.

In thinking about my father's almost ethereal fragility, I'm reminded of a kind of trance that Bruno once wrote would take over the mind as the magus ascended to contemplation of the All: this was a mental state whose intensity had to be carefully controlled by the use of magical images or else the ascending soul could be lost in the All—the result being that the body, bereft of the soul, would perish. Yet I recognize that this loose analogy between the soul's ascent to gain knowledge and my father's wooziness before a blood transfusion is my own mind looking for some escape from the inevitability of my father's death. The very fact that I'm trying to link my father's death to this kind of mystical notion implies a kind of magical thinking: I remember trying to control the panic I felt as my father's condition worsened by focussing on an image of air molecules gliding into his lungs. Talk about faith in images!—

at such moments, who was guiltier of magical thinking, me or the heretical, Messiah-magus Bruno?

Perhaps my deepest impression of this kind of magical thinking was inspired by watching my dad's dialysis. Grafted beneath his forearm was a tube sewn into his artery through which his blood left his body and then returned. Three days a week for four hours a day while his blood was being cleansed, he would sit uncomplaining in an easychair among other patients in easychairs, a small-screen television available for him to watch, an earphone plugged into the console, just as it was for all the other patients. When I would drop my father off or pick him up in the reception room, a sense of ordinary human activity pervaded the place. But if I passed beyond the reception room door into the clinic itself, the sight of the patients' blood flowing beyond their veins through a clear tube, then passing through a filter attached to the dialysis machine, always stirred in me a profound unease at seeing what should remain invisible made visible—rich, red, and almost painfully vital in comparison to the patients sitting passively in their chairs.

Low red blood cell counts, deficient auto-immune reactions, kidney dysfunction, fluid imbalance, the numbers for creatinine and ph . . . But how to say beyond the numbers and medical jargon the interior mystery that hid behind those numbers and that jargon! My father and I were linked by what at every moment was attempting to dissolve us, to carry us beyond the ministrations of these machines crouched human-sized next to each chair, metal boxes with gauges and dials routinely checked by the nurses scribbling down a few numbers and comments on the patients' record sheets, taking blood pressures, the inflatable cuff expanding, then deflating with a sudden sigh.

My father, who matter-of-factly had made his living by projecting gigantic images on a screen, and then helped create the thrust needed to break a rocket loose from the earth's gravity, was now at the mercy of the machine beside him, its physical presence weirdly blending in my mind with his own. If my tricycle had once made me feel that my body was larger and more powerful, now the dialysis machine made my father's body seem like a vestigial, soon to be discarded part of its own functioning. And yet I had other intimations that ran counter to my sense of medical technology beginning to erase my father's presence. They weren't as grandiose as Bruno's, but from a scientific point of view, equally hermetic—that my father's life and my life were borne on a current (animal magnetism?) that also passed through the other patients in the room. Our fates were permeable and mutual, but also irreducible. I don't know how to explain it, but it was like the arc of each life, in all its unrepeatable difference, was nonetheless contained in the arc of my father's life. In looking at him, I'd passed behind a mirror into a place that certain gnostics call Adocentyn, mystic city of the sun, from whose glass towers and flashing beacons emanated all the images and representations that human beings are capable of conceiving.

Perhaps this strange conjunction of dialysis machines and quasi-mystical intimations struck a momentary truce between what Stevens once called "the pressure of reality" and the poetic imagination. My dad's physical frailty and my own hopes and fears for him seemed part of a necessary exchange, death pushing back against life, the two achieving an uneasy equilibrium. At such moments I found it easier to accept that my dad was soon going to die. But these moments came infrequently. More often than not, I had less comforting intuitions: the dialysis machine tending to my visibly failing father made his weakness that much more pronounced—and though I fought against such feelings, I'm ashamed to admit that my dad's wasting flesh, in contrast to the machine's seeming indestructibilty, sometimes made me a little afraid of him. Hooked up to the machine, he seemed both more and less than human. Eventually I'd reach the limit of my ability to project onto the machine benevolent intentions—and while I was grateful to the technology that kept him alive, the machine slowly came to dwarf him.

But during those moments when the sinister relation between his body and the machine was transformed into a strange communion between me, my father and his machine, and the other patients and their machines, I felt a spooky joy: joy that I could feel so connected to my father, regardless of whether he felt it, too. Despite his unfailing gentleness and devotion to us, he was always a shy man, not easily demonstrative; and the constant exhaustion he suffered because of his illness made him even quieter and more distant. From childhood on, I had been haunted by his remoteness, which I experienced as fear of losing him—a fear that, as a child in Texas, I had controlled by an almost magical belief in the protective powers of the comedic duo we showed so often at the drive-in theater, Jerry Lewis and Dean Martin. Always rising unhurt from bizarre pratfalls, their mutual loyalty prevailing over all dangers, they were my slapstick guardians, their power to make me laugh as protective in its way as Bruno's star demons moving harmoniously throughout the living universe as they kept watch over their respective corners of infinitely expanding space. So Lewis and Martin watched over my sleep while my father and mother were off attending to the popcorn machine or rewinding the first reel so that they could start threading the second.

But there in the clinic those guardian powers seemed neutralized by forces of equal magnitude. My father's physical fragility made it hard for me to separate the lifesaving function of the dialysis machine from my sense that he was flickering out right before my eyes. His ruddy coloring had been extinguished by a creeping pallor. No amount of medical technology was going to keep his flesh steadily burning. But in another, more animistic part of myself, I believed that I could keep him alive by sheer force of will. If I kept his image firmly in my head, charging it with my own animal magnetism, I could keep him from gradually vanishing from sight.

There were times when my animism and the operations of the dialysis machine seemed weirdly parallel, the physical work of the dialysis machine in keeping my father alive transmuted into the mental work of preserving his image. So the same tubes, pumps, and filters which I found dehumanizing also served as an imaginative springboard, a creative impetus that partially patterned my mental response to my father's health. The adaptability of the imagination, first to generate the technology on which the dialysis machine was based, and then to transform it in this idiosyncratic way, shows just how omnivorous and unpredictable its powers are. But from a more personal perspective, at bottom what I needed was a sense of control over my father's fate. As he gradually grew sicker and his need of me increased, I discovered in the imaginative work of trying to preserve my father's image a source of solace and some small measure of control—fragile, illogical, but as vital to me emotionally in a quiet day-to-day way as the dialysis machine was to my father physically.

From a less magical vantage, I can see that witnessing my father at the clinic routinely put me in those extreme states of mind that thinking too much about death induces. Although I experienced that state over and over, each time I passed behind the waiting-room doors the mystery and reality of the clinic seemed always new, even as it came resistlessly closer—the most unfathomable part being that every few weeks a patient would suddenly stop coming. I'd notice a new patient sitting in the dead patient's easy chair. And I knew with a helpless desolate shock that one day the dead patient would be my father, another patient quietly usurping what I'd come to think of as his chair.

And so it's fallen out. On my desk, kept ziplocked in a plastic Baggie, pure product of technology, is all that remains of my father—a half handful of ashes I saved out from when our family scattered them on my mother's parents' graves, on my father's parents' graves. At first I thought of making a box for his ashes, but in the years since his death the plastic pouch of the Baggie, in its cruelly casual, utilitarian indifference, has come to seem a more effective goad to memory. Just as mystics like Bruno took to suspending a colored figure of the cosmos from the ceiling so that the figure of the universe and not just single things would meet their eyes, so the plastic Baggie brings to my inner eye the image of my father superimposed on the myriad surfaces of the world.

~

As I've mentioned earlier, Bruno's absolute faith in the power of images to transform us seems to me similar to the poet's desire (at least the poets I admire) to give each passing thing its living name, to illuminate inside our abstract technological web the face of each particular. It's tempting to speculate about the fate of art in our time, launching into jeremiads against that web's accelerating autonomy from moral reflection on the one hand, or singing dithyrambs to it accompanied by electronic synthesizers for its attempts to ameliorate human suffering. Instead, let me say that technology's essence as the ability to create and organize freely could also describe the making of art: given such a definition, art and technology are mutually entailing, each suggesting to the other new directions.

In other words, I'm not so much worried about technology as such as I am about our loss of human presence as the primary factor in how we think about technology's purpose: the uses of technology threaten to usurp our images of ourselves, which in part explains my unease with the benevolent workings of my father's dialysis machine. But I could gladly live with such ambiguities if, in its less benign manifestations, technological utility, and the social and economic forces that sustain it, didn't keep shifting the spotlight of history away from the human face, and onto their own ever more abstract, increasingly autonomous processes. In contrast, poetry as I conceive it is a way of illuminating that face from the inside so that the subjective life of each individual in a world community can add its own peculiar luster to that spotlight.

That's why as poet I find so appealing the manner in which Bruno's mystical images work on the imagination, a specific image channeling a celestial force to bring a particular benefit to the human mind. The sensory concreteness of his system insists that images aren't empty shadows that can be arbitrarily manipulated, but are as physically real as the divine properties that they have the power to attract, the *materia* of the world able to capture and store the *spiritus* material emanating from the stars.

This power to draw down the divine seems similar to what I experienced when, as a child on the verge of sleep, I watched the gigantic actors up on the screen. The parking lot with its hundreds of speakers all whispering at once, the images succeeding each other so rapidly that the frames seemed able to register each least detail of human life, the flickering projector like the flashing towers and beacons of Adocentyn endlessly inventive in shooting out images across the night, all these influences, plus the exhilaration of being at a drive-in movie while other children were tucked in at home, my bedtime story literally filling the horizon, gave me a sense of familial connection to the giants before me who were working out their black-and-white fates while my parents were busy working the projector and the snackbar.

In my mother's and father's absence, I linked the voices coming from the speaker with my reverie of flying in a rocket ship built by my father, my technological/poetical version of Bruno's aspiration to penetrate the armature of the spheres and show to nature the beautiful form of God. At this moment, the moment when sleep and the projector's power to make images operated on my imagination as strongly as Bruno's magical diagrams, I would feel myself drifting among the stars shining on the rear window's curved glass, and slowly turn my head away from the lit screen to make the constellations show up more brightly against the wide sky. Since I never saw more than a few minutes of a movie before I fell asleep, plot and dialogue dissolved into the comforting sensation of the actors on screen accompanying me through the night.

As I said before, I know now that I must have used this reverie to quiet my anxieties about being abandoned by my parents, especially my father, lost not in the All but in the warm night of Texas, the parking lot deserted, every car gone home but ours while they shut down the snackbar and cashed out. I remember how even through my dreams I could sense their voices and footsteps, and how their approach freed me to let myself go even farther into space, the immense Texas panhandle shrinking to nothing from my vantage among the stars. But perhaps this anxiety also added fuel to the sense of well-being I experienced during those moments just before sleep when I lay in the back window-well, the shadowy images of Martin and Lewis so protective of me in their superhuman size and goofy benevolence. At such moments even my fear of losing my parents temporarily receded into the distances I traveled through, the blackness opening and opening to my closing eyes.

Bibliography:

Collier, Michael. *The Neighbor.* London and Chicago: University of Chicago Press, 1995.

Koestler, Arthur. *The Sleepwalkers.* London and New York: Penguin Books (Arkana), 1989.

Yates, Frances A. *Giordano Bruno and the Hermetic Tradition.* London and Chicago: University of Chicago Press, 1964.

Part II

Proteus as Poet

~

A beach, nothing on it, a sort of Beckett beach. And then out of the waves come seals, tapering to flippers at one end, dog noses at the other, their middles shiny black and streaked by gray scars, the pack shimmering and ominous, moving boulders. What at first looks like a seal sprouts two legs and walks among them. He holds a trident in his hand. He counts them up nose by nose, and then lies down to take a nap.

His body from the waist down keeps changing as the sun changes, almost like a cheap religious card, the kind that shows Jesus smiling, then wearing a crown of thorns, forehead bleeding for the world's sins. In the case of the sleeper, though, his nether part transforms back and forth between human and fish, so that sometimes he seems like an old man asleep on the beach, and sometimes like a merman, human to the waist, all fish below.

A wit would say that we've all run into such people at parties, but this doesn't seem like the time for joking, there's a feeling of desperation in the air despite the apparent serenity of waves running in even grooves and the backwash percolating down into the sand. Whence this desperation, why this sense of limit being reached, who or what is projecting such an aura?

This old man of the sea, this sea god called Proteus, his eyelids are flickering, just what is he dreaming? Is he dreaming that he's some man or woman's inner Homer, a modern, literate, workaday person who sits in meetings all day, but gets up early every morning before work and sits down at the desk to write, scratching away with a pencil or staring abstractedly into a computer screen? This inner Homer is struggling to find a word, a phrase, a line that then finds an emotion that then finds a thought: this is a poet's form of ritual action, this is poetry as transformation, this is a poet's version of coming into contact with the divine.

The poet writes and rewrites, the poet is writing about Proteus, the beach, seals on the beach, but Proteus keeps changing, under the poet's grip the words themselves are Proteus, language itself is another of Proteus's disguises. But the poet too is protean, the poet shifts shape to keep up with the way the words shift theirs, so that each time they change the poet changes too and gains a fresh perspective: at each new transformation of Proteus, the poet learns more about the beach, the seals, the sleeping god whose dreaming is a ritual that the poet too must dream so that each new line the poet writes is a new aspect of whatever aspect the dreaming Proteus is just this instant now revealing.

On the beach there are three seals that don't quite look right: and when the poet brings us closer, we're rewarded in our suspicions. For these are men disguised in sealskins that have gone undetected by the sleeping old man, shepherd of the deep. But our inner Homer knows who they are, they are Menelaus and two of his lieutenants becalmed on their way back to Sparta from man-destroying Troy.

How desperate they are to get home if they are willing to risk a battle with the divine. Pirates, vocational killers, resembling their gods in ways that our inner Homer finds both comical and moving, these hard-bitten men know how dependent their own fates are on the gods' crooked and devious ways: proper observances must be paid the gods if a human being is to prosper. And now, at a signal, they rise up and rush the sleeping old man, they seize him by the arms and legs and hold on.

Terrified, they cling ever tighter as his body transforms under their very hands: they feel fire scorch their palms and singe their faces, they feel the rough nap of a beast's fur and smell its funk, they jerk their heads away from snapping teeth, dry scales slither in their hands and poison spits in their faces.

The poet's words jerk and slither and scorch and spit. The poet feels the men's hearts beating hard in terror, but still the men hold on. To let go is to die on this beach. To let go is to have fought for ten years all for nothing. For our inner Homer knows that if the men can grip hard enough long enough, at last the old man will resume his true shape, and answer their questions about how to get home. He will tell them what rituals and sacrifices need to be performed to obtain a favoring wind.

The adrenaline high is pumping in the men's veins. Voices in their heads dictate to them what to do, voices whose orders their bodies execute flawlessly: grip here, here, now grip even harder. As the body of the old man shifts, so does their knowledge of his body, the tricky old man's body, now beast, now fire, now water: this is firsthand knowledge of every order of being, from the inanimate to the animal to the human to the divine. The poet feels the men submitting to the changes of the god, just as the poet submits to the changes of the words that describe the men, the poet's at the limit of endurance—spark—flare—a hole opens in our inner Homer's head and the men rise out of it like ritual smoke, zoom in for the close-up, and on the men's faces and on the poet's face are slashes of light that signify *terror pain wonder* and we who are watching get to see how mixed our earthly lot is, and above all to experience it in an objective, if ever changing, form.

~

Proteus has awakened and dived back into the sea, and as he dives, the hole in the water he dove into pulls the beach in after it and the water in after it so that all that's left is a blank white space like a piece of printer paper. On the outside, quiet; on the inside, our inner Homer is getting to work again, trying to sum up what can be learned from this encounter. We rehearse the story of Proteus, the all-knowing sea god, the shapeshifter who sees the past, present, and future. Proteus, the reluctant seer who fights shy of telling what he knows, and for that very reason seems all the more like a figure of wisdom.

But also a paradox-monger who resorts to disguises of his own to escape the hands of truth seekers, who takes on his original form when he is willing to answer questions. Our inner Homer knows that writing poetry, revising poetry, can be a frightening venture because of the unpredictable nature of Proteus: he can assume terrifying shapes and those shapes may convey a truth that, as we hold onto him, isn't easily reconciled with what Proteus tells us when he resumes his original form.

In other words, his disguises are also a kind of truth that affects how we think about his answers. Our struggle isn't simply passive endurance of his shape shifting, but also changes us. In that sense, for each transformation that Proteus enacts, we also are required to shift our assumptions about our own mental and emotional life—what we call our "material." This is appropriate to his nature as a sea god: the sea, after all, is a metaphor for the unconscious life, and that unconscious life is both his care and his dwelling place.

The nature of Proteus is ambiguity—fruitful, frightening, but always vital. But through that ambiguity we understand that Proteus is like a shadow of our own ambiguous inner life: contradictory in the ways we see ourselves, dynamically unfolding even as we are blocked by habit. The conviction that there are serious limits to our self-knowledge may be at the root of Valery's assertion that a bad poem is one that disappears into meaning; or Stevens's insistence that poetry shouldn't make things "too near, too clear"; or Pound's comment to Williams that what saves him as a poet is his "opacity." All these statements suggest the ways that a poem can resist its author and its reader, though without simply remaining in the realm of potentially endless process: then the eternal shape shifting of Proteus would be frivolous, a kind of hyperkinetic spiritual torpor.

And so each shape Proteus takes on is valued for its inflection of how the god appears when he at last comes to the end of his transformations and will answer our questions—though after such transformations, that moment may well feel ambiguous, provisional at best: so much so that our inner Homer may be reluctant to say that it occurs at all. Valery's assertion that a poem is never finished, only abandoned, takes on an even more mordant quality when seen from this perspective: "to finish" a poem is in fact to finish it off by insisting on too much closure, by imagining that a poem can be anything more than Frost's "momentary stay against confusion." In other words, the moment when Proteus comes to the end of his transformations remains ambiguous, more a possibility hovering above the poem than a possibility the poem enacts.

But whether or not Proteus takes on his original shape, and whether or not we would still perceive that shape in the same way after witnessing so many transformations, the nature of the questions that we must ask Proteus has changed. The unconscious life saturates the language of the poem, and that saturation makes for proliferating meaning.

By proliferating meaning, I don't mean murk and blur: I mean the resonances of ambiguity conveyed by a clear expression of mixed emotions. I mean the way myth goes beyond the myth's literal events while remaining grounded in those events. I mean the way a poet's pleasure in language can refute or subvert his more overt intentions, revealing inside the most straitlaced moralist the sensualist eager to follow Proteus into unexpected waters.

The burden for the poet is not that Proteus has an infinite repertoire of shapes, but discovering which of these shapes will release him to speak of despair and hope, pleasure and pain in a way that feels definitive, at least in the provisional way that the world of a poem can provide. By release, I mean the moment when the poet's imagination and Proteus's transformation suddenly come into alignment, regardless of whether that moment may give way to another moment and another in the process of composing and revising a poem.

The distinction between "finishing" a poem, as I defined it earlier, and the process of discovering a poem's language as it attempts to capture the shining and sounding surfaces of the world, or trusts itself to the currents of language to reveal the forms of reality, is like seeing a glassblower spinning his iron rod while blowing a gather of hot glass into a cylinder that can then be worked by shears and tongs into a recognizable form. As you watch the glass take shape, the potential forms of the glass change moment by moment: and that sense of excitement in the possibility of transformation is what the poet, in attempting to align his imagination with the shape shifting of Proteus, is attempting to capture.

It's as if all the possible shapes that a poem can take on are summed up by the manifested poem. Those shapes are still active beneath the surface of the poem as a kind of spectral field against which the definite outlines of the poem are starkly drawn. In other words, the poem is an achieved identity, but replete with latent, inexhaustible potential for further transformation that the fecundity of Proteus offers up to us, although not without a struggle:

At noon the Old Man came out of the sea
and found his fat seals and counted them up—
and we were among the first he counted.
. . . Then he too lay down . . .
We rushed him, shouting, and locked him
in our arms, but the Old Man didn't forget
his wily art; he turned into a great, heavy maned lion,
a snake, leopard, a huge boar, then he shimmered
and overflowed and ran like water through
our hands, then fountained up into a tree
with waterfalling branches, but we held on to him,

tightening our grip, holding on desperately.
But when the devious Old Man finally tired,
he spoke to me, asking, Which of the gods
put you up to this, son of Atreus, just what do you want?

—*The Odyssey,* Book IV, *450–463*

Self as Self-Impersonation in American Poetry

As a boy, I remember one of the few Sundays that our family went to church. Our regular attendance was partly hampered by the fact that one Easter Sunday my older brother, on a dare from Weegee Hansen, hit Reverend Fox in the back of the head with a water balloon: you can imagine the withering effect this might have on tender religious feelings, especially when Reverend Fox turned up at our house later that afternoon, seeking, as he put it, "to wring that little sinner's neck." But on the particular Sunday I have in mind, Reverend Fox recounted the story of Saul on the way to Damascus, in which God knocks Saul, the Christian persecutor, off his horse and he rises up from the dust as the apostle Paul. The miracle of the conversion went right by me. All that I could think about was the fate of the horse: Was Paul a better master than Saul? When God knocked Saul into the dust, did the horse also feel the blow? What kind of fodder did the horse get that evening in Damascus? The fact that my mind focussed on the horse first, and Saul second, indicates how far I am from comprehending the mind of a truly religious sensibility, for whom Paul's conversion would have been a template: the fallen consciousness is brought to God's light by the fire of faith, and the self that suffers the flames is all the better for the scorching.

Although my sympathies may lie with the horse and not with God's implacable heat, implicit in this conversion story are questions about identity, how it gets established, and what forces are sufficient to sponsor it. In the realm of poetry cocktail parties, you get to hear your share of conversion stories: cocktail parties being what they are, no one is under oath. And so I once witnessed a poet undergo multiple conversions in a single evening: depending on the confessor's faith, this Paul/Saul claimed to be an autobiographical poet one moment, a L=A=N=G=U=A=G=E poet the next, a narrative poet after that. Totally apart from whether or not these professions were sincere, is the question as to why a poet shouldn't be able to inhabit all these positions at the same time. And it's an interesting question as to why this kind of fluidity causes such unease in the poetry world, as well as in the realm of cultural debate. If you claim to be in league with the aesthetics of poet X, then you can't possibly like the work of poet Y.

One aspect of this unease is the ongoing and inevitable debate about the place of subjectivity in art. What are its limits and possibilities, its responsibilities and risks? The varying camps of cultural and critical theory in which "I" is both a grammatical project and projection of systems of power, and the almost preliterate hostility that some poetic scribblers feel toward any attempt to call the authority of "I" into question, makes for a lot of noise—some of this noise is what a friend calls "a tempestio in a teapotio," the usual jockeying for audience that every generation is heir to, while some of it harks back to a reigning and basic question that underlies American imaginative writing from its beginning in Anne Bradstreet and Edward Taylor. Emerson formulated it when he asked what was "American" about American poetry, and what and whom should American poetry serve. But it exists in embryo in Bradstreet, when she declares that she wants no "Bayes" of laurel as handed down by tradition, but is content with a home-grown "wholsome Parsley wreath."

In a poem entitled "Here Follows Some Verses upon the Burning of Our House July 10th 1666," Anne Bradstreet exhorts herself to see God's hand in the flickering flames, presumably as part of the murky working out of His Divine will.

In silent night when rest I took
For sorrow near I did not look
I wakened was with thund'ring noise
And piteous shrieks of dreadful voice.
That fearful sound of "Fire!" and "Fire!"
Let no man know is my desire.
I, starting up, the light did spy,
And to my God my heart did cry
To strengthen me in my distress
And not to leave me succorless.
Then, coming out, beheld a space
The flame consume my dwelling place.
And when I could no longer look,
I blest His name that gave and took,
That laid my goods now in the dust.
Yea, so it was, so 'twas just.
It was His own, it was not mine,
Far be it that I should repine;
He might of all justly bereft
But yet sufficient for us left.
When by the ruins oft I past
My sorrowing eyes aside did cast,
And here and there the places spy
Where oft I sat and long did lie:
Here stood that trunk, and there that chest,
There lay that store I counted best.
My pleasant things in ashes lie,
And them behold no more shall I.
Under thy roof no guest shall sit,
Nor at thy table eat a bit.

No pleasant tale shall e'er be told,
Nor things recounted done of old.
No candle e'er shall shine in thee,
Nor bridegroom's voice e'er heard shall be.
In silence ever shall thou lie,
Adieu, Adieu, all's vanity.
Then straight I 'gin my heart to chide,
And did thy wealth on earth abide?
Didst fix thy hope on mold'ring dust?
The arm of flesh didst make thy trust?
Raise up thy thoughts above the sky
That dunghill mists away may fly.
Thou hast an house on high erect,
Framed by that mighty Architect,
With glory richly furnished,
Stands permanent though this be fled.
It's purchaséd and paid for too
By Him who hath enough to do.
A price so vast as is unknown
Yet by His gift is made thine own;
There's wealth enough, I need no more,
Farewell, my pelf, farewell my store.
The world no longer let me love,
My hope and treasure lies above.

While the poem seems like a form of obeisance to God's inscrutable will, the poem seems to hint that all is not right in the New World's dunghill mists. Bradstreet's admission that the voices calling out "Fire" dovetail with a secret desire of her own makes one wonder about Bradstreet's hidden tendencies toward the community: Is she a kind of spiritual pyromaniac wrestling with her more saintly self over how best to burn down God's house? Of course I realize that one of Bradstreet's aims is to use her own persona as a vehicle to proselytize. And from that point of view, her self-admonishments are both exemplary to others as well as sincerely felt. I suppose what I'm talking about is a kind of historical sixth sense that the poem exudes to a secular reader like myself. In Bradstreet's New World, the tenor of religious feeling is undergoing a subtle shift: because there are no rose windows and high-flying spires to buttress your belief, to a sincere Puritan like Bradstreet, God's personal presence begins to imbue everything, from a chest or a trunk to a burning house. And as God's personal involvement in your life increases, so too does His responsibility for your fortunes. And that level of personal intimacy is bound to have serious psychological consequences.

As I said before, I realize that my horsy loyalties may reflect my own secular shortcomings in understanding an intelligence like Bradstreet's. Nonetheless, when Bradstreet shifts from "I" to "thine" toward the end of the poem, I sense the ground of being shifting as the pronouns shift: this division of soul is finding expression on the level of grammar. Bradstreet's ambivalence about losing "that store I counted best" is subtly signaled by her use of the second- and third-person pronouns to address the "mighty Architect" and keep him at a slight grammatical remove. In contrast, she lavishes affection and regret on her burned-out house by addressing it as "thee." And in the final couplet, Bradstreet's teeth-gritting resignation is likewise undercut by a subtle shift in pronouns in the last third of the poem. Once she learns that her house is on fire, she goes from addressing the Lord as "my God" in the eighth line, to calling on God in the third person, even while she tries to bless "His name that gave and took." Of course, one wonders why she should need to bless His name at all. Shouldn't she be the one asking for His blessing?

Further evidence of this psychic strain is the way she addresses herself in a strangely disassociated second person, which at first seems like a form of self-address, but in fact is an address to her house. When she says, "Under thy roof no guest shall sit," the psychic blurring between herself and her "pleasant things" that "in ashes lie" signals the spiritual depths in which she now burns. It's as if the shift in pronouns signals a clandestine desire to cut loose from the Puritan God and explore her own peculiar psychological mechanisms. She splits off from the sorrowing self in order to admonish that self, and in the process the "I" sanctioned by the divine principle has begun to split along the grain. The more Bradstreet exhorts herself to see in her personal tragedy a divine lesson, the further she ventures into her own subjective wilderness. Apparently obedient, her mind may be the horse ridden by God, but it harbors animal tendencies to rear up and throw Him.

Abstracted further and further from its divine source, Bradstreet's version of a religious self gives way to the Emersonian self, the Whitmanian self. For the self in American poetry has usually been dependent on some sponsoring transcendental source, even in a poem like *The Waste Land,* with its reflexive inclusion of personified spiritual qualities of Datta (give), Dayadhvam (sympathize), and Damyatam (control) from the Upanishads, not to mention the weird, oneiric Christ-like figure wandering in the desert who sinisterly invites the reader to "Come in under the shadow of this red rock." Since its inception in Bradstreet, American poetry has never been content to let the self hang in the wind, subject to the uncertainty of its own status, but able to experience that uncertainty in its own independent way. And this seems as true to me now as it was to those in the seventeenth century.

When I mentioned this view to a friend of mine, he thought it was a pretty strange claim, since in his mind any poetry that wasn't overtly devotional more or less had to be based on epistemological uncertainty. And I don't disagree. Maybe what I'm talking about is more an attitude of inquiry, a special attentiveness to this metaphysically weightless condition. The image I have in mind is of a poet in a spacesuit, crossing the void with a little jet pack, and when that fails, behaving like Milton's Satan as he fights his way through chaos, who "With head, hands, wings, or feet pursues his way." In other words, to make that uncertainty a place to explore so that the poet doesn't try to vanquish it by falling back on universalizing abstractions—which are, as always, in abundant supply. In our age, God the supreme authority has been displaced by secular abstractions like "hegemonic discourse"; or if you are a semiologist, the "transcendental signifier." And the poetic doctrine of "deep image," which saw consciousness as a set of images pre-existent to tainted history, looks to Jung's notion of the collective unconscious as its sponsoring, transcendental authority. Even theories of poetry that stress language's primacy seem based on a displaced passion for the assertion in John: "In the beginning was the Word." And aesthetic stances like objectivism, imagism, and followers of projective verse tend to treat the world's surface as a kind of phenomenological absolute. We may give lip service to human subjectivity as its own self-sufficient cause for being, but even the scientific assumptions surrounding neurological research, such as the right-brain/left-brain structures of consciousness, have been enlisted as a way to root the self in something outside its own waveringly subjective force field and experiential flow. This scientific way of explaining consciousness as brain function resembles a kind of Cartesian variant: "If my mind is structured like this and perforce must think like that, therefore I am the projection of that structure that I think of as if it were my self." Clearly, the self on its own is a difficult proposition to accept.

Shifting from an epistemological to an historical perspective about the place of the self in American poetry, we return to the questions Emerson asked: What makes American poetry "American" and not European; and whom or what should American poetry serve? Frost's half-joking line, "The land was ours before we were the land's" points to not only the irony of a colonial situation in which the colonists, fleeing the oppression of their mother country, feel alienated in the promised land, but their unconscious arrogance in assuming that the land is theirs while being blind to their own murderous intention to take the land by force from its Indian inhabitants. Of course the ironies I'm deploying here are more mine than Frost's, since he did read the poem at John F. Kennedy's inauguration, hardly the venue for revisionist thoughts about the United States' westward expansion.

But if you squint at those lines from a certain historical perspective, Frost's repetition of "we" implies a queasiness about who this "we" really is, in which ethnic and class divisions are elided so that "we" may possess, and become possessed by, the land whose price "was many deeds of war." The answers to these questions about American poetry's status as American—which seem narrowly chauvinistic at worst, and at best a goad to make a "nation language" that isn't cowed by what Seamus Heaney once called "the Absolute Speaker" of bureaucratic and technocratic officialdom—don't seem to have included the notion that American poetry could be a force in its own right, a self-sufficient category of human consciousness. Either its purpose was to serve God in the New World theocracy; or, as democracy replaced theocracy, it must serve, according to Whitman, as a prophetic source for the ever renewing energies of democratic experiment.

But to return to Bradstreet: as Puritanism became less and less the attempt to fathom the mystery of God's grace in the New World wilderness, and more and more focussed on individual salvation and self-scrutiny for the purpose of exposing sin, the native skepticism of such scrutiny inevitably turned against its transcendental author, the hitherto unimpeachable "I am that I am." Belief becomes nonbelief through Puritanism's own genius for self-scrutiny and self-doubt, and so the grounding authority of the self is forced to find new ground: Emerson floats the concept of the Over Soul, a version of God as human and human as God, but all so undifferentiated that the self begins to blur into universal consciousness: it becomes wispy, thin, fog that mists a mirror. And then Whitman attempts to clean the mirror by focussing on the body: this seems like a promising direction, to ground the self in the universality of sexual feeling; he calls this "adhesiveness," but his missionary zeal about eros as a democratic force doesn't take into account how oblique sex is, how opaque, how irremediable to generalization—people actually having sex in Whitman is too often a question of hygiene, physical and mental, and too seldom a matter of "sharp-toothed touch." Whitman's intuition of the self grounded in sexual pleasure smudges out into his proselytizing zeal to make us all into mothers and fathers of clean-limbed sons and daughters of the Republic.

After Whitman's vision of democracy based on the body gets trampled under by the Civil War and the national psyche splits into North and South; after the Robber Barons who endow our major museums cement the divisions between the classes; after advertising seduces the language of private desire into the language of consumerism; after Eliot and Pound explode the remnants of the self into the many voices of *The Waste Land,* and the historical perspectives and personae of the *Cantos;* after New Criticism puts pressure on the work and begins to displace the author as the subject of literary study; after autobiography becomes just another form of psychological and historical projection; after "confessional poetry" becomes simply a blanket term of disapproval of certain kinds of done-to-death subject matter; after the death of the author, both as a joke and as a serious challenge to the myth of authorial mastery over language; after rereadings of cultural icons like Shakespeare, such that Shakespeare's heroes are removed from the realm of action in the world, and made into specular instances of various schools of psychoanalytic and cultural critique; after media conglomeration and the proliferation of "real-time" "real-life" news coverage and television shows, such that the self observing the self impersonating the self becomes the most current form of naturalism; after a sense of time as serial begins to fragment into a sense of time as discrete, so that the actual moment of writing becomes part of the drama of writing, as in Beckett's speakers who make the phenonemon of their own vocalizing the focus of the story; after all this, who would dare claim that the "I" isn't a phantom and a projection of language, a mere grammatical convenience? Add to all this the lingering prestige of the Tel Quel group declaring that writing (as Italo Calvino informs us in his essay, "Cybernetics and Ghosts") no longer consists in "narrating but in saying that one is narrating." According to this idea, the immediate claim of sympathy on the reader by an "I" confident of its status as not only a linguistic entity, but as a flesh-and-blood speaker whose fate is of intrinsic interest, has come to an end. What one says becomes identified with the act of saying. The psychological person is really a grammatical person, defined by its place in the discourse.

But I balk at this—there is something a little canned about all of it, a little too symptomatic of a kind of expected, "with it" theorizing that ignores what I feel when I write. And so I don't quite know how to take my own list . . . is it merely poetry gloom, culture gloom, spleen? Or in a more serious vein, could the list be symptomatic of a desire to make up stories that would join in the weave of stories that blanket all earth's creatures in an atmosphere of compassion and intelligent concern—what Teilhard de Chardin called the noosphere? If this notion seems a little too idealized, its hardheaded corollary would be a pluralist, quasi-anthropological way of understanding the world, in which there are many different cosmologies and cultures all functioning with equal authority, if not equal in their political and economic status.

Both of these models pose a quiet challenge to what vestiges of the Whitmanian self remain. After all, when Whitman says, "I do not ask the wounded person how he feels, I myself become the wounded person," underneath the well-meant identification, a certain violence is being done in that omission to ask. Yes, the poet is identifying with the wounded, but the identification is also a kind of erasure of that person's local cultural and historical circumstances. So is there a way of allowing the voice of the wounded to speak through the poem, while preserving the right of the poet to make the kind of confident self-assertions that Whitman makes? In other words, how can the poet make the partiality of "I" into an interesting formal feature among many, as opposed to the be-all end-all of lyric utterance? More importantly, how can the solitary singer's story participate in the larger story, as Wallace Stevens puts it, "of the planet of which it was part . . ."?

My notion of the "I"'s partiality depends to a certain extent on understanding the range of solutions to the problem of solitary singing and its potential participation in the larger story of the planet. One of the most prevalent solutions has been to favor dissolution of the teller of tales into a tale that tells itself, language out on its own space walk, floating through referentiality, as opposed to being anchored in it. You might call this a constructivist perspective, in which words have their own autonomy and plasticity, and meaning doesn't depend upon a solitary singer, but is the result of the poet's exploratory relationship to many different lexicons, ranging from the slogans of advertising to political rhetoric to the whisperings of private feeling. Of course the danger here is relegating the singer to a language prop, or what one critic dubbed the "subjectivity effect."

And then there's Allen Ginsberg's notion of poetry as "first thought, best thought." This approach makes the solitary singer's song the by-product of a meditative practice of mindfulness that would release us from the world of illusion to the eternal truths behind the veil of Maya. To further that recognition, Ginsberg was willing to sacrifice what he called "the whole boatload of sensitive bullshit" that undergirded the myth of poetic mastery. A poem's *raison d'être* is to serve as a prayer wheel whose mind-expanding spin helps us contemplate the inexhaustible forms of reality, and of the unity behind those forms. His poetry of swift notation proposes that the self is nothing more—or less—than the ebb and flow of perception, in which perception is a springboard to comprehending the Oneness of the universe.

Another tack is Robert Duncan's practice of poetry as composition by field: the page is a field of possibility and the words are actions on that field. That the actions are of consequence becomes a matter of knowing when the self is at the right spiritual pitch to plot a significant course in words, the words open to the accident of inspiration at every moment of composition. There is no perfected "form" for the poem to take on, no conventional adherence to beginnings, middles, or ends. Every poem the poet writes is really the sign of a continually unfolding revelation that only comes to an end at the poet's death—and not even then, because the story is taken up by other poets, and in Auden's phrase, "modified in the guts of the living."

And now I hesitate. My sense of the dilemma that faces contemporary poets and how they represent "I" might simply boil down to this: no matter how fragmented words appear on a page, they will tell a certain story, if only as the trace of the mind that willed them onto the paper. And so the "I" is still intact, if not as a personality in words, then as words diffusing the traces of a personality, a doppelgänger projected outward from the page. And so the mere presence of a poem suggests that the poet is also a subjective presence, if only as a projection of the operations of language. Well, and so what? Who didn't know that if you saw marks on a page that someone put them there? But is that really as obvious as it sounds? Well, yes—provided that you're willing to grant those marks the provisional status of "author"—but if you aren't, or if your initial reaction is to think this is writing, *l'écriture,* an inheritance of the tribe's codes and customs, as opposed to thinking this is the texture of an individual mind, then the question of the authority of who is speaking becomes important in our experience of these marks.

Most serious readers float somewhere halfway between these two shores and reserve judgment about the issue of authority until they are well into the experience of reading. But this very reservation of judgment is also a hesitation that effects writers: I can identify at least three tendencies in American poetry that this self-consciousness has engendered: the fact that "I" has been impeached as too confident in its pronouncements has forced some poets to adopt the tone of self-reflexive irony and jokiness that undercuts the commitment of the voice to any particular tone, stance, or provisional stab at truth. This is an extremely popular stance, and amounts to a widespread period style. Another strategy is to adopt the tone of phenomenological inquiry, but to do it in such a way that suggests an obsessive temperament relentlessly interrogating perception: the stance here is that the obsession flows from an obsession with "truth"—a truth that may already be discredited as merely a projection of human desires, but is better than nothing. When this stance amounts to more than a surface manner, it can produce poems of great power and integrity, as in the work of Frank Bidart, or in the best poems of John Ashbery. But all too often, it degenerates into the third tendency: an armored, "smart" sounding vocabulary that steers back and forth between the referential and the hiply nonreferential, a kind of brainy, process-is-all surrealism that at its best promises verbal innovation, and at its worst feels utterly formulaic in its disjunct leaps of association—a more complex variant of the above-mentioned joky ironist, but who as an undergraduate read a smattering of Lyotard and Baudrillard and picked up their tone of philosophical inquiry.

But let me put my cards on the table and suggest another way of thinking about the impeached "I." What I'm proposing is not to be taken as a manifesto, but a speculation on how the self in poetry is a kind of self-impersonation, the subject of a voice, or voices, that are always aware of their own provisional status. As I mentioned earlier, I want to incorporate that provisionality into the poem's formal structure. The shortcoming in Whitman's stance toward the wounded, in which Whitman desires to be the wounded person, is that he seems unconscious of his own limited subjectivity. The verbal formulas Whitman resorts to, the catalogue, the relentless parallellisms, speak to the automatic nature of Whitman's response. And the difference between a poem like *The Waste Land* in its multiple voicings and many-eyed perspectives, and my speculation, has to do with Eliot's manipulation of the voices in the poem.

Great a poem as it is, there is something faintly imperious about Eliot's virtuosity, the sense of a puppet master deploying the materials of his poem with just a touch too much certainty. The material, for all its portents of chaos, never really seems on the verge of spinning out of control. And it's precisely this sense of the material beginning to get away from the poet, the sense that the voices in the poem have an autonomy beyond the authorial presence, that interests me. And from a reader's viewpoint, I mean more than the fact that poems often bear contrary meanings to their authors' overt intentions, as in the case of Blake reading Milton and saying that Milton was of the Devil's party, but without knowing it. In my scenario, the poet is deeply attuned to the paradoxes and contradictions inherent in having both devils and angels whispering in his ear: the poet must express, simultaneously, the many ways that such opposing and unruly recognitions might function in a poem.

Many contemporary writers have responded to this question of self as self-impersonation, but what do I mean by that phrase? Of course, it's a truism that the first thing any writer does is impersonate whoever the "I" is that does the writing. Italo Calvino, in an essay on the levels of reality in literature, creates a flow chart that starts with Gustave Flaubert, the author of various books who then impersonates the author of the book he is currently working on, in this case, *Madame Bovary,* who then projects himself into Emma Bovary who then projects herself into the Emma Bovary she would like to be. The salient thing about this flow chart is that it works in reverse as well, with each link in the chain reaction transforming, both forwards and back, all the other links. So when Flaubert says, "Madame Bovary, c'est moi," the question arises as to how much of the "I" who shapes the characters is, in fact, an "I" who has been shaped by the characters. In American literature, this way of thinking has been taken to an extreme point by a poet like James Merrill in *The Changing Light at Sandover,* in which the poem's author, James Merrill, is also the speaker of the poem who also becomes a character denominated in his speeches by the initials, JM, even as the entire poem's cosmological machinery is made present to the author/character through the oracular voicings of a Ouija board. This is obviously a radically different and mischievous way of thinking about writing than the myth of the writer as a little god or as a master of language who "treats" his material by giving it style. But you don't have to go as far as Merrill does in order to see that this flow chart notion of intersubjectivity upends the traditional hierarchy of author set above his so-called "characters."

How seriously do I mean all this? I don't for a moment imagine that anyone will sit down with this model in their head and apply it systematically. But what I'm interested in is finding a way of talking about the slippery transactions that go on between whoever "I" is and the words that "I" is putting on the page: the old model of revision as the writer working toward a formal unity seems to me far too limiting a description of the possible ways of writing poems. And since one of the crucial determinants in how you think about the art is the way you envision embodying the self in language, I'm interested in putting forth a new description that opens up the old model, if not exactly exploding it. The various levels of reality that interact in the creation of art, the empirical, psychological, supernatural, aesthetic, mythic, all of which sort together in a play like *Hamlet* (*e.g.*, the political rottenness of Denmark; Hamlet's state of mind; Hamlet's father's ghost; the play within the play; and the actors killed off as characters and resurrected as themselves at the curtain call), suggest just how insufficient and blinkered this all too settled notion of "I" is.

But how would a poet actually write the kind of poem I envision? Let's imagine P walking down the street to do some shopping, his own internal monologue fissioning off in various directions: PTA, long-ago memories of late-night heroin parties, a fantasy about the Medal of Honor being given to John Waters, a plan to set aside certain hours in the afternoon to reread Paul Valery's musings on the character of Monsieur Teste, that monster of abstraction who knows the plasticity of thought because everything Monsieur Teste thinks his mind obligingly performs. P has a little notebook in his pocket, and suddenly these random thoughts begin to suggest words: the words keep getting distracted by a not-too-original erotic fantasy, a sort of bookmark that marks off the page of desire that P is currently perusing. But brushing away the thought, P sits on a bench, takes out the notebook, all the while feeling a little foolish to be doing this outdoors at a bus stop rather than at home at his desk: but the words are beginning to announce themselves: "The window is stuck. First tragedy of the day." And suddenly P is no longer P, he is stretched between his various thoughts and roles, he is stepping out of his skin and plunging into the currents of language. As P scribbles though, he begins to be aware of other P's that want to say things: the P that doubts that windows are tragedies, the P that wants to salvage that sense of tragedy by turning it into a joke, the P that begins to feel despair that any of these words will ever make it into a finished poem, let alone get published in a book of poems. And then P has a savage turn against the "I" that is writing the poem and puts down the notebook in disgust, suddenly torn between his sense of real tragedies, what he knows is the political awareness of the poem, and his desire to insist on the window's stuckness as indeed feeling like a tragedy, a metaphysical condition he can't escape from. And so the poet is stretched between politics and transcendence, and feels a growing hostility toward any settled position, and more and more desperate to be affected by, and responsive to, all positions at once. In Seamus Heaney's words, the poet is disposed to be "negatively rather than positively capable." And then he begins to pull away from the window and to try to view it from the farthest reaches of space, or to view it from as great a temporal distance as possible, in order to give that negative capability free play. Now he is channeling the spirit of George Herbert in which a human being "is a brittle crazie glass"; and as he peers through that glass he's also looking through Larkin's high windows, meditating on the "sun-comprehending glass,/And beyond it, the deep blue air,/that shows/Nothing and is nowhere, and is endless," and suddenly he is taking out his pencil again and writing a very different kind of poem: a poem that might say "I," but in which a "self-forgetful, perfectly useless concentration," in Elizabeth Bishop's phrase, has taken over all the anxieties, the hesitations and squirmings. And what to say about his concentration except that it seems neither an act of the self or the product of the many different voices that consciousness is woven from. It speaks, as Kafka says, with the voice of an alien stranger, but a stranger whose voice seems to resonate inside P, if not exactly belonging to P. And of course that voice keeps diffusing into voices: the voice of tradition that Herbert and Larkin represent, the voice of the social world that P inhabits, the voice of English itself in the way it inflects, reflects, and projects outward the words flowing from that "self-forgetful, perfectly useless concentration," in which will and imagination are involved in a call and response of completely mutual entailment.

I realize that this description can be dismissed as mere soft-focus blur—but that blur seems more true to the actual process of writing a poem than a more coherent laying out of terms and principles based on a myth of mastery of language. Of course, allowing yourself such permeability is its own talent. I see in that talent a kind of transcendent achievement that nevertheless has nothing to say definitively about the transcendence of the self. Of course, much contemporary academic criticism has focussed on calling into question the notion of a transcendental self, and in the process tries to eliminate the concept of individual authorial genius as a necessary criterion of literary and cultural value. These attitudes are expressed in the various HOW TO READ theories, in which an interpretive grid is laid on top of a poem so that it produces certain kinds of meanings in relation to that grid. My focal point is somewhat different, in that I am not so much interested in how we read, as in the experience of understanding what happens to us as we read. And since I'm a writer, I take the further step of trying to account for what happens to us as we write. If that's your point of entry, then what you are doing is trawling through your own unconscious processes for some glints and gleams that might prove useful to others when hauled up into the light. So when I say that the myth of mastery over language is insufficient and blinkered, I'm not doing so to undermine the difficulty of the art of poetry, and how the genius of individual poets negotiates that difficulty. What I am doing is hoping to find some inklings and intuitions that will suggest a more comprehensive model of subjectivity for the working artist.

I want poetry to be as complex, as resistant to easy generalization, and as humanly capacious as Proust's *Remembrance of Things Past* (one of the obvious models for Merrill's *The Changing Light at Sandover*). The many levels of reality the novel occurs on are paralleled by how the "I" can be split into a number of voices, all working under the aegis of the Argus-eyed Marcel: the narrator who writes the work (or rather complains about not writing the work), the sufferer of the narrator's tale who lives out what the narrator is nerving himself up to write, the social commentator of drawing rooms and bedrooms, the cultural historian of a bygone era. This many-eyed way of seeing many-leveled reality suggests, for poetry, the obvious analog of many different kinds of speech sorting together, with no self-consciousness about juxtaposing wildly differing lexicons and forms of diction. And this is precisely the procedure of John Ashbery. But Ashbery's is not the name that seems to exemplify in the fullest way possible the potentialities of a multiply overlapping "I." In fact, Ashbery's multivocal, multiperspectived way of writing a poem isn't so much a form of provisionality as a settled stance. In other words, the formal inventiveness in Ashbery has crystalized beyond the point where the formal structure of the poem is being called into question. Despite the associative movement that Ashbery has perfected, his poems as formal structures are fairly static. A reader knows more or less the linguistic territory Ashbery will inhabit, and from that settled perspective there is capacious, often brilliant insight into the "solving emptiness" that underlies daily life. But despite the standard critical line that Ashbery is a poet of ceaseless transformations, what I feel in his poems is a fatalist at work. Ashbery's ingenuity as a rhetorician doesn't extend to wanting to ground the "I" in a unitary identity, so as to call that identity into question, to explode it, to deny its existence, to diffuse it into the quietly rebellious pronouns at work in Anne Bradstreet's poem, or the myriad other operations you can perform. In other words, Ashbery assumes the multiplicity of "I," but never does that enter into his poems as a process of ongoing revelation. Consequently, Ashbery represents what Elizabeth Bishop once called "the mind at rest," as opposed to "the mind in motion."

Dissonance of feeling, the disrelation of "I" to any settled viewpoint, which is a way of being that seems foreclosed to the "mind at rest," is a quality in poetry that over the years I've come to prize more and more. As the "tale of the tribe" grows ever more complex, and the notion of subjectivity ever more vexed, I want to feel that every time the poet sits down to write is the occasion of what John Crowe Ransom called "a last ditch ontological maneuver." And while I admire Ashbery's fidelity to his stance, and the melancholia of his habitual irony, there is nothing "last ditch" about his amiable, and wholly admirable relation to this issue of self and selves. In fact, the difficulty of pinning down Ashbery in his poems as anything other than the medium of language is one reason why he is such a bad model for other poets interested in the slippery relations of "I" to "the tale of the tribe." The positing of a unitary identity is crucial to a process of questioning that identity. Ashbery's associative movement is too strictly linear in what it is obliged to leave out: the sense that we are getting "the real John Ashbery," illusory and as much an effect of language as that may be, is simply not one of the formal burdens that Ashbery's poems are willing to take up.

And the winner is: Robert Lowell. Robert Lowell again? The Robert Lowell of *Life Studies?* The "I" writer to beat all "I" writers? How does Robert Lowell begin to exemplify, even remotely, the provisionality of the self, let alone many selves interacting under the aegis of multiple voices? But there are many ways in which Lowell and Ashbery are "near allied," especially late in Lowell's career in a book like *Day by Day.* The mode of these poems is the lateral movement of a highly associative mind that finds its generative cues as much in the synapse fire between words as in narrative or idea. But even a book like *Life Studies* has its own form of indeterminacy. What is it but a gallery of family portraits in which the faces, at first highly defined, by degrees begin to blend together into the composite face of a crucial cultual and historical moment in Cold War American life? But more narrowly, the question remains as to who is being portrayed. I would say that each of the characters in the book—from the mad black soldier in "A Mad Negro Soldier Confined at Munich" to Czar Lepke of Murder, Inc. in "Memories of West Street and Lepke"—are in fact aspects of the author's fractured sensibility, thinly veiled alter egos held together under the myth of the self as unitary. When you look at the personages in the poem, they begin to resemble a hall of mirrors in which the speaker keeps hoping to see in others' faces the lineaments of his own face in order to firm up his extremely shaky sense of identity. Of course, one could speculate on the relation between Lowell's mental illness, and the literalness of his desire to make writing a place where his identity would be fixed, stabilized between the pages of a book. And what I see as the course of Lowell's relation, or disrelation to the lyric self, is that early in his career he clung to the myth of the self as unitary, and late in his career, abandoned the myth but without losing his deep need to believe in it. And this shifting relation to the self in part accounts for why Lowell, of all the poets of his generation, was the most protean stylistic shape shifter: from the formal grandeur of *Lord Weary's Castle* and *The Mills of the Kavanaughs* to the Chekhovian texture of autobiography in *Life Studies* to the loose-limbed omnium gatherum of *Notebooks* and *The Dolphin* to the final, elliptical, digressive meditations in *Day by Day*, you can see the poet adopting and modifying to his own purposes the different ways of handling "personality" that I've sketched out.

You can feel Eliot's penchant for collage, Ginsberg's love of the immediate, Duncan's trust in process, and the constructivist's faith in language all operating throughout the years that he wrote his version of the sonnet, and on into the autumnal greatness of *Day by Day*. But there are indications of all these temperaments at work in earlier poems: in a well-known interview, Lowell credits the Beats with having led him to the seemingly more informal, if no less formidably composed, poetry of *Life Studies* and *For the Union Dead*. Of course, to link Lowell with Ginsberg, Duncan, and constructivist aesthetics is to yank Lowell by the hair out of his own milieu: but rather than apologize, I think it's high time to get rid of blinkered notions about what it means to be "beat," "confessional," along with all the other noxious ready-made terms of literary journalism. The continuities are there, just as the discontinuities are unignorable. Only no critics to my knowledge have bothered to suggest the continuities, while the hobbyhorses about "confessionalism," "objectivism," and many another contending "isms" have been ridden into splinters.

Lowell's late work is a treasure house for other poets in a way that *Life Studies* never could be. Elizabeth Bishop once wrote Lowell that the mere circumstance of his being a Lowell gave his autobiographical impulses a certain edge over less illustrious family sagas. Although Bishop meant this as a compliment, it feels like an oversimplification. The flood of autobiography that attended the publication of *Life Studies* may have over valued the aesthetic of sincerity, but it ratified a fundamental shift in American poetry that, although Bishop and Lowell would come to abhor its more sensational aspects, dramatized the fundamental instability of "I" as a source of authority. The wide canvas of Eliot and Pound and the other Modernists, and their confidence in abstract forces outside the self (what Randall Jarrell once characterized as the monumental certainties that go perpetually by perpetually on time) had come to seem overweening. And the uncertain authority of the self even to speak about its own experience became more and more a part of the formal explorations that *Day by Day* testifies to, both in the associative way in which the poems build and disperse, and in the way they seem famished for the perspective of other voices.

In this late work, as in a poem like "Home" from *Day by Day*, Lowell dramatizes the self as a kind of self-impersonation in which the poem as a place of many different voices—there are no fewer than six different voices in the poem!—enacts the provisional nature of those voices that are always aware of their own subjective limits. And even though the self had first to be established in the early work before it could be taken apart, amplified and diffused over the immense terrain of the poet's intellectual and emotional life, the multiple selves that those voices in the later work imply are far more inclusive of the reader and the world precisely because of their instability and overlap.

In other words, Lowell interrogates in these quietly heartbroken, deeply meditative poems the many different selves reflected back from his work. The Christian agonist of *Lord Weary's Castle* becomes the secular householder and public-minded citizen in *Life Studies* becomes the kaleidoscopic, many-selved chronicler of private and public lives in *Notebooks* and *Day by Day*. There would seem to be many different poetic tongues speaking through the medium of "Robert Lowell." And the voices that speak through this medium are only incidentally concerned with autobiography: it's as if history were conceived of as an immense composite personality, one personality overlaid on another until the world of myth and the present day world of whatever poem Lowell was writing fused inseparably together. Lowell's central concern with the shape shifting of identity, and the burden that imposes on us as moral and social beings, led to his obsession with history as the lens he would use to explore this burden: but not history as large, impersonal forces working themselves out above and beyond mere human beings, but history as the concatenation of many human personalities caught up in their own intensely personal struggles.

So for Lowell, history is a kind of phantasmagoria of collective human strivings, folly, and aspirations. You could say his obsession with autobiography is an historical obsession with first person, eye-witness accounts that give back to history the feel and texture of flesh and blood experience—for Lowell, history and biography were seamless, as a book like *Life Studies* or *Notebooks* amply demonstrate. Seen from this perspective, history becomes the communal interweaving of the many different voices that inhabit us, none of them authoritative over the others, all vying and colluding to present experience as unique, unrepeatable, fleeing constantly ahead of all attempts to codify it.

This feeling for history as intimate detail led Lowell to invent ways of writing about the self that, if he were better understood, would illuminate and, more importantly, ground much of the previous thirty year's intellectual and artistic debate over the status of the self and its relationship to history. His generosity as an artist extends not only to putting our everyday concerns on an equal footing with strutting abstractions like History. Lowell also dramatizes how individual lives and history are as much about the shadowy colloquy between our own obscure inner voices and the world at large, as they are about verifiable subjects with names like Alexander the Great, Marcus Cato, Joinville, Robert Frost, and of course, Robert Lowell.

In keeping with this sense of history as a projection of liminally shifting identities, what Lowell's example so generously teaches younger poets is how to use antithetical conventions—whether Eliot's, Ginsberg's, Duncan's, a constructivist's approach, or the equally difficult ones of lyric narrative—to make a poem too messy to be thought of as an artifact, and too wrestled with and considered to be condescended to as process. Lowell, a compulsive reviser, wanted the labor to show: effortlessness and ease, a kind of spurious, surface perfection went against his impulse to roughen things up, to break down the expected boundaries between life and art. In pushing these boundaries, Lowell succeeded in making his poems hospitable to perspectives and voices other than his own. And so the "real" Robert Lowell and the Lowell of the page, the history-obsessed chronicler of his own so-called autobiography, in which autobiography is the sieve that strains his verbal genius, becomes the most synthetic of poets: in his developments and creative swerves, you can witness how "one life, one writing" is a response to the shifting authority of the self as it refracts into language and is shadowed forth into the world as a reputation and a name.

Space Composition in Two Poems by Robert Lowell

~

Let's begin with a hunch and a quotation: the hunch is eccentric—eccentric as in Euclidean geometry, off center: it concerns the intuition that poems describe certain shapes, and that those shapes can be reduced to simple geometric concepts: point, line, spiral, vortex. What kind of poem forms a line? And if a poem that is a line begins to curve into a circle or spin out into a spiral, then what properties of narrative and what kinds of materials, social, psychological, and spiritual, get set in motion? Moving from outward form to inward matter, the quotation has to do with the space created by the poem. Bernard Berenson once defined art as the process of "space composition," which "woos us away from our tight, painfully limited selves, dissolves us into the space presented, until at last we seem to become its permeating, indwelling spirit." When you add together my hunch and Berenson's intuition, you get a model for the complexities of narrative impulse in relation to the poem's materials, a way of talking about form as spirit and spirit as form.

When I was a boy, I used to love the puzzles that led you to connect dots one at a time, each dot numbered so that as your crayon or pencil raced numbered dot to numbered dot, a picture of a face would begin to appear—and as that face sprouted a nose, and the lips formed up, you began to imagine the kind of person it was whose face you were conjuring out of the dots. That, in its simplest form, is what I take Bernard Berenson to mean by "space composition": the creation of a space where human personality finds a way beyond its point-to-point outline to express what Berenson unself-consciously, and without any hedging, calls "indwelling spirit." And if we think to ourselves how that process of connecting dots makes us aware of how straight lines begin to bend into the arc of the cheek, or curve of the jaw, so that as we draw the face, the face is constantly changing, revising our assumptions and guesses about whether it's the face of a man or woman, the features hinting at kindness, impatience, calm—then I think it becomes clear how I'm using point, line, circle, spiral, vortex to suggest the process of telling a story. So "space composition," whether the medium is language or the plastic arts, is a way of making in space a significant shape that unfolds in time: in the case of my follow-the-dots puzzle, the lineaments of eyes, nose, and mouth that suggest the peculiar qualities of that face's indwelling spirit.

Of course, the way that story is told has profound implications about how we think of that vexed concept, "indwelling spirit." I realize that the confidence of Berenson's definition, it's old-style humanist faith in the power of art to create a sense of communion, may seem a little too easy—though Berenson also knows that art is a "seeming" kind of experience: it only *seems* as if we become the indwelling spirit, it only *seems* that we permeate the space created. So as a way of upping the spiritual ante, and calling Berenson to account for dissing, however therapeutically or kindly meant, "our tight, painfully limited selves," here is a quote by Czeslaw Milosz from "Ars Poetica?":

> The purpose of poetry is to remind us
> how difficult it is to remain just one person,
> for our house is open, there are no keys in the doors,
> and invisible guests come in and out at will.

Obviously, Milosz puts a higher priority on the difficult integrity of having a self at all. In comparison, Berenson tends to view the self as a kind of tight, painful knot, a sort of charley horse that needs to be massaged by art into cloud-like pliancy. Two poems by Robert Lowell, both recounting sojourns in mental hospitals, illuminate these competing speculations about the self. Written almost twenty years apart, "Waking in the Blue," published in *Life Studies* in 1959, and "Home," collected in his final book, *Day by Day,* in 1977, reflect such wildly different attitudes toward language and the experience itself that it seems as if different poets had written them. What I hope to show is how Lowell, at least as a persona in his poems, transformed himself from a tight, painfully limited self to the wider consciousness and more embracing humanity implied by Berenson's notion of art as a way to dissolve identity into the space presented, until we seem to permeate the space with our shared but also separate subjective lives.

I also hope to provide a practical example of how one artist took his art to another level by giving himself latitude to experiment, to the point where he seems to demolish every move in his stylistic playbook, and finds a new way to write. Whatever part his mental illness played in his sylistic shape shifting—and certainly it enlarged the range of his experience, and, who knows? perhaps crossed his lexical wiring in bizarre and interesting ways—he was the kind of writer who could only go forward by changing his stylistic spots. By this, I don't mean the standard "breakthrough" narrative, in which a poet suddenly "finds his voice" and writes happily ever after; this gives the poet's labor short shrift, especially when that labor is dedicated to finding ways to embody many different voices and vocal registers. In fact, the very notion of "finding your voice" is too static, too neat, too overweeningly certain that we can summon from the deep "The Voice." It leaves out the struggle of having to unlearn a style, a process every bit as important and difficult as acquiring one. As if artistic achievement could ever be made reliable—Ovid can tell you how to apply makeup, but beauty isn't guaranteed. I remember a poet once telling me that by throwing off the influence of Modernist X, he had "found the voice by which posterity will know me." To listen to him talk, he seemed in complete control of this "catch-all, do-all" voice: I could imagine him laying out his subjects like corpses in a mortuary, intoning over each of them in the same "signature-style" rhetoric, and generally reducing them to clods. It's a little depressing to think "finding a voice" can even be a goal for a poet. And so I hope Lowell's struggle to embody, in new and resourceful ways, "the invisible guests" that "come in and out at will" can inspire, as well as admonish us, to avoid the worst dead end of all: complacency.

There is nothing complacent about "Waking in the Blue," a grimly humorous dramatization of a tight, painfully limited self, which shows in spades what Milosz means about the difficulty of being just one person. You could say that the Lowell persona in the poem is like a line—a tightrope, say, stretched out over an abyss—but that the shape of the poem's dramatic action describes a circle:

Waking in the Blue

The night attendant, a B.U. sophomore,
rouses from the mare's-nest of his drowsy head
propped on *The Meaning of Meaning.*
He catwalks down our corridor.
Azure day
makes my agonized blue window bleaker.
Crows maunder on the petrified fairway.
Absence! My heart grows tense
as though a harpoon were sparring for the kill.
(This is the house for the "mentally ill.")

What use is my sense of humor?
I grin at Stanley, now sunk in his sixties,

once a Harvard all-American fullback
(if such were possible!),
still hoarding the build of a boy in his twenties,
as he soaks, a ramrod
with the muscle of a seal
in his long tub,
vaguely urinous from the Victorian plumbing.
A kingly granite profile in a crimson golf-cap,
worn all day, all night,
he thinks only of his figure,
of slimming on sherbet and ginger ale—
more cut off from words than a seal.

This is the way day breaks in Bowditch Hall at McLean's;
the hooded night lights bring out "Bobbie,"
Porcellian '29,
a replica of Louis XVI
without the wig—
redolent and roly-poly as a sperm whale,
as he swashbuckles about in his birthday suit
and horses at chairs.

These victorious figures of bravado ossified young.

In between the limits of day,
hours and hours go by under the crew haircuts
and slightly too little nonsensical bachelor twinkle
of the Roman Caholic attendants.
(There are no Mayflower
screwballs in the Catholic Church.)

After a hearty New England breakfast,
I weigh two hundred pounds
this morning. Cock of the walk,

I strut in my turtle-necked French sailor's jersey
before the metal shaving mirrors,
and see the shaky future grow familiar
in the pinched, indigenous faces
of these thoroughbred mental cases,
twice my age and half my weight.
We are all old-timers,
each of us holds a locked razor.

In an interview, Lowell once said that the secret of autobiographical and historical writing—and for Lowell, they were the same—is to give the reader the impression that you're getting "the *real* Robert Lowell." And as the poem demonstrates, the patient's voice and Lowell's voice are constrained into one speaker: the reader is meant to believe that the solitary, suffering consciousness of the patient is identical to the suffering consciousness of the poem's author. And so you could say that Lowell as author and Lowell as subject make up a linear self, a self in which all the points line up into a single identity. What this linear self dramatizes is the conscious mind wrestling with the seduction of the animal vitality of mania; this accounts for the proliferation of animal, or animal-related, imagery: catwalks, crows, seals, harpoons, whales, cocks, thoroughbreds, even a phrase like "turtle-necked." That vitality is cut off from language and contact with others, as evidenced by Stanley, "more cut off from words than a seal." None of the characters in the poem seem able to reach beyond their own much reduced linear selves: Lowell's focus on Stanley's, Bobbie's, and his own physique holds the suggestion that their bodies are really one body, the composite body of the old-timer locked away with a locked razor. And his half ironic, half rueful recounting of Stanley's and Bobbie's former Harvard glory days make them seem like points in a line that lead directly to the "real" Robert Lowell whose "shaky future" threatens to reduce his illustrious family name to a mere "Bobbie." Former fullback, ex-clubman, and madhouse cock of the walk, their concerns aren't exactly world historical. Limited to slimming on sherbet and ginger ale, or swashbuckling in one's birthday suit while horsing at chairs, or strutting about while observing the figure you cut in the unbreakable metal shaving mirrors, for these "thoroughbred mental cases" the outside world of "Azure day" only makes Lowell's "agonized blue window bleaker."

The temporal shape of the poem is similarly circumscribed, turning round and round in a circle: the poem describes a specific moment in the present, dawn; then depicts a generalized present, a day in the life at McClean's; then closes the circle by returning to a particularized present in the final stanza. This is a parodic vision of a well-breakfasted Lowell trying to look macho in his "turtle-necked French sailor's jersey," seemingly at home with the other "thoroughbred mental cases," but also terrified by their "pinched indigenous faces." In these lines, the use of "turtle-necked" and "thoroughbred" as adjectives ricochet back to the earlier suggestions of encroaching animality. And in this stanza's last two lines, which circle back around to the opening evocation of "the house for the 'mentally ill,' Lowell comes up with the central insight of the poem: his inclusion of himself in the category "old-timers," a recognition overlaid by a sense of doomed futurity. This "Cock of the walk" will descend into animality just as surely as Stanley and Bobbie have. So you can see how all the characters in the poem tend to become aspects of Lowell's stricken consciousness: the "shaky future" he sees in the "pinched, indigenous faces/of these thoroughbred mental cases" is very much his own. Lowell's bravura use of physical description differentiates one patient from another, but underneath the wonderfully concrete surfaces of the poem, they link up like points in a line.

If we step back from the poem's hepped-up drama though, the character of the speaker is slightly more complex than what I've allowed: the isolated, anguished patient in the first stanza becomes a social commentator in the parenthesis that ends the stanza. Lowell's concern to make this statement parenthetical distances himself from his own avowal that "this is the house for the 'mentally ill.'" He is desperately trying to maintain a difference from his surroundings, even to the point of putting "mentally ill" in quotes, as if the punctuation itself were a way to ward off the contagion of madness. All the evidence to the contrary, he wants to think of himself as an outsider, not a full-fledged member of the Bowditch Hall club. In the next stanza, too, after ruefully acknowledging that his sense of humor may well be useless in helping him cling to his outsider status, he nonetheless presents a grimly comic vision of ruling class, Boston blue blood gone sour. But the humor feels strained: he can joke all he wants, pointing out the incongruity of a "kingly granite profile" wearing "a crimson golf-cap"—but such joking can hardly short-circuit the seductive electricity of mania.

Part of the mania is the subtle way that Lowell tries on each identity in the poem in turn, as if Bowditch Hall were a hall of mirrors, and Lowell were searching among the faces reflected for his own. The portraiture that goes on in "Waking in the Blue"—night attendant, Stanley, Bobbie, and their ghost image, Robert—presents one face on top of the next, as in an Old Master subjected to X rays, where you can see different versions of Christ's face superimposed. The relentlessly Dutch still-life manner of detail piled on detail has for me a frantic quality of holding on: as if physical description was a rock to found a paper self on; a self that might help firm up the poet's shaky future; a self that will stay the same every time you read the poem, even though that self is purportedly "mad"; a self that the covers of a book will keep from sliding off into chaos. How high the stakes are for the poet, as if he actually were attempting to anchor his identity in the substrate of words! No other writer of his generation could claim such an unliterary, quirkily personal aim for their work. And when the self that the words conferred on him no longer held firm, Lowell dismantled his "self" by dismantling his style. No wonder the teeth-clenching intensity Lowell brought to his writing—the poet makes himself up out of words until the words begin to crack under the strain. Of course part of that strain is the spectacle Lowell makes out of his own and the other patients' suffering. The "real" Lowell's deep identification with this suffering is heightened by his status as a Boston Brahmin among other mentally ill Boston Brahmins. Their shared sickness becomes an emblem of social decay, their privilege of birth and circumstance linked to spiritual ossification.

Now, let me reverse directions and circle back to an earlier draft of "Waking in the Blue." After the finished poem, this may seem like hard dealing: but it's also heartening to see how such a serious artist can also write like a klutz: if Lowell had not been such an obsessive, as well as intelligent reviser, it would have been a public service to literature to keep him locked up in McClean's. However, what is fascinating about these drafts is that the style Lowell would adopt twenty years later is already there, in embryo. Though he may have made the poem resemble a line inside of a circle, you can see by the twists and turns in these early drafts that Lowell's linear self and circular construction were always on the point of warping into a spiral and starting to spin like a vortex. As one can see in the drafts that follow, the way he places abstractions so that they break up the linear continuity of the narrative is precisely the formal impulse that he rejects in "Waking in the Blue," but which he embraces in the later poem, "Home." In fact, this kind of speculative and associative drift becomes in his later poems one of the most enlivening features of his style. What seem at first like non sequiturs are, in fact, the currents of the mind as it launches itself out on ever-widening reaches of sensation and experience, which it funnels down to a focal point so that everything Lowell sees and feels can suddenly find its way into his poetry: as Lowell once said, you can say anything in a poem, provided you can place it right. Yes, and provided that you have the courage and artistic panache to twist the linear brilliance of your old style into the poetic equivalent of a pretzel.

These drafts were written during his first two weeks in a locked ward at McLean's Hospital. Ann Adden, the poem's dedicatee, was a young woman that Lowell was infatuated with. The first draft bears the title, "To Ann Adden (Written during the first week of my voluntary stay at McLean's Mental Hospital)":

> Like the heart-toughening harpoon,
> or steel plates of a press
> needling, draining my heart—
> your absence . . .
> What use is my sense of humor,
> basking over "Jimmy," now sunk in his sixties,
> once a Harvard all-American (if such were possible from
>   Harvard)
> still with the build of a boy in his twenties,
> as he lolls, ram-rod
> with the luxuriance of a seal
> in his long tub,
> vaguely sulphurous from the Victorian plumbing.
> His bone brow is crowned with a red golf cap
> all day, all night,
> and he thinks only of his build,
> gobbling ice-cream and ginger ale—
> how to be more shut off from words than a seal.
>
> Thus day breaks in Bowditch Hall at McLean's;
> it ends with "Hughey" 29,
> looking like Louis XVI
> released from his white whig *[sic]*,
> reeking and rolly-polly as a sperm whale,
> as he careens about naked,
> horsing down chairs.
> This fine figure of bravado ossified young.
> In between the limits of day, here,
> hours and hours go by under the crew haircuts,
> and slightly too little non-sensical bachelor eyes
> of the R.C. attendants

(there are no blue-blooded
old Boston screwballs in the Catholic Church)
Ann, what use is my ability
for shooting the bull,
far from your Valkyrie body,
your gold-brown hair,
your robust uprightness—you, brisk
yet discrete *[sic]* in your conversation!

And here is a draft written a week later:

The night attendant, a B.U. student,
rouses his cobwebby eyes
propped on his Social Relations text-book,
prowls drowsily down our corridor. . . .
Soon, soon the solitude of Allah, azure day-break,
will make my agonized window bleaker.
What greater glory than recapturing the moment of glory
in *miseria?*
Snow's falling. Farther off in time,
a more illuminating snow:
on the slopes of the Mittelsell,
near Franconia, topped by Mount Washington,
you loom back to me, Ann,
tears in your eyes, icicles on your eyelashes,
bridal Norwegian fringe
on your coat, the wooly lining of a coat.

Your salmon lioness face is dawn.

The bracelet on your right wrist jingles with trophies:
The enamelled Harvard pennant,
the round medallion of St. Mark's School.
I could claim both,

for both were supplied by earlier,
now defunct claimants,
and my gold ring, almost half an inch wide,
now crowns your bracelet, cock of the walk there.

My Goddess. . . . But where in literature
has a goddess been able to stand up
to flesh and blood?
A lioness, then. With Descartes
I can almost lower animals to the realm of machines.
Ann, how can I charade you
In a lioness's wormy hide?—
massive, tawny, playful, lythe *[sic]?*

God be thanked, I now weigh 200 pounds,
have been a man for forty years;
You are 19,
see me still a St. Mark's sixth former,
my symbol the Evangelist's winged lion!

The first draft seems like a fairly credible effort, until it goes seriously off the rails when Ann Adden enters the poem. And in fact, the excision of Ann Adden is the single most important revision, not simply because she never never emerges as anything but a vaguely sketched goddess figure, but because her presence complicates the clean line Lowell draws between his identity and the identity of the other patients. Lowell seems to realize this when, in the first draft, he changes "your absence" to "Absence!" a metaphysical and psychological category—absence of self, perhaps?—derived from Ann Adden's presence. And when you look at how she's described in both drafts, her "Valkyrie body" and "gold brown hair" and "robust uprightness," "her lioness's wormy hide" complete with "icicles on her eyelashes," she begins to seem like a Goth goddess, as much kitsch and comic-book erotic daydream as she is a stereotyped version of "sanity" who wears school-spirit gewgaws from Harvard and St. Mark's School on her wrist, and is "brisk/yet discrete" *[sic]* in her conversation. Her portrait, so wildly at variance with Jimmy and Hughey (and it ought to be remarked that "Jimmy" becomes "Stanley," a more proper Brahmin name, while "Hughey" becomes "Bobbie," a diminutive of "Robert"), displays none of the satiric, intimate detail that makes the poem's anguish so concretely felt. And the lines about "defunct claimants"—a truly awful, so-bad-it's-almost-good phrase that seems to have escaped from a probate court brief—and the ring that is "cock of the walk" of poor Ann Adden's bracelet, are in the same McGonigle Hall of Fame for bad writing as the legendary opening of this undergraduate story about a concentration camp inmate: "Dawn came early at Auschwitz. But John didn't mind, he had always been an early riser."

And yet everything isn't dross in these drafts. The surreal "Your salmon lioness face is dawn" is splendid in its sheer weirdness, though there is nothing in the lines surrounding it to give it presence. And the lines about Descartes and his notion of animals as machines; the recasting of the famous lines that Francesca speaks in Dante's *Divine Comedy* (*"Nessun maggior dolore . . ."* to "What greater glory . . .") to give them a positive charge instead of a negative one; and even the loopy but fascinating "[. . .] where in literature/has a goddess been able to stand up/to flesh and blood," all point to a style in embryo. These verbal gestures, so abstract and riddling and speculative in comparison to the full-bore, descriptive blast of "Waking in the Blue," give off the aura of the uncanny, the paradoxical and incommensurate, that become central to the spooky sense of "solving emptiness" and transmogrification that underlies Lowell's later poems. As I said before, "Waking in the Blue" is so deeply rooted in this-worldly physicality because the poem attempts to found an identity in the midst of psychic disturbance. And that's why, in the finished version, he gets rid of the abstractions, speculations, and surreal touches that crop up in the second draft. In the most literal way possible, Lowell is creating a self on paper that will firm up his identity in the world. In order to make that self hold steady, he needs as much concrete physicality as he can muster. Posing real questions, such as "how can I charade you," or speculating about Descartes' view of animals, interferes with Lowell's need to invest himself in the concreteness of the crow, the night attendant, Bobbie, and Stanley—and when Lowell realizes his common lot with them, that recognition could be said to be the therapeutic gesture of the poem.

That gesture, in which Lowell the outsider becomes an insider—almost as if he were being initiated into a post-Harvard secret society—is ambivalent. While his sense of isolation gives way to the odd solidarity in thinking of himself as an old-timer, that solidarity is a fearsome one, fraught with the suggestion that Lowell will become one of McLean's lifers, a permanent fixture like Bobbie and Stanley. Yet bizarre a consolation as that may seem, to be an old-timer is at least to be part of a community—and one can sense a hint of grim pride in Lowell's identification. Underneath the social analysis and comedy, Lowell seems intoxicated with the extremity of his own experience. And rather than question that extremity, and put at risk his hard-won sense of solidarity, the only question Lowell allows into the finished version is a rhetorical one: to ask, "What use is my sense of humor?" is of a different order than the philsophically searching questions Lowell poses in the drafts. In "Waking in the Blue," his sense of humor is no use at all, just as it's no use at all to destabilize, by posing real questions, the self he's wrested from his suffering.

That self that Lowell establishes in the poem is like the locked razor in the final line—static for the moment, but capable of violence and harm. Yet when you realize that Ann Adden in the drafts is, in fact, a sort of lens that reflects back to Lowell the distance between himself at forty and an idealized, saner, younger version of himself that he hopes she sees, the "St. Marks sixth former,"

Lowell's eventual fate isn't as bleakly overdetermined as at first it seems. To see that you are what you are attempting to deny is a first step toward change. And while the struggle for Lowell in the poem is to produce the illusion of a single self—even a "mad" self is better than indeterminate flux of constant shape shifting—that self may have in it seeds of possibility for further transformation. And so to call it a "mad" self may be too narrowly linear. After all, this is a poem of memory in which a breakdown in the past is being dramatized as "the present," a fact that hints at more complex structures than the linear self and circular architecture I've been describing. While the poem hints at the nature of the future, nevertheless Lowell's act of self-removal from the actual present of McClean's Hospital to the imagined present of the poem, is a counter-prophecy to his permanent descent into animality. To put it differently, Lowell won't simply remain a locked razor, but as he says in another poem, he'll be "freelancing out along the razor's edge," freelancing suggesting a much looser formal relationship to his material than the one that he so brilliantly develops in *Life Studies.*

Now, let's jump forward almost twenty years to the later poem, "Home," published in *Day by Day* in 1977:

Home

Our ears put us in touch with things unheard of—
the trouble is the patients are tediously themselves,
fussing, confiding . . . committed voluntaries,
immune to the outsider's horror.
The painter who burned both hands
after trying to kill her baby, says,
"Is there no one in Northampton
who goes to the Continent in the winter?"
The alcoholic convert keeps smiling,

“Thank you, Professor, for saving my life;
you taught me homosexuality is a heinous crime.”
I hadn’t. I am a thorazined fixture
in the immovable square-cushioned chairs
we preoccupy for seconds like migrant birds.

“Remarkable breadown, remarkable recovery”—
but the breakage can go on repeating
once too often.

Why is it so hard for them to accept
the very state of happiness is wrong?

Cups and saucers stamped with the hospital’s name
go daily to the tap and are broken.
In the morgue and hospice of the National Museum,
our poor bones and houseware
are lucky to end up in bits and pieces
embalmed between the eternal and tyrants,
their high noses rubbed rough.
How quickly barred-windowed hospitals and museums go—
the final mover has all the leisure in the world.

We have none. Since nature,
our unshakable mother, will grow impatient with us,
we might envy museum pieces
that can be pasted together or disfigured
and feel no panic of indignity.

At visiting hours, you could experience
my sickness only as desertion . . .
Dr. Berners compliments you again,
“A model guest . . . we would welcome

Robert back to Northampton any time,
the place suits him . . . he is so strong."
When you shuttle back chilled to London,
I am on the wrong end of a dividing train—
it is my failure with our fragility.

If he has gone mad with her,
the poor man can't have been very happy,
seeing too much and feeling it
with one skin-layer missing.

~

The immovable chairs have swallowed up the patients,
and speak with the eloquence of emptiness.
By each the same morning paper lies unread:
January 10, 1976.
I cannot sit or stand two minutes,
yet walk imagining a dialogue
between the devil and myself,
not knowing which is which or worse,
saying,
as one would instinctively say Hail Mary,
I wish I could die.
Less than ever I expect to be alive
six months from now—
1976,
a date I dare not affix to my grave.

The Queen of Heaven, I miss her,
we were divorced. She never doubted
the divided, stricken soul
could call her Maria,
and rob the devil with a word.

In comparison to the simpler, line-within-a-circle development of "Waking in the Blue," the shapes "Home" describes are radically different. The linear self has become a vortex of selves and the circular temporality has gone fourth-dimensional. The voices in the poem include the other patients, such as the infanticidal painter incongruously speaking bored socialite chitchat ("Is there no one in Northampton/who goes to the Continent in the winter?") and the lugubriously earnest alcholic convert ("Thank you, Professor, for saving my life;/you taught me homosexuality is a heinous crime."); Dr. Berners, a sort of head doctor-cum-hotelier ("A model guest . . . we would welcome/Robert back to Northampton anytime,"); an interior spokesman who articulates the metaphysical views of the committed voluntaries *("Why is it so hard for them to accept/the very state of happiness is wrong?");* the voice of society gossiping about the reasons for Lowell's breakdown, and linking it to marital unhappiness (*"If he has gone mad with her/the poor man can't have been very happy,");* a social commentator in the museum passage; the devil that Lowell confuses with himself and who causes him to say, instead of "Hail Mary," *"I wish I could die."* And then there is Lowell's own voice, the voice of the "Professor," sorrowing, rueful, gently self-mocking. In its humorous quietude, that voice humanizes Northampton, and makes it seem just another part of the world, as opposed to McLean's, a place set apart from the world, "the house for the 'mentally ill.'" At Northampton, it isn't that the "Professor" and the others are out of their minds, but that their madness is nothing out of the ordinary, a form of immunity "to the outsider's horror." And so, unlike "Waking in the Blue," in which the poem's pivotal moment was Lowell's recognition of himself as an insider, in "Home" Lowell and the others are merely "tediously themselves."

As committed voluntaries, they talk about mundanities that clash with the extreme behavior for which they've asked to be hospitalized. In recording this clash, Lowell's sense of humor has darkened considerably from "Waking in the Blue." In "Home," his deadpan presentation of the painter who "burned both hands/ after trying to kill her baby" is both more consequential, and much harder to fathom, than the buffoonish antics of Stanley and Bobbie. The incongruities of character are still there in the way Lowell contrasts the painter's horrific actions with her numbed-out boredom at being in Northampton rather than someplace more exciting on the Continent. But the humor underneath the deadpan, the dead-level voice in which he recounts his and the other patients' suffering, is both creepier and more casual, sadder and wiser and more heartbreakingly despairing than "Waking in the Blue." It has about it the aura of a deeper knowledge, a mellowed, compassionate, all-the-way-to-the-bottom look at human fragility, physical and mental. The genius in the poem is the genius of Chekhov in Sonia's speech at the end of *Uncle Vanya,* in which human striving has come up against ordinary, but absolute limits. The patients in Northampton have been swallowed up by the immovable chairs of their separate and unavoidable fates, chairs that, in a genuinely surreal passage, "speak with the eloquence of emptiness." And that emptiness isn't the nerved-up "Absence!" of "Waking in the Blue." It's more a sense of ground-to-sky, dull gray cloud cover that you can't fly above or beyond, but is the constant element in which daily life goes on and inevitably expires.

And the temporality of the poem is similarly cloud-like, no longer the circle in "Waking in the Blue" of immediate present, generalized present, immediate present. It's evolved into something much more amorphous: a present which doesn't posit that time will ever get tired of changing shapes, as if time itself were an extension of that fated, hard-to-see-your-way-through miasma of daily life, in which

> In the morgue and hospice of the National Museum,
> our poor bones and houseware
> are lucky to end up in bits and pieces
> embalmed between the eternal and tyrants,

This is a sense of time in which "barred-windowed hospitals and museums" last only for a blink of the eye, in comparison to "the final mover" who "has all the leisure in the world." It's what the present would look like if you regarded it from the multiperspectived viewpoint of eternity encompassing every aspect of private and public life: mental breakdown is one of the permanent features of that present: "Remarkable breakdown, remarkable recovery."

In that sense, the feared prediction in "Waking in the Blue" has come true—Lowell is an old-timer; but this hasn't reduced him to unthinking animality. On the contrary, the poem is marked by a loose-limbed, quiet, speculative drift—the hyped-up exhilaration and acute physical anxiety of "Waking in the Blue" has been transmuted into a rueful, ironic, heartbroken meditative calm. The Romantic implications of madness as access to heightened intensity has given way to a darker sense of breakdown as simply another feature of quotidian life. The human world is particularly susceptible to breakdown and stands in ironic contrast to the world of things—the furniture in the clinic, the artifacts in the museum that are indicative of "the eternal and the tyrants," show how breakdown is a general condition. Whereas in "Waking in the Blue" breakdown was a hook to hang your identity on, in "Home" it's simply the psychic version of a general, ineluctable process of decay in the human and nonhuman world.

The final section of "Home," in which Lowell freely admits that he can't tell the difference between the devil and himself, suggests that his capacity for belief in a linear self to deliver him from the curse of his illness has been undermined: Lowell experiences a profound sense of despair ("the trouble is the patients are tediously themselves") when he imagines a fixed identity—the linear self has become a tombstone inscribed with his date of death, as opposed to a rock on which he can rest; and it certainly is not a stepping-stone toward further transformation. Even his nostalgia for the Queen of Heaven, which recalls Ann Adden as a principle of sanity and faith, but this time not as kitsch or erotic daydream, has bottomed out: "I miss her,/we were divorced" has a kind of anti-eloquence about it, it's clunky, plainspoken directness pitched against the mystique of Maria. In another eon of Lowell's life, she could have robbed "the devil with a word." But now her confidence in "a word" to save "the divided, stricken soul" is accorded the respect of a one-time believer in miracles who no longer can believe but desperately wants to: Lowell, after all, has become the indwelling spirit of the hospital, incapable of distinguishing himself from the devil, a diffusion of self into his surroundings that seems irreversible.

And yet the shape of the poem—drifting speculation, anecdote, differently voiced meditations from the world outside the hospital—moves with a fluency that you might call "freedom." At least this seems true when you compare it to the narrative shape of "Waking in the Blue." And "Home" also seems more cognizant of the world beyond the clinic, its meditative calm contrasting with the pumped-up, teeth-gritting intensity of the earlier poem, in which you feel the speaker in the poem is half enamored of the demon faces of mania. However, unlike Berenson, who finds solace in the dissolution of personality into the contemplated space of art, I don't sense much comfort in Lowell having become "the permeating, indwelling spirit" of this hospital that is the double of the world. "Home" as a title is ironic—the domestic hearth seems anything but home; the speaker's estrangement from Mary folds back into his estrangement from his wife; his own soul has open doors to the devil—home seems like a state of permanent exile, rather than a place to rest. And yet the poem does have a kind of richly orchestrated complexity of tone that convinces me that yes, despair is despair, but despair is knowledge, too.

So solace in the poem is not for the poet—whereas in "Waking in the Blue" at least Lowell came to the realization that he, too, is an old-timer. But because of the relative calm of "Home," and the way Lowell takes pains to puts our ears "in touch with things unheard of," the poet succeeds in "placing" not only his own personal troubles, but shows their wider connections to the world. In other words, he implicates the reader much more directly in the narrative shape shifting and the minute fluctuation of emotion as it unfolds, beautifully plotting the sine wave of his own mind's undulating pulse and surge. As readers, we aren't kept at manic arm's length from the mental anguish of the poem—which is a further example of how a vortex's pinwheeling perspectives can give a wider, more inclusive feel to what can seem like a fairly insular experience. And the wayward, unpredictable narrative structure of "Home," in comparison with the much simpler organization of "Waking in the Blue," reflects that broader, more humane perspective.

And so the despair the poem expresses isn't only the despair of mental cases, but shadows forth a communal recognition that makes one feel what Wordsworth meant by "the still, sad music of humanity"; a music mixed up with the quotidian desire to go on holidays and the murderous desire to kill one's own child; to say "Hail Mary" and find yourself saying instead, "I wish I could die." And yet Lowell's apparent despair in the poem, and his nostalgia for the certainties promised by the Queen of Heaven, becomes an instrument of intellectual and emotional inquiry, and in that sense a release from despair. The imaginative space that Lowell creates in "Home," so wide and inclusive in its sense of shared suffering, embodies both Berenson's hopeful sense of a collective, permeating, indwelling spirit, and Milosz's need to honor the privacy and incommensurability of pain.

"Some Measure of Insanity"

Let's imagine a comic strip in which T. S. Eliot and W. B. Yeats meet in a bookstore: Yeats dresses in a fur coat and calls even more attention to himself by wearing a red shirt. Eliot is dressed in immaculately tailored grays. They go over to the shelves to see if the bookstore carries their books. Neither Yeats or Eliot appears on the shelves. Eliot says, with a parson-like, self-deferential shrug, "It looks as if this bookshop doesn't carry my books." Rubbing his hands together in self-satisfaction, Yeats says, "God bless us, it looks like my books just sold out!"

Well, as we all know, the problem with criticism is that it makes points. So here is the story's point: it suggests to me two temperaments that are at the heart of how contemporary American poets think about their art—their art, not their reputations. The story comments on that as well—that's the manifest content—but what I'm interested in here is how the story suggests two conflicting impulses, the desire to communicate, but also to remain hidden: although both poets seem to want their books to be read, might the absence of the books suggest a certain ambivalence about being delivered up into their readers' hands? The fact that neither poet's book appears on the shelf could be the joke's subconscious wish. And I want to suggest ways in which this wish goes deeper than Yeats's apparent egotism or Eliot's diffidence. After all, Yeats's red shirt could be as much of a disguise as Eliot's grays. (As Eliot's tailor was reputed to have said about the poet, "Remarkable man,

Mr. Eliot: never anything to excess—quite.") So what is the nature of this ambivalence about wanting to communicate, and what are some of the potentialities for poetry that this ambivalence suggests?

I'd like to use as a springboard some notions from the child psychologist and pediatrician, D. W. Winnicott, notions about selfhood and its connection to the desire to communicate. As with much of Winnicott's terminology, its lack of specialization makes it flexible, but also a little obscure, if not downright vague. But since this is a speculative essay, perhaps a certain oracular looseness in terminology will get us farther than a well-mannered grid. I also want to propose that this conflict between wanting to communicate and remain hidden works itself out in both Yeats's and Eliot's styles, and that it accounts for the movement back and forth between relative stylistic obscurity and surface transparence. Furthermore, that some poets favor making the world a little hard to see, while others insist on proclaiming, in Stevens's words, "The near, the clear," accounts for most of the spleen vented among warring aesthetic camps over the last half century. Finally, I want to suggest that this spleen is being vented in a good cause—namely, in the fight against the erosion of privacy and the subtle creep of fascism—or at least that part of fascism directed against the inalienable right to maintain a certain solitude and distance from media intrusion through advertising, the cult of celebrity, and government surveillance.

But to return to the first question concerning the desire to communicate, but also to remain hidden. One way to address it is to establish a link between Eliot's famous little dictum about poetry and personality—that poetry should be an escape from personality, but that only those with personality would know what it is to want to escape from it—and Winnicott's views on privacy and the self. Eliot's comment makes personality seem like a kind of prison from which art has the potential to release him. This attitude toward personality has a certain associative relation to this statement by Winnicott: "In the artist of all kinds, one can detect an inherent dilemma, which belongs to the co-existence of two trends, the urgent need to communicate and the still more urgent need not to be found." Eliot's need to escape personality through art, and Winnicott's cryptic phrase about the artist's "still more urgent need not to be found" chime off each other in interesting ways.

What Winnicott means by not being found has to do with his notion of the self as needing a private space where the self cannot be exploited. By exploited, Winnicott means being forced out of what it means to each of us to feel what he simply called "real." Not feeling "real" has to do with the kinds of psychic accommodations that a person is forced to make when the nurturing environment is either insufficient or hostile to the development of the feeling of "a true self."

The experience of art, the deep absorption it can create, is part of what Winnicott means by real, and the artist is the exemplary figure who strives for that integrity of being that Winnicott so deeply values. Winnicott's somewhat rose-tinted view of the artist and artistic process would seem to be related to that deep absorption a child experiences when happily playing by itself in the presence of what Winnicott called "the good-enough Mother," who protects the child but doesn't stifle its creative play. The child's experience of separateness together is the emotional foundation for what Winnicott means by feeling real. To go beyond Winnicott, I'd like to speculate that this form of separateness together is akin to what poets, each in their own way, experience when engaged in the solitary act of writing a poem. And so the process of making art becomes a stand-in for the maternal figure hovering beneficently in the background as the child discovers the world through play. That is, the poet is kept company by the actual process of doing the writing. The artist experiences solitude as a form of connection with that process, as opposed to isolation, alienation, and all the other ways of being alone. J. Alfred Prufrock may be lamentably lonely and complain "I grow old . . . I grow old . . ."; but Eliot, at least during the time he's writing the poem, is absorbed in coming up with the pleasurable rhyme in the next line: "I shall wear the bottoms of my trousers rolled."

Of course I still haven't adequately defined "real" or "true self," but maybe that inadequacy can be thought of as a kind of speculative space for wide-ranging mental play. So part of the play I'm involved in now is to say a word about Winnicott's concept of self, as opposed to Eliot's distaste for personality, and the political implications of that concept. For Winnicott, the self is essential, and not a Foucauldian interweaving of various forms of discourse: what Eliot might plausibly have meant by personality. As I said before, to have a self that feels real means, in Winnicott's terms, the capacity to be happily alone. In a suggestive phrase, Winnicott speculates that feeling real means a sense of self that is not distorted or invaded by "communication seeping through the defences."

The reason why communication can be so damaging to the self's inviolability is a big subject: on a private, domestic level, it has to do with molding your sense of self to the demands of others. On a societal level, you might say that Winnicott's passionate espousal of the privacy of the self was an intuitive response to Foucault's obsession with the coercive nature of forms of discourse, and how those discourses, in their ramifying minutiae of rules and protocols, lead to a society obsessed with the domination of individuals and their bodies, to the inculcation of a political docility that is both internalized and coercively applied, and to ever more sophisticated systems of surveillance—in short, a subtle and pervasive form of fascism. It's as if Winnicott instinctively understood that the cultural symptoms of this fascism are a hostile attitude toward the privacy of individuals and the collective value that that privacy should be protected: a nation of happy solitaries is wildly opposed to fascism's goal of total societal control, especially if that control is exercised through forms of consumerism. In a true fascist state obsessed with buying things, the only time a person should be allowed to be alone (whether happily alone or miserably is of no matter), and thus unavailable to the blandishments of advertisers, telemarketers, and government propaganda—is when they are asleep.

In that case, you could say that truly creative individuals do their part against this goal by communicating with others in a way that reflects their true selves, but that also allows them to remain securely nested in that privacy of self where they cannot be found—either by fascism's fantasy of total domination, or the formulations of mass media, or even the deformations of self that the intimacies of domestic life can impose. As I said, Winnicott saw the artist as the exemplary figure of this profound ambivalence about communication. According to this conception, the artist both invites and wards off communication seeping through to the artist's most private self. Self might be said to be the core, while personality might be said to be the artist's adaptations to keep that core inviolable: Eliot's quiet, though studied elegance in dress, and Yeats's relative flamboyance, are equally forms of camouflage.

The paradox is that personality threatens, as a defense of the self, to also distort the self. Eliot's need not to be found is the need to sidestep formulations about the self, and that can lock the self into place, so the self can be found—and in Winnicott's view, once the self is found, it is there to be exploited. My hunch about Eliot's view of the relation between language and self is this: a poem is a form of communication in which the self must remain private, isolate even, and it must in some measure be oblique, a form of disguise as much as disclosure.

In contrast to this way of thinking about personality in poetry is the mode of much first-person, lyric autobiography, in which so much rides on the reader feeling the coherence and force of personal identity as sufficient cause for a poem. In this mode, it would seem that the artist longs not only to communicate, but to have that communication be a form of self-revelation. Of course, this predilection to be found can show forth forms of reality that go beyond what Eliot calls, somewhat disparagingly, personality.

W. B. Yeats's patently lyric speaker in "The Wild Swans at Coole" may partake of navel-gazing, but the quality of Yeats's attention to the "swanniness" of the swans reminds us that they are indeed wild swans, seminally alive, and a rudely honking rebuke to the poet's melancholy. As the swans "paddle in the cold/Companionable streams or climb the air;" the "bell-beat of their wings above my head," the poet goes beyond his anthropomorphism and seems to acknowledge, as Simone Weil once said, "It is better to say that I am unhappy than that the world is ugly." A poem of private sensibility, it also dramatizes the dangers of that privacy; and in its knowledge that the swans will delight other men's eyes once they have flown away, the poet would seem to yearn after a state of reality "cold and passionate as the dawn." For Yeats, the narrow focus of self-regard becomes a wide-angled lens, an instrument of "worlding," as Heidegger might put it.

These two impulses, or temperaments, seem to lie at the heart of how contemporary poets think about their art. L=A=N=G=U=A=G=E poets and those who are influenced by them are obviously partial to Eliot's need to keep the self hidden. Poets who are interested in lyric autobiography, and the self as a sign of the real, are partial to Yeats's desire to be found. The arguments between these two temperaments are generally conducted with all the finesse of Catholic Youth Organization boxers. I want to bypass these polemics, and instead make some speculations that seem to me to be of crucial importance in how contemporary poets think about their own artistic development, and the current cultural conditions in which artists both need to communicate and not be found.

In our media-glutted age, personality suggests the stink and blaze of a Hollywoodish public persona that is irremediably emptied out, one that opposes surface to depth, psychological interiority to manipulated façade—a façade that, as Keats put it, has designs upon us. "How beautiful are the retired flowers! how would they lose their beauty were they to throng into the highway crying out, 'admire me I am a violet! dote upon me I am a primrose!" The skepticism we might feel about Yeats's poetic candor is similar to Keats's mockery of a self-consciousness that can never see past its own marvelous petals. Yet Eliot's rueful recognition that only those with personality would know what it is to want to escape it, tacitly acknowledges that the act of writing poetry is in part a form of petal preening. A certain amount of self-display (or in Winnicott's terms, the need to communicate) comes with the territory of making art. Every poet, no matter how oblique their writing selves' relations may be to their own workaday selves' experience, is in the position of the primroses and violets!

The aesthetic controversies that roil between L=A=N=G=U=A=G=E writing and its spinoffs, and lyric autobiography and its spinoffs, seem not to have taken into account that the bloodiest rose of autobiography, the gaudiest orchid of surrealism, and the ghostliest lily of L=A=N=G=U=A=G=E writing are all forms, in one way or another, of self-disclosure. And because the artist also wants not to be found, the act of self-disclosure is always risky. This is true even if one subscribes to the view that the art of poetry is mainly a combinatorial operation that mixes and matches dictions, images, and styles of discourse, such that the self of the poet is subsumed by writing, diffused and absorbed into the quality of the language itself: ". . . Increments of routine/disinterest disabling trapezoids: trampolines of the/spleen." In these lines, the way Charles Bernstein plays with the prefixes, and rhymes "routine" with "spleen," opens up a space for the self to make its appearance, despite the surface obliquity. So the question of the private core, of what to do to protect "self" from the eyes of ready-made formulation, is of great concern, no matter how rigorously the pronoun "I" may be suppressed, or the conventions of fragmentation and syntactic indeterminacy, or the pinwheeling perspectives of distracted consciousness, are adhered to. To think that that risk can be avoided by resorting to certain methods of composition, no matter if your aesthetic predilections are with Eliot or Yeats, is to ignore just how insidious "communication seeping through the defences" can be.

An intriguing comment on this seepage can be construed from Wallace Stevens's poem, "The American Sublime," a poem that speculates about the place of spirit in a utilitarian society that regards with suspicion or indifference any claims to sublimity, either in art, Nature, or humanity itself:

How does one stand
To behold the sublime,
To confront the mockers,
The mickey mockers
And plated pairs?

When General Jackson
Posed for his statue
He knew how one feels.
Shall a man go barefoot
Blinking and blank?

But how does one feel?
One grows used to the weather,
The landscape and that;
And the sublime comes down
To the spirit itself,

The spirit and space,
The empty spirit
In vacant space.
What wine does one drink?
What bread does one eat?

The sublime, and its connection to fullness or emptiness of spirit, dovetails with Winnicott's concerns about the conditions under which a true self can be formed. The mickey mockers, hostile to any wavelength of feeling that vibrates at higher frequencies, resemble not only the eyes that would fix Prufrock "in a formulated phrase" and leave him "sprawling on a pin," but Yeats's almost identical fear of the "defiling and disfigured shape/The mirror of malicious eyes/Casts upon his eyes until at last/He thinks that shape must be his shape?" And since feeling real about one's emotional life is so crucial to the formation of a true self, and so to an artist's (or anyone's) inner integrity of feeling, in a world of plated pairs and bad statues of General Jackson, ". . . how does one feel" becomes a fundamental question. If you're the kind of temperament that wants more than "The empty spirit/ In vacant space," then emotion itself, as well as knowing how to experience emotion, depends on both spirit and space not being empty. To go barefoot, blinking and blank feels impoverished, especially when the empty spirit in vacant space clearly craves the wine and bread of communion—though not communion with some transcendent divinity, but richness of inner feeling.

What wine and bread to use (or buy—ours is a brand-name culture, after all) in order to commune with one's own heart underlines the melancholy of Stevens's hunch that "the sublime comes down" to "The empty spirit/In vacant space." Without access to what Stevens once called "the interior paramour," the spirit becomes empty, the inhabitant of a void. And so "The American Sublime" presents a cultural situation in which the feeling of real has been seriously undermined—and not just for Stevens, but for all of us. And I would say that this sense of emotional impoverishment is of deep concern to contemporary poets, and is one of the reasons why our current aesthetic controversies are so polarized and passionate. If integrity of feeling is threatened, then poetry as a category of consciousness is also threatened. Again, the examples of Yeats and Eliot shed a clarifying light on the various aesthetic strategies that contemporary poets have come up with to counter this sense of threat to feeling real.

In response to this threat, Eliot has chosen an ironic approach to emotion in order to more surely lay claim to it. Eliot's use in *The*

Waste Land of multiple viewpoints and the pinwheeling perspectives of fractured sensibility means that a reader is more aware of his poem as a literary construct. The poem's linguistic inventiveness, and Eliot's trust in the currents of language run counter to the impoverishing void of spirit and emotion that Stevens speaks of. In contrast, Yeats has approached emotion as if it were unimpeachable, and made language serve that confidence in the face of such impoverishment. The Echo of "Man and the Echo" may speak of grim truths that await all of us when we pass "Into the night," but there's no doubt that those truths aren't the ones of empty spirit in vacant space.

The contemporary poets who are most interesting to me are those who have taken into account Eliot's trust in words, and Yeats's trust in emotion, and used this accounting to resist Stevens's diagnosis of spiritual and emotional impoverishment. One way to deal with this impoverishment is to understand the "self," not so much as a linguistic construct, but as a kind of informal essence: an essence that Winncott insists on when he says: "A word like 'self' naturally knows more than we do; it uses us and can command us." Winnicott's canny understanding of the difference between our ability to talk about the self, and what the self actually is, flies in the face of most postmodern assumptions about the nature of language and the self. That selfhood is the trace of language is a truism for most postmodern thinkers, but Winnicott believes that the self is anterior to language. I find his insistence on our unknowing about how we actually are to ourselves immensely refreshing. His ordinary usage of words that other psychoanalysts go to great lengths to define suggests that "self" has as much reality for him as John's insistence that "In the beginning was the Word."

And there are contemporary American poets for whom this also seems true—notably David Ferry, Alan Shapiro, Michael Collier, Robert Polito, Anne Winters, James McMichael, Robert Pinsky, Frank Bidart, Rosanna Warren, Lloyd Schwartz, Gail Mazur, Donna Masini, Louise Glück, Anne Carson and others, as well as younger poets like Josh Weiner, Catherine Barnett, Tom Ellis, Victoria Redel, Peter Campion, and Dan Chiasson. That doesn't mean that they aren't uncritical of how to talk about that essence: none of them evinces the confidence of Yeats, or has the faith that Eliot did in language to substantiate emotion. Instead, their varied modes of address and intelligent skepticism draw attention to the at times appalling grandiosity and self-dramatizing hokiness that lyric autobiography at its worst can engender.

To take just one example, David Ferry's poems about street people are scrupulous in acknowledging the limits of what he can know about their subjective lives. In his version of the sestina, "The Guest Ellen at the Supper for Street People," the speaker of the poem is as other to Ellen as she is to him. At the same time, this poet's committment to not being found doesn't sacrifice emotion to that barefoot, blinking blankness. Ferry is again exemplary in how he handles the issue of the speaker's authority in relation to the poem's ostensible subject, the tormented Ellen:

> One has to keep thinking there was some source of torment,
> something that happened someplace else, unclean.
> One has to keep talking in a reasonable voice
> about things done, say, by a father's body
> to or upon the body of Ellen, in enchantment
> helpless, still by the unforgotten event
>
> enchanted, still in the old forgotten event
> a prisoner of love, filthy Ellen in her torment,
> guest Ellen in the dining hall in her body,
> hands beating the air in her enchantment,
> sitting alone, gabbling in her garbled voice
> the narrative of the spirits of the unclean.

What emerges is that the speaker's suppositions about why Ellen is the way she is becomes a tactful imagining of the speaker's own veiled sense of degradation, shame, and helplessness before the spectre of some enchantment that is nameless and all powerful. Ferry's subtle self-implication is what makes his emotional investment in Ellen's plight credible.

In contrast to a poet like Ferry is the straightforward FEEL poet—or to put it more accurately, that poet's tendency to keep pressing the FEEL IT IS BEAUTIFUL TO FEEL button. What "self" knows is assumed from the beginning of the poem to be identical with what the author knows. This is a type, of course—every artist to some extent wants to press the FEEL button. Let's imagine such a poet writing about the guest, Ellen. Instead of Ferry's tact in keeping his speculations about Ellen tentative, and acknowledging that they are his projections, a FEEL poet might write something like this:

> The source of her torment
> was a place that was unclean;
> things were done to Ellen by a father's body,
> yes, a father did such things to Ellen in her enchantment,
> Ellen made helpless by the unforgotten event,
> and made a prisoner of love, poor filthy Ellen lacking voice

and so forth. This mangling of Ferry's poem strips out all the self-implicating strangeness of the speaker's construal of the events that led to Ellen's tormented state. In my version, Ellen's privacy is being violated by the confidence of the poet's assertions. Since Ellen lacks a voice, the poet, in the guise of speaking for her, only succeeds in reducing her to his own formulations. In Winnicott's terms, Ellen's core has been found and is now being doubly violated: once by the father, and the second time by the poet who thinks that he knows what only "self" knows. My hypothetical poet seems utterly unconscious of having pinned Ellen to the wall. As I said, this is a tendency in poetry in which the inviolable core isn't allowed speculative space between what "self" knows and what the poet knows.

The opposing tendency—or rather the same tendency, just a different manifestation of it—would be a type that wanted to nail down what "self" knows with a self-reflexive irony coupled to nonlinear techniques—the kind Eliot pioneered in "The Love Song of J. Alfred Prufrock" and developed into *The Waste Land*. This type relies mainly on every poet's interest in the formal strategies of language, and the kinds of experience—linguistic, emotional, and intellectual—that formal possibilities open up to an artist. I remember a poet friend going on and on about Rilke's famous dictum, "You must change your life," and how he ought to go to Africa, go to India, work in hospitals, work in banks, in order to shake up his poetry. I was with another, mutual friend of ours, and as we walked away from the meeting, the mutual friend said, "He doesn't need to change his life, he just needs to change his line length."

The moral of the story is that what "self" knows and can command us to do may grow out of the experience of words, as much as experience of the world: that words are also a form of experience is probably the most valuable insight that the nexus between L=A=N=G=U=A=G=E writing and certain forms of critical inquiry have to offer to younger poets, especially those who attend writing programs. Maybe it's lack of experience, or maybe it's because anyone who offers you instruction in how to write seems to promise what, in fact, can't be delivered: a reliable way to write interesting poetry. At any rate, there are a lot of poets who seem intent on pressing the WORDS ARE GOOD ARE GOOD ARE GOOD button to the exclusion of the FEEL button. This may avoid certain clichés of feeling by committing clichés of rhetoric equally as noxious.

At the beginning of this essay, I speculated on Winnicott's notion of the privacy of self as an intuitive response against cultural symptoms of creeping fascism. Of course, my reliance on Winnicott bypasses the question of how Yeats's stylistic choices reflect his conservative nature; and the attempt to make these kinds of linkages has been one of the reasons why contemporary poets often seem to be in warring aesthetic camps. If your style and your politics are one, then that ups the ante on aesthetic choices as something that goes beyond formalism, or mandarin concerns with "standards." The consensus view of most artists is that art is supposed to foster forms of political organization that are inclusive, democratic, nonhierarchical—an ideal, obviously, and some would say a softheaded kind of Cloud Cuckoo Land ideal. And if you're a skeptic as well as a liberal, who can argue with either of these views? In effect, that consensus makes it hard to say anything of value, or at least interesting, about stylistic choices and the politics of contemporary writing—NEWSFLASH: Fixed forms are a form of fascism applied to your own subconscious! The only way to the future is to write in nonreferential language using lots of murky abstractions! Vatic mumbling is good! Reason is bad! And the mandarin side of the debate is equally silly: Tradition is what counts! Clarity above all! Rhyme and meter link us to the Great Ones! We stand on the shoulders of giants! All originality is a return to the Source! One can't help but think of Goya's painting of two berserkers clubbing each other to death in a bog. And so rather than talk about contemporary writers in this context, let me simply say that how we write and our political affiliations run deep. Simply put, Yeats's affection for Ireland led him to advocate for Irish independence, and this desire for a public voice fostered a proclivity for what he called "a passionate syntax," thus producing the vernacular compression of the later poems. But the relation between Eliot's style and his politics is far more complicated, especially because his stylistic affinities and the drift of his politics are so frequently at odds. The many dimensions of Eliot's voices, and the uncategorizable nature of *The Waste Land* in its use of contradictory aesthetic conventions, makes it a perpetual and vital challenge to Eliot the critic's authoritarian notions about culture as Christian, hierarchical, and aristocratic.

In trying to account for the conservatism of Eliot and Yeats,

I've touched on cultural conditions and trends that have only accelerated in our own day. These conditions were both addressed by Yeats and Eliot, Yeats in his directly stated fear that "the center will not hold," Eliot in his more skeptical, formalist's way of making the poem in its structure reflect that lack of center. The fact that *The Waste Land* has no central narrator, but what might be called tonal centers or nodes of sensibility sending out various complementary and competing signals, speaks to a contemporary unease with what Seamus Heaney calls the Absolute Speaker: the voice of undisputed authority that speaks in the dominant accents of the ascendant imperial power of the moment—in Heaney's case, the voice of the BBC radio announcer. The Absolute Speaker is the Big Brotherish incarnation of Prufrock's "eyes that fix you in a formulated phrase." It's interesting to note that Eliot, the conservative critic, would be in the guise of Eliot, the revolutionary poet, the purveyor of literary techniques that suggest ways of resisting the Absolute Speaker's univocal coerciveness, its desire to assert that what it knows is what every "self" knows—period. In that sense, Eliot's example would seem to have been a more useful one than that of Yeats—though it needs to be said that in the Ireland of his own day, Yeats was an infinintely more political poet than Eliot ever dreamed of being.

But given the circumstances of our own day, in which the Absolute Speaker has joined forces with mass media, how does a poet inside the empire express opposition to this co-opting voice? Of course, one way is to directly inveigh against power, in the manner of protest poetry that has a fixed viewpoint opposing a fixed imperial viewpoint. The problem with this stance is that it repeats the phenomenon of the Absolute Speaker, so that you have two Absolute Speakers shouting each other down, though of course the power differential inevitably means one voice will be louder than another. You might say that this strategy follows a Yeatsian approach to pitting the self against history. And who can deny that in the age of political activist artists like Vaclav Havel,

Seamus Heaney, Grace Paley, Czeslaw Milosz, and others, that a single voice can't pose a vital challenge to the eyes that want to pin "self" to the wall?

Another strategy, and one that would seem to follow Eliot's example in *The Waste Land,* has been to make language no longer serve the Absolute Speaker, to destabilize its speaking apparatus by short-circuiting all the usual assumptions about the logic and reliability of language. This method is extremely popular at the moment among young poets who have picked up some of the stylistic moves of L=A=N=G=U=A=G=E writing—for better and worse, these techniques have been detached from any overt political agenda, and are now just available rhetorical moves employed for their own sake. (This in itself could be seen as a political gesture, in which one generation re-imagines the aesthetic conventions of the previous one, depending on how "self" uses and commands it.)

If there is a silver lining to these polarized ways of responding to the Absolute Speaker, it's to be found in the widespread unease among poets about the underpinnings of aesthetic procedures and attitudes toward language that tend to support the Absolute Speaker's dominance. And yet it has to be acknowledged that the oppositions I've been making between the Absolute Speaker's dominance and the practice of poets aren't as simple as they seem. As Eugenio Montale points out in his sardonic little essay, "The Intellectual," the most insidious collaborators are the ones who would seem to connive at aiding and abetting the cultural conditions they decry:

> [. . .]
>
> "The intellectual thinks modern poetry is lacking in humanity, but has a weakness for abstract painting.
>
> The intellectual decides in the end that modern poetry is full of humanity; and the disaster is irreparable.
>
> [. . .]

> The intellectual defends freedom, leaving for Prague and Warsaw; when questioned he says that "they made him do it."
>
> [. . .]
>
> The intellectual thinks it would be a good thing to re-establish the Academy, provided that he is included, and above all, that A, B, and C are not . . .
>
> The intellectual is against planning in the arts but is of the opinion that A, B, and C should be prevented from writing.

As Montale intimates, to chastise the Absolute Speaker while ignoring the collusion of the literati in that Speaker's dominance is to ignore how difficult it is to keep your hands clean. Consumerist trends of taste and fashion, in which liquor and clothing ads might feature writers and artists in an attempt to "brand" their product as hip/smart/bohemian, are obvious danger signs. What is celebrity, after all, but offering yourself up to eyes that are all too eager to pin "self" down and rob it of any vestige of privacy?

You can see this desire for celebrity-branding extending itself to the branders themselves: talk about violets and primroses thronging into the highway! More and more, the tendency of media is to shift the spotlight away from the people who actually make the art and write the books to the people who distribute them, or to the products that the cachet of hip/smart/bohemian might sell. One can imagine Yeats and Eliot looking down from the slopes of Parnassus with looks of mock horror and bemusement on their faces. However, in a hopeful moment, as Italo Calvino intimates in his essay, "Literature as Projection of Desire," one might think of this as Mikhail Bakhtin's notion of "permanent revolution": "a society that regularly alternates between periods of destructive consumption and carnival spirit" and "periods of productive austerity." The consumption part of the cycle would correspond to the artistic desire to be known, and the austerity part, the desire not to be found. If we look at the intersection between media and artistic production from that angle, then we needn't despair just yet about the progressively more media-savvy nature of the arts, or break out into rants about self-prostituting artists.

And by the same hopeful token, this mixing up of celebrity image and highbrow culture has tended to promote hybrid cultural forms, and characterizes some of the best work that is being done right now: in her first two books, *Glass, Irony, and God,* and *Plainwater,* Anne Carson's work is often a highly inventive fusion of the academic essay, the literary celebrity interview, and autobiography, just as Eliot's *The Waste Land* was a fusion of different philosophical traditions and literary styles. And in the visual arts, the work of a polymath like Ellen Driscoll incorporates early film technology, puppetry and shadow play, traditional techniques of sculpture and the domestic arts like knitting and sewing, and the exploration of texts as various as Harriet Jacob's slave narrative and nineteenth-century texts on phrenology, and combines these with video, advertising banners, and state-of-the-art LED and photographic mosaic techniques. Both of these artists have a rich, complex notion of what "self" commands them to do in the face of what Philip Larkin once called "cascades of monumental slithering."

Of course, Larkin's cascades are the downside of this hybrid mix of highbrow and "celeb." There are myriad examples of the opposite result of the effects of taste and fashion on literature and the visual arts—the attention paid to an artist like Vanessa Beecroft, who takes photographs of models wearing only Manolo Blahnik shoes—demonstrates how carnival spirit coupled to social critique can be made palatable to a consumerist mindset that is becoming harder and harder to resist, no matter what your political and economic status. What "self" the naked models possess is eclipsed by the total package, the spectacle of self that Vanessa Beecroft is projecting: whoever Vanessa Beecroft is for real, what we understand is her insider position in an exclusive world that is equal parts art world star, fashion consumer, and social maven. Perhaps social maven is the most prominent of these selves: this piece would seem to be about the power of Ms. Beecroft to put naked models, Manolo Blahnik shoes, and her own artistic intentions in the same frame. The consumerist mindset that such art is geared for is always purveyed as critique of same, but the formulating eyes of mass media overwhelm any such critiques. The artist's desire to be known is, in fact, obscured by the inevitable hype that surrounds such a spectacle.

Of course, it's easy to be a finger-wagger at how the arts and individual artists are regularly co-opted by mass media and by the means of distribution, even as they participate in those systems, in most cases because there are so few alternatives. But if the practice of an art is going to amount to more than jockeying for grants, jobs, and inclusion in Academies that A, B, and C are excluded from, then artists will have to pay better attention to what it means, in Winncott's sense, to feel "real" in both their lives and their art. Just as in Yeats's and Eliot's work, if not their politics, this may mean finding ever more complex ways to keep the eyes of formulation from pinning "self" down. In Adam Phillips's book on Winnicott, Phillips concludes by saying that "The self, by definition, is elusive, a player of hide and seek." He then goes on to quote a review Winnicott wrote of Jung's autobiography, *Memories, Dreams, Reflections:* "If I want to say that Jung was mad, and that he recovered, I am doing nothing worse than I would do in saying of myself that I was sane and through analysis and self-analysis I achieved some measure of insanity." By the same token, if I want to say that poetry is a means of provoking us to "some measure of insanity," I am doing nothing worse than saying that poetry is a vital counterforce to the ready-made phrases of "sane" formulation that threaten the inmost privacy of self. Furthermore, the ability to experience solitude as a source of creative refreshment and joy, and as a form of resistance to consumerism's fascistic undercurrents, is one of the most important human qualities that poetry can foster. Artists have the unique opportunity to display just how fundamental to our personal and collective well-being this privacy is, as well as the responsibility to use all their ingenuity and resolve to secure it.

Eleven Scenarios for the Avant-Garde in the New Millennium

~

1

Pretend we're living in a movie made by someone like David Cronenberg. Our bodies are like leaky bags of unpredictable fluids, squirting out in great gushes of goo and ooze. At the edges of consciousness, we're constantly being infiltrated by the promise of sex, the sort of pornographic video sex that is all *this this this that that that* and barely any faces. We're also aware of hints of violence emanating from behind chainstore doors and discount-outlet basements, as if a pit of vampires were waiting to suck our blood just behind the rack of on-sale windbreakers. And then there's the paranoia-inducing menace of totalitarian surveillance, in which nothing is private: video monitors are hidden everywhere, even, we suspect, in our own brains.

Into this aura of voyeuristic sleaze and near hysterical threat and promise, a poet enters, declaiming Wordsworth:

> No motion has she now, no force;
> She neither hears nor sees;
> Rolled round in earth's diurnal course,
> With rocks, and stones, and trees.

But where is the poet? You look for the speaker of the words, but all you see is a cloud of language, a kind of dirty mist ebbing and flowing all around a veiled center: Is it the poet at the heart of the mist? Or is this mist of language autonomous of the poet, speaking itself, asserting once and for all the primacy of language over those who speak it? Language itself become corporeal, abstractions made material, a little the way Milton thought of the bodies of angels as ethereal matter that needed to eat and drink and have sex: complete interpenetration of body into body like vapor passing into vapor?

By now, you're losing all track of what is movie and what isn't, you're getting more and more disoriented about what is and isn't real—for right there in front of your eyes, words hover in the air, freed from the flatness of the page to disport themselves: words not as signs, but as entities in themselves, corporeal as your own body.

You wonder if this isn't the new sublime, the new key to an avant-garde that will be the ultimate avant-garde: no gap between word and thing: a sort of poststructuralist sublime. A form of the sublime Kant could never have envisioned because the words are, in fact, the cellular/granular/atomic substance that literally embodies the transcendental real. And if that's the case, then who needs all those messy, oozy, leech-gathering human referents grubbing away for existence in a poet's poem? It's as if Wordsworth put on the best virtual-reality glasses ever made while reading a seed catalogue and saw spring up in front of him "A host of golden daffodils,/Beside the lake, beneath the trees,/Fluttering and dancing in the breeze." Under such conditions, who needs anything but language?

The rules these new words follow, in which each utterance, or move in the game, is to create a new reality, may be language having the last laugh on that notorious language gamester, Ludwig Wittgenstein, who derailed philosophy for half a century by his mischievous assertion that the mystical is "the inexpressible," and so beyond the bounds of philosophy. You think of W. B. Yeats's censure of William Blake for being "a too literal realist of the imagination." Because Blake believed that the figures seen by the mind's eye, when exalted by inspiration, were "eternal existences," Yeats takes Blake to task for hating every grace of style that might obscure their lineaments. But if words themselves were eternal existences, what need would Blake have for style?

After all, these words do what gods do: they not only see eternity in a grain of sand, they conjure up new worlds in their very state as words. You hold up your arm to hail the words, to salute this ultimate manifestation of abstraction turned concrete, of language's triumph over the gray matter that produced it! But without quite knowing how, you find in your hand a switchblade—and before you know it, you've eviscerated the cloud of words . . . and guts, real gory guts are spilling all over the sidewalk. Are these the guts of the unseen poet? Is this the equivalent of the return of the repressed, the body wreaking its havoc on what threatens to supplant real blood, flesh, and bone?

So, you mutter to yourself, maybe this isn't the new sublime—and you begin edging away from the gathering crowd, wondering how many camcorders, video monitors, and helicoptering Eyes in the Sky have seen you commit this murder: the cloud of words by now has drained into the gutter into an inky pool, and you hear a plaintive last gasp: "We murder to dissect." And then you realize that Wordsworth's caution against analytical reason's power to destroy the sublime and the beautiful is, in fact, part of an elaborate plot to frame you of a murder you've committed, but only virtually committed: you start shouting that this is all just a performance in language, a set of images begetting other images. You haven't really cut the guts out of a poet, this is just writing, *l'écriture,* the guilt you feel is just dream guilt: what Berryman feels in one of his *Dream Songs,* where he knows he's hacked someone up, but every time he counts up his acquaintances, "nobody is ever missing."

But the Language Police don't see it that way. *Words are real, motherfucker, and we're taking you in for first-degree homicide.* And then it dawns on you: that cloud of words, words which you used to think referred only to the surface of the world, have slipped loose of their moorings and are invading the planet. And there's nothing you can do about it, the tide of abstraction is unloosed: but as they handcuff you and shove you into the squad car, you feel a huge sense of relief: at last you don't have to feel guilty anymore about never doing justice to the surfaces of the world, about hacking them up every time you try to put them down in words. You can exist now in your cell, away from the world, away from your antiquated need to make the shining and sounding surfaces of the world stand forth. At last you are free to become wholly a creature of language.

2

You sense inside yourself a longing to make art without precedent, without thought of the past or foreboding of the future. And yet you worry about the fate of art under these same conditions, you suspect yourself of nostalgia for an old-style Enlightenment dispensation, in which human beings were at the center of history, and history meant human progress, however slowly, working its way to a glorious conclusion that art would both express and help bring about. But what was thought glorious, as many a post-structuralist has pointed out, has led straight to totalitarianism of every sort: human beings are mere creatures of self-perpetuating systems of power and enslavement, and battles of ideology have all but replaced the old debate about sacred impulses working in concert with historical destiny.

And so what are you to do with these useless feelings of divinity and fated futurity? You begin imagining a time of "avant-garde" transition: every work of art must take on itself the burden of showing just how it is made; there will be no more magical illusions that don't openly reveal that they are illusions. You see in this a gesture of honesty—but you worry that it's only the honesty of the cigarette pack, the Surgeon General's warning easy to ignore. And of course how can you guarantee that this gesture itself doesn't become simply another convention, another trick up the artist's sleeve? When you think of Yeats wanting to lie "down where all the ladders start/In the foul rag and bone shop of the heart," you have to ask yourself what would be lost if Yeats got rid of the rhyme between "start" and "heart," got rid of the declamatory, spell-weaving rhetoric in the name of disenchantment? Then you really would have rags and bones—but aren't rags and bones just another kind of rhetoric?

Rhetoric is not so easy to escape. Would it were as easy as it sounds to bypass the self by displacing the lyric "I" onto the operations of language. But you still have the web the operations of language weave, and that web is the result of a personal, deliberate, ego-driven hunger to trap flies. The fly may not see the spider when it blunders into the web, but the fact remains that the spider spun the web and will eventually eat the fly. Visible as a lyric "I," or invisible as an effect of language, the prime mover is still everywhere present in the filaments it spins.

When Rimbaud said, "*Je est un autre*" (I is an other), he wasn't only referring to self-estrangement, or the magical sense of shedding the self, or what is least likely for so self-referential a poet as Rimbaud, the act of taking up residence in the subjectivity of someone else. He might also have been saying that "I" is a convention established by its relation to an "other." This reciprocal nature of an "other" and "I" is a grammatical property as well as a personal one: and only from that perspective does it make sense to talk about the autonomy of language, the free play of language, as a way to write poems. Hovering in the background, giving this free play a shape and purpose, are the agreements in the language game that distinguish "I" from an "other." And Rimbaud, despite his espousal of a "*dérèglement de tous les sens*," understands that the grammatically anomalous "Je est" only takes on meaning in relation to the grammatically expected "Je suis." Without conventions, there would be no "I" to derange from, and no "other" to derange into.

Rimbaud's progress from poet magician to Abyssinian gun runner highlights the unexpectedly prophetic nature of "Je" becoming "un autre." A generation before Rimbaud traveled east to French colonial Africa, Baudelaire sailed west to Martinique. Baudelaire was at the beginning of his career as a poet, and mythologized what he saw into a kind of Eden. Rimbaud inherited this mythology and tried to convert it into a reality. "Je," as the dirty soul of Europe, could become, through the magical rites of poetry, "un autre," the instinctive, unashamed, latter day Adam. When Rimbaud lost faith in poetry as a magical rite, he also abandoned the hope of transforming "Je" into "un autre." As a colonial merchant, "Je" would end up writing carefully observed and highly practical business letters complaining about his botched dealings with "un autre."

3

Baudelaire is often seen as the first true modern, the avant-garde *poète maudit* who prophesies to the bourgeousie the coming soullessness of the new age, the poet as outsider who forges the new consciousness that resists the fusion of human beings into a mass society, a "public." Damned by his sensibility and his historical inability to accept technology as the arbiter of human life, Baudelaire longs for traditional religious feeling, he wants to be one of Milton's angels—but instead, he is the apostle of human vice, for principally through vice is a human being brought into contact with ultimate realities: ". . . we can plunge/to Hell . . .—any abyss will do—/deep in the Unknown to find the *new!*" In the Paris that the nineteenth-century urban developer, Baron Haussmann, was creating, in which the city resembled an immense construction site, the old neighborhoods are razed to make way for the grand boulevards. As old Paris is swept away by urban grandiosity that dwarfs the people living in its shadow, Baudelaire sees how ineffectual God is in this man-made world in which relentlessly changing fashion becomes the guiding principle of modernity. Thrown back on himself, he subjects himself to experiments of living at the edge of his nerves: absinthe, wine, opium, hashish, sadism and masochism as forms of sublimity and power.

Of course what partly fueled Baudelaire's attraction to the margin was his intense desire to make *maman* and his stepfather notice him, even if it meant being an intellectual exhibitionist. On his gravestone in Père-Lachaise Cemetery is the inscription "Charles Baudelaire, good son of General Aupick"—a man Baudelaire admired, but also scorned for his lack of imagination, tightfistedness with money, and worst insult of all, for his lack of soul, his Belgian soul—Belgian denoting the worst possible insult Baudelaire could muster for a person's lack of any distinctive inner qualities. To have a Belgian soul was to believe in Second Empire values of respectability and conformity, to hum martial tunes and believe fervently in Progress. But Baudelaire's nostalgia for God, for some form of the absolute, was an inheritance from the Belgian side of himself that he couldn't escape: and so he attempted to replace traditional religious feeling with his own intuition of what a divine principle might be under the conditions of Man and Woman being forged into a public, the mass society of mechanized life.

This positing of a divine principle turns out to be more a shadowy intuition of evil than a principle, more spookhouse décor than hellfire: skeletons, vampires, ghosts, whores, gamblers, the world a façade of poses to mask gigantic boredom and a primal sense of terror. Behind the façade, there lurks an inchoate but palpable sense of some omnipotent malevolent will working through each human destiny to bring us face to face with our own evil natures. And yet in that encounter was our only hope for salvation: evil would be the lens through which we would see what Baudelaire called "the new."

This notion of "the new" was intimately connected in Baudelaire's mind with death as a voluptuary's hope to be released from dirty, shitty Paris into a reality at once atrocious, banal, but also sublime: the décor of a rich art collector's steel-lined bathroom, with urinals shaped like human mouths and the toilet bowls staring up at you with elongated, heavy lashed Cleopatrine eyes. But this longing for sublimity, this hunger for the authenticity of the new, no matter how absurd its form, shows a deeply conservative streak in Baudelaire's nature. It represents a displacement of traditional religious feeling, an adaptation to the conditions of modernity—no matter how kitschy this longing may seem to our postmodern eclecticism in which we eat sushi and listen to Beethoven's *Eroica* while watching a director's cut video of *Blade Runner.* See how Baudelaire treats the phrase "avant-garde" in his little book, *Mon Coeur Mis En Nu (My Heart Laid Bare)*—a book of squibs, pensées, and fierce misanthropic "fuck yous" to his age. It was inspired by Poe's suggestion that any writer who wrote exactly what he thought, no matter how painful to self or others, would of necessity write a masterpiece:

> To be added to the military metaphors:
> The fighting poets.
> The literary vanguard.
> This use of military metaphor reveals minds not militant but formed for discipline, that is, for compliance; minds born servile, Belgian minds, which can only think collectively.

To use military metaphors for the operations of art was the height of vulgarity for Baudelaire. Still, such an attitude strikes me as a little odd, coming from a man who revered an authoritarian thinker like Joseph de Maistre. No wonder Rimbaud, who saw himself as a soldier of new sensations, and of the new forms those sensations would give rise to, denounces Baudelaire for his formal grace, while praising him for his understanding of the age. And doubtless

Baudelaire would have tried to disenchant the young mage who believed in the power of words to literally change the world.

What kind of artist would be created from their fusion, in which Baudelaire's grace is married to Rimbaud's visionary faith in language as magic? One unconcerned with such trivial matters as style? Who needs style when, like the gnostic demiurge, your words have the power to incarnate worlds? You would have transcended what Baudelaire calls "the forest of symbols," the divine correspondences between ineffable sensations and the words that attempt to describe them. The history of styles would wither before such a poet! But if you aren't a demiurge, then not to have a style is to do without a body, which is unthinkable for Rimbaud, obsessed as he was by the equation of poetry with his own shit. And for Baudelaire to be bodiless, he would have had to embrace the optimism of his age and done without his most powerful subject: the destruction of every human tie to the past.

4

Perhaps avant-garde as a term only makes sense as a strictly historical plotting of movements, each one generating the next, precursor and foreseeable influences linked in a chain in which a single link cannot be missing. Art would seem to spring from art, from the history of styles, as much as from experience. Romantic though he was in his experiments with vice, Baudelaire knew that smoking hashish didn't guarantee you could write convincing poetry about smoking hashish. And yet I resist the thought that all artistic action is merely mental action.

I have a nightmare in which, because of the pressure of random bombs, state-sponsored terror, the weird way disturbing images of sex and destruction invade our always open heads, we will all suddenly explode into torrents of automatic writing, words as an orgiastic flight away from the operations of reason, logic, all the conscious workings of the will. Creatures of pure intuition, your words will mingle with mine and all the others, until nobody knows whose words are whose, our minds a collective effortlessly expressing our passions and desires so directly that we are like water acted upon by wind. But when I come out of that rapturous orgy of words, I wonder: How will we recognize ourselves in those artworks that we will spontaneously create with our every breath? Unlike certain artists of today who believe that we are moving into the realm where, to quote Eugenio Montale, the task "of involving the reader is the purpose of the absolute work of art," I worry with Montale that perhaps we ought to consult this reader first: perhaps this reader has had quite enough of "absolutes" of every kind.

But this Orwellian vision, in which we are overwhelmed and reduced to sameness by language, is only a fantasy, and in a few years may seem like a utopian fantasy at that: the real situation is that languages are going extinct faster than rare birds and plants, and that the market's utilitarian relationship to language tends to flatten language to meet its needs. Under such conditions, my nightmare may begin to look like the sail that shipwrecked sailors fix their hopes on as they more and more desperately scan the horizon.

5

If ever there was a formulation that seemed bent on obliterating boundaries between life and art, as well as word and thing, it is Robert Lowell's violence of mind when he says, "I want words meathooked from the living steer." This will strike some as damning evidence of Lowell's imperious will, his desire to dominate language as opposed to being a creature of language. But there is a way of being literal that is infinitely more brutal than Lowell's *Grand Guignolish* use of "meathook." Consider this *bon mot* from Comrade Stalin: "A single death is a tragedy, a million deaths is a statistic." Stalin was a fearsome literalist whose relationship to language made him a man of his word—the kind of fellow who only mentions meathooks if he's certain he'll be using them. Of course, Stalin was a notorious liar, and perverted language no end. But his muse was power, and language was always subordinated to power. Nothing could be more artificial and far from the dependability of a real meathook than Lowell's violently unstable, exploratory relationship to metaphor.

But what will happen to such slippages of meaning between meathooks in poems and meathooks in real life when that exploratory space is closed up by the fear—a fear that is radically reshaping contemporary notions of civil liberties—that violent words incite violent action? Will there be a flattening out of language? Or will poets react by becoming ever more zealous to preserve their words from too dependable a relationship with a fearsome literalist like Stalin? To judge by the interest in fragmentation—what certain academic critics would call the cultivation of "indeterminacy"—as a means to elude dependability, many poets are trying to respond to historical conditions in which systems of power have replaced the myth of the dictator strongman. Rather than write poems directly denouncing the dictator, the poet uses strategies of discontinuous language as a way of challenging the language of officialdom. But when Jean-François Lyotard, the French philosopher, makes the claim that postmodern art is art that forsakes in its means the solace of formal wholeness, he seems to have had in mind the notion that an artistic work based on fragmentation, collage, or other nonlinear methods can somehow escape the history of styles. Such ahistorical thinking seems to assume that there is a mainstream and an avant-garde, and that the two are always easy to distinguish from each other. Or are there many avant-gardes, and only one mainstream? But what about a poet who is a traditionalist in his use of verse forms, but avant-garde in his subject matter? And since the majority of American poets write free verse, should we think of free verse as mainstream and verse avant-garde? Or is this focus on techniques of composition incidental, and are we really talking about a special quality of poetic sensibility?

One problem with the way Lyotard characterizes the avant-garde is to suggest that it always constitutes a radical break with tradition. But consider the case of the Russian poet, Osip Mandelstam, one of Stalin's statistics: his widow, Nadezhda, a great historian of Stalin's terror, and a shrewd critic of poetry, says of her husband's work:

> Mandelstam had no poetic forerunners . . . there is no discrepancy between the form and the content . . . both of them always new . . . with no great disparity between them—and where the ego of the poet is always strikingly felt. Marina Tsvetayeva said she could write as Mandelstam did . . . but she was greatly mistaken. She could be influenced by Mayakovsky and Pasternak . . . because they were innovators and therefore easily aped. But Mandelstam composed verses in tradition, which is far more difficult to imitate.

The claim that Mandelstam had no poetic forerunners is puzzling: nobody writes in a vacuum. But perhaps what Madame Mandelstam means is that the poet's originality derives from tradition. In relation to poetic originality, Borges once observed that an image that seems wholly unprecedented is almost certain to be banal because it very likely will not derive from basic human concerns. Originality is an originality in understanding and using the conventions, formal, intellectual, and emotional, that define and extend a tradition. Then the avant-garde myth of breaking with tradition to achieve originality becomes only another function of tradition: a sort of strategy of renewal, and when necessary, of repudiation of formal elements that seem exhausted. To compose verses in tradition, then, means that words are allowed their instability, but against a recognizable grid: the rules of the language game agreed on between reader and writer. Stalin's words are stable and flow in a single channel, that of political utility, hence there is no mutual agreement, or possibility of agreement. Whereas Lowell's relationship to a word like "meathook" is unstable, and that instability is an invitation to the reader to hold a dialogue about the game's rules. The violence of Lowell's rhetoric may indeed give the effect of having been meathooked from the living steer, but that violence is an effect of the rules negotiated between reader and writer.

6

Or consider the extravagant sensibility and rhetoric of the ultimate avant-garde Russian poet, Vladimir Mayakovsky, so different from his more classical, but equally innovative contemporary, Mandelstam: In his fondness for violent metaphors, Mayakovsky resembles Lowell. But because of the difference in their historical conditions, when the Russian poet writes that the "line burns to the end/and explodes,/and the town/is blown sky-high/in a strophe," the exhilaration and playfulness of that dynamite-laden strophe reverberates with more ominous overtones. In Mayakovsky's case, language as play collides head-on with the mass arrests and executions of Stalin's purges. The man who called himself "a cloud in trousers," who celebrated impulse as if it were subject to Hegelian laws that would deliver a world free of class conflict, finds the trousers ultimately constricting: to write, to hunt, to farm and not be reduced to a writer, a hunter, a farmer, that's what Marx envisioned as freedom.

But Mayakovsky the free man who at first saw his muse and the Revolution as one would find it difficult to reconcile himself with Mayakovsky the Soviet who wrote jingles in the service of the Revolution. This divided creature claimed in a poem that he had "stamped his heel/on the throat/of my own song." A more complex example of Mayakovsky's self-division (one that throws in sharp relief the difference between the private man of Eros, and the man marching to the tune of history) is the story the poet tells about how he first used the phrase, "a cloud in trousers." He said he used it as a kind of anti-pick-up line, "to prove the purity of my intentions to a young woman I met on the train by telling her that I was not a man, but a cloud in trousers." But when he uses it as the title of a poem, it loses its whimsy and becomes "a catechism for the art of today . . ." "Down with your love!"; "Down with your art!"; Down with your social order!"; "Down with your religion!" "The cloud in trousers" suddenly finds himself holding up the banner of the Revolution. And given the Revolution's penchant for meathooks, it would seem a short step from Mayakovsky's sloganeering to using real dynamite to literally blow the town, and all the citizens in it, sky high. As Baudelaire foresaw, the use of a military metaphor like "avant-garde" can come back to haunt you: this is especially the case when a dictator like Stalin begins to take a personal interest in your poetry: the advance guard may seem out in front of history, leading the rest of humanity on—but to what and to where?

On April 14, 1930, the day Mayakovsky played Russian roulette for the last time, a single bullet in the cylinder of his revolver pointed at his heart, he had made plans with a friend to visit a fashionable Moscow tailor. In observance of a Russian superstition that before death a man should wear clean linen, he had put on a fresh shirt: whatever Mayakovsky's personal reasons for pointing a revolver at his heart, it would seem that impulse and the inexorable laws of history were fatally at odds. By 8 p.m., a mere 9 hours and 45 minutes after he pulled the trigger, the State Institute for the Study of the Brain sawed through his skull cap and extracted Mayakovsky's brain: "the cloud in trousers," that mercurial creature of impulse, had become a grimly reasonable Soviet statistic. His brain weighed 1,700 grams—a full 300 grams heavier than the average 1,400 gram brain—and was placed in the Institute's "Pantheon", the Soviet brain Hall of Fame.

7

What would happen if you took Mayakovsky's impulsiveness, and Lowell's resolute will to make language measure up to the living steer, and channeled that into a mode of composition in which art is the by-product of an absolute faith in process: then you would get an artist like Giacometti painting the portrait of James Lord day after day, ruining the painting, bringing it back, then ruining it again, the paint building up and up on the canvas until finally Lord snatches it off the easel and pronounces the painting "finished."

Or imagine a mode of composition that is purely rational, the ratiocinative method Poe describes in his essay about writing "The Raven," in which his every aesthetic choice is a conscious choice of taste, subject to the operations of logical deduction and of an impeccable knowledge of past literary styles, decorums, conventions. The old dream of doing without a style, of writing a poem that would not only take the place of a mountain, but be a mountain, becomes, under the spell of Poe's method, the ultimate artifice.

And if both of these methods of composition—Poe's use of reason, Giacommetti's committment to process—were to be fused into one method, what kind of poetry would result? One whose process would lead inexorably to the perfect realization of a Platonic form? Like Mallarmé without the aporias, the air of transcendence that makes you wish, after while, that Mallarmé had spent more time describing things the way Hemingway would describe them? Just how durable is Mallarmé's little slogan, *"Peindre non la chose mais l'effet qu'elle produit"* (Don't paint the thing but the sensation it produces)? A combination, then, of Mallarmé's suggestiveness and Hemingway's precision, suggestiveness accomplished through precision?

And yet, despite Hemingway's dogs-and-cats realist claim that, for him, composition was the process of writing one true sentence, the truest sentence you could write, and then writing another, and another, Hemingway uses syntax like Mallarmé, as a species of almost mathematical pleasure in which the formulary symbols take precedence over the solution to the equation. In both Hemingway and Mallarmé, the syntax tends to float among meanings, the possibilities ramifying in relationship to the repetitions in cadence, vocabulary, and sentence structure:

> The world breaks everyone and afterward many are strong at the broken places. But those that will not break it kills. It kills the very good and the very gentle and the very brave impartially.
>
> (A Farewell to Arms, *Ernest Hemingway)*

> nothingness questions the broken man . . .
> . . . here is the only lasting light
> where the poet's casual, broken gesture ends
> the dream that breaks with his humanity . . .
>
> *("Toast Funèbre," Stéphane Mallarmé)*

Both passages are wonderfully wayward and unpredictable in how sense ultimately becomes just another element in the self-delighting play of language.

8

What sort of life should an avant-gardiste live? Mallarmé, whose poetic Truths were ineffable and could only be suggested by means of symbols, led a home life that was resolutely petit bourgeois, complete with overstuffed Second Empire furniture. What would Mallarmé make of Hemingway's romance with experience, his love of the physical and the sensuous?

At Finca Vigia, Hemingway's home outside Havana, which since his death has been turned into a state-run museum and monument to the writer, Hemingway's devotion to truth with a small "t" clashes rather wonderfully with the laid-back glamour and luxury of the Finca's grounds, complete with swimming pool, tennis court, and boathouse—luxury that seems amazingly out of keeping not only with the living conditions of Havana's proletariat, but with the subjects of Hemingway's fiction: outcasts, losers, those who die or are destroyed by their loyalty to outworn codes.

The state museum guide told me, with obvious affection, that Hemingway was a man who drank at least fourteen cocktails a day, kept a huge menagerie of cats and dogs, so many in fact that they took over the tower his wife built for him to write in. Of course the tower happened to be her idea, not his: I can imagine Mallarmé wanting his poetry to read as if it had been written in a tower; but then, Hemingway also had his sense of writing as a magical operation, though he preferred writing, as he always had, in the humdrum ordinariness of his bedroom. But a photograph in his bedroom shows him standing on the skin of a kudu he had shot on safari and which, he claimed, gave him inspiration. When I visited, the skin was still there, as was his typewriter, and numerous photographs of Fidel shaking hands with Hemingway, the white-bearded writer and the black-bearded revolutionary smiling warmly and naturally at one another on the occasion of Fidel having won the fishing contest Hemingway sponsored every year. The magical power of that kudu, though, links Hemingway as much to Mallarmé as to the quintessential man of action, Fidel.

Mallarmé once said that to name an object is to take away three-fourths of the pleasure given by a poem. When you consider his unfinished poem, "A Tomb for Anatole," in which his grief for his dead boy frames the poem in the most literal way imaginable, it seems clear that Mallarmé had a horror of experience that his poems attest to in their very attempt to evade it. So perhaps Mallarmé's relationship to experience was as fraught and complex and immediate as Hemingway's: perhaps his encounters with the invisible were as emotionally intense as Hemingway's need to fish and hunt and test himself in war. So many of Hemingway's best stories are expressive of this complex horror of experience, the way it degrades and destroys human beings, no matter how noble their actions, by its sheer capriciousness and chanciness. Surely Hemingway would have felt the rightness of Mallarmé's poem, "A Throw of the Dice Will Never Abolish Chance."

Of the two, Hemingway was clearly the less worldly writer, if by worldly we mean a sense of disenchantment with the sights and sounds and textures of the world. What Hemingway so vigorously pursued, and found, in Paris was the particularity of passion and a style to match it. Mallarmé was like a sedentary oyster, producing pearls by closing around a particle of grit. I suspect they would have detested each other's company and yet they believed in grammar and syntax the way an alchemist believes in magic spells—rock-solid gold was their aim: for them, art was an objective fact, with acknowledged limits to its spiritual reach. Hemingway was a celebrant of human action, Mallarmé a rhapsodist of its futility. Yet they both believed in an objective reality (if rarefied, in Mallarmé's case) that transcended the structures of their own minds. You could say that both men fought against the lush invention of their minds, and the remains of that battle are what we call their styles.

9

Parnassus may be a place of many mansions catering to all different aesthetic persuasions, but behind the surface politeness, it has always been a messy place. Take the war between William Carlos Williams and T. S. Eliot, both vociferous exponents of "make it new," at least early in their careers. *In this corner, the American grain! And in this corner, the "universal mind of Europe!" At the bell, come out swinging!* If either notion ever had much credence, the grain has long since been chopped to splinters by pluralism, and Euope's mind reduced to nightmares of "ethnic cleansing." Eliot's cultural myopia, Williams's sour grapes over Eliot's success—in this light, neither poet appears at his best. Yet Williams's sense of being the underdog during Eliot's ascendance no doubt helped create a taste for his work in younger writers eager to see themselves as underdogs: Williams has since been lionized, so that for a time in the 1960s and '70s, his style almost became what he imagined it, a sort of all-purpose, utilitarian style grounded in the local conditions of American English.

Meanwhile, Eliot's idiosyncratic cultural conservatism has demoted him in the ranks: "And the fire and the rose are one" or "All shall be well, and/All manner of thing shall be well" are inviolably beautiful phrases, and possibly true in the context of Eliot's poetry. But the poetry and the donnish image Eliot projected—an image that has largely faded by now, so that most people know him as the man who wrote the poems on which the Broadway hit *Cats* was based—are separate things.

And that's not necessarily bad. The sheer goofiness of Eliot's decision to paint his face green before going to visit the notoriously snobbish Bloomsbury crowd is an aspect of Eliot's sensibility that violently clashes with the image of the poet as London's literary dictator. Anyone who has ever heard the recording of Eliot declaiming "Sweeney Agonistes," in which he chants in a screechy falsetto, *"Under the bam/ Under the boo/ Under the bamboo tree,"* won't be fooled by Eliot's own self-characterization as a "classicist in literature, royalist in politics and Anglo-Catholic in religion."

Or maybe these contrasts are exactly what you'd expect. Eliot's famous dictum that poetry "is not the expression of personality, but an escape from personality," is followed by the qualifying statement: "But, of course, only those who have personality and emotions know what it means to want to escape from these things." The irony with which the second statement undercuts the first seems to me part of the basis of Eliot's Modernist experimentalism. "Let us go then, you and I,/ When the evening is spread out against the sky . . ." is pure late-Victorian pastoral, a lulling Tennysonian assertion of the harmony between you and I as personalities and our harmony with the world. But the next line—"Like a patient etherized upon a table"—is self-reflexive Modernist irony that is suspicious of all merely personal feelings, especially feelings that posit an unselfconscious reciprocity between self and world. *"Je est un autre"* is a Modernist article of faith.

Williams would also subscribe to this faith, though it would be no big deal, if he worried about it at all. For Williams, the personal and the impersonal, perception and what it perceives, aren't, as in Eliot, dissonances to be exploited for poetic effects. In fact, when you read Williams, you realize, as Randall Jarrell said, that Williams doesn't suffer from what Eliot called "dissociation of sensibility," but feels what he thinks and thinks what he feels. Heart and head aren't of necessity contentious opposites, but just another product of Williams's beloved "local conditions." The "American Idiom" springs from those conditions, heart and head speak it, hence Williams's acceptance of personality as being part "of the American grain." But for Eliot, who found personality itself an oppressive local condition, the way out was to find in high culture an alternative set of conditions to his own neurasthenic's "wherever-you-go-there-you-are" syndrome—conditions that would allow him to commune with "the universal mind of Europe." Personality comes to seem like a sign of morbidity to Eliot, and his response to that morbidity was to embrace "the tradition" as a kind of psychological, and then upon his conversion to Anglicanism, spiritual corrective. But Williams regarded personality as possessing the same interest and the same exciting possibilities as a flower pushing up in his backyard: Why not put the two together in a poem, like chemicals in a test tube, and see what happens? For Williams "local conditions" and personality were mutually entailing, and so poetry and personality were inseparable.

In our own day, the debate about "personality" and what its place is in poetry, is an updated version of the debate between Williams and Eliot. Essentialism aside, phrases like "the American grain" and the "universal mind of Europe" point to a persistent anxiety about the authority of the self in relation to the word and world that surrounds it. Autonomous language or autonomous selves? The poem as a celebration of language's structures or of the poet's subjective relationship to language? According to these antinomies, John Ashbery lines up to duke it out with the lingering influence of Robert Lowell.

Since his death, Lowell, an infinitely various, inventive, and splendidly difficult poet, has been forced to wear a sandwich board, one side declaring "Madman salad—all you can eat!" while the other panel reads, "Brahmin Boston beans *à la* John Crowe Ransom and Allen Tate." But *Day by Day,* Lowell's last book, is as laterally associative, many-voiced and many-eyed as anything in Ashbery. Language-driven and permeable to different kinds of discourse, told from multiple perspectives and identities, Lowell's last poems exemplify Charles Bernstein's suggestion that one goal for poetry is to have the opposite reaction from Elizabeth Bishop's exclamation in her beautiful poem called "Poem": "Heavens, I recognize the place, I know it!" When Lowell's earlier work is read through the lens of *Day by Day,* I am constantly made uneasy and exhilarated by the sensation, *I'll be damned, I don't recognize the place, I don't know it! Whoever thought this stuff was confessional, or even personal: his verbal genius is out on its own spacewalk!*

And what you notice, too, in *Day by Day* is just how Pop Lowell's work can seem—if you define Pop sensibility as an unembarrassed conviction that life's shadowy meanings or non-meanings lie in its ordinary terrors and troubles, objects and appetites. (Andy Warhol's electric chair would be right at home in Lowell's poem about Murder Inc.'s Czar Lepke, Warhol's deadpan mirrored by Lowell's self-deprecating humor, and the artist's Day-Glo colors by the hard edge of Lowell's style.) Lowell's candor about daily life was out of step for his time, but what did he actually confess to that hasn't been trumped by any reality-TV show? And yet certain critics still read Lowell, both detractors and admirers, as if his use of language were incidental to his subject matter. Why don't people talk about Lowell's weird associative logic that follows more the muse of language than the muse of experience? One current take on Lowell is that he's this square who writes about his aunt as if she were a real person—and shouldn't the writing be writing Lowell? But the writing *is* writing Lowell, he is almost entirely a creature of language by the end of his career. Which is Ashbery, which Lowell?

> . . . The trees close branches and redden,
> their winter skeletons are hard to find;
> a friend seldom seen
> is not the same—
> how quickly even bad cooking eats up a day.
>
> *("Suicide," Robert Lowell)*

> Some of these houses are startlingly old.
> Other, newer ones seem old too.
> Only when a line of trees ends in something
> Does it resemble the model of progress glimpsed once
> In a bottle as a boy . . .
>
> *("Avenue Mozart," John Ashbery)*

But the suggestion that Lowell and Ashbery are near aligned, both in their embrace of a Pop sensibility and language as muse, would blow a hole in both their critics' and defenders' academic boats!

Obviously, there is ugliness all through Lowell's work, instances of cruelty, at times a massive insensitivity to other people. But there is also a preternatural sweetness and concern and love for other people, and a heartbroken yearning for an unattainable world of sweetness and concern and love, that makes Lowell's world an amazingly wide, comprehensive one. Besides, if Lowell is a confessional poet, then why isn't Ginsberg, who talks openly in his great poem "Kaddish" about wanting to have sex with his mother? It's time to scrap the term "confessional": it's been so debased as a term that all it really signals now is unthinking, blanket disapproval of the conventions of autobiography. But everyone, no matter if they believe language is referential or nonreferential, works from conventions. The truism that we live in an era of pluralist approaches to art is given almost no credence in practice. A truly pluralist world is a difficult world to keep your bearings in, which is why there is so much sniping, so much fervor about "aesthetic correctness" as a brand of political engagement. Exhibitionism and egomania—what people really mean when they say "confessional poetry"—aren't restricted to the conventions of autobiography. I was once told by a self-described "constructivist poet" that the line "And and and and & and" was an indictiment of the Cartesian tendency to hierarchize experience and reduce it to coercive binaries.

But aesthetic wars between schools of poetry aside, isn't it insensitive of Ginsberg to characterize his mother in "Kaddish" as "fat"? Or in his hilariously defiant poem, "Ave Maria," should Frank O'Hara espouse kids going to the movies so they can have their first sexual experience? Why is Lowell outré and Ginsberg and O'Hara not? Who knows, perhaps on Parnassus, Lowell prefers O'Hara's company to Allen Tate's. But why choose? Why not embrace Lowell and O'Hara and Ashbery and Ginsberg? Well, this is a luxury that readers can afford, but what about writers? Aren't writers forced to choose this way of writing over that if the poem is going to amount to more than an intention? So all this sniping and jockeying and sour grapes may serve a purpose, if only as a spur to the ego to get work done. But don't be fooled or fool yourself into thinking that your style is the one style that will evade the history of styles.

Of course, some will object that Lowell's style was a highbrow style, an elitist style, whereas The New York School was firmly based in the quotidian. But doesn't the quotidian need as many footnotes as the highbrow? How many twenty-year-olds have even heard of *Picayunes* (a kind of cigarette), *New World Writing* (a journal of foreign literature), or Mal Waldron (Billie Holiday's accompanist), all details in O'Hara's splendid elegy, "The Day Lady Died"? Surely these references are now every bit as obscure as Lowell's allusions to what Alexander the Great was like after he'd been on a bender (a large, dangerous drinker who once killed one of his lieutenants, but was sick with remorse after he sobered up.) Of course, Alexander was an anointed killer king and would be thought of as a madman in our day—and rightly so. And his name is freighted with a sense of imperial dominion that seems like a harbinger of totalitarian regimes. But in Lowell's poem in his book, *History,* Alexander is a cautionary figure, not exemplary; just as the speaker in O'Hara's poem is difficult to pin down about how serious he really is about children having sex with strangers.

But objections to Lowell or O'Hara on moral grounds are most likely a cover for the inchoate conviction that only one kind of style can have authority in our time. The Russian painter, Malevich, wrote in 1917, "the only meaningful direction for painting is Cubo-Futurism." "True art like true life takes a *single road,*" said Piet Mondrian in 1937. "The one thing to say about art is that it is one thing," said Ad Reinhardt in 1962, firmly convinced that his paintings—black, matte, square—are what art essentially is.

The notion that great art embodies transhistorical essence, everywhere and always the same, but that essence only comes to light in the working out of history, is a notion I would like to believe in . . . but on most days, I can't: my experience of art is so particular that I can't extrapolate beyond a certain point of abstraction. But what I know is false is to identify this transhistorical essence with any one style: Clement Greenberg, the art critic who laid the theoretical groundwork for the appreciation of the Abstract Expressionists, was wrong when he insisted that all art is essentially abstract. And in the realm of poetry, no matter how often poets dismiss the work of other poets in the name of their politics, ideologies, jealousies masquerading as principles, these little *autos-da-fe,* or enactments of faith, fall prey to the same fallacy as the grand historical scheme that identifies history with a chosen people, or class, or part of the world. Hegel's assertion,"What we properly understand by Africa, is the Unhistorical, undeveloped Spirit" reminds me of Greenberg's claim that "the imperative [to make abstract art] comes from history" and that the artist is "held in a vise from which at the present moment he can escape only by surrendering his ambitions and returning to a stale past." But the future has a way of thumbing its nose at what the present imagines the future will look like: there are many reasons to link James Schuyler and Robert Lowell as closely as Ashbery and Schuyler—Schuyler's precision, his quiet way of writing about madness, which is so similar in tone to the way Lowell writes about it in *Day by Day,* may make Schuyler seem, in twenty years, as close a cousin stylistically to Lowell as to Ashbery. Again, which is Lowell, which Schuyler?

> . . . How
> many trips
> by ambulance (five,
> count them five),
> claustrated, pill addiction,
> in and out of mental
> hospitals,
> the suicidalness (once
> I almost made it)
> but—I go on?
> Tell you all of it?
> I can't. When I think
> of that, that at
> only fifty-one I . . .
> . . . am

still alive and breathing
deeply, that I think
is a miracle.

("Trip: The Payne Whitney Poems," James Schuyler)

I cannot sit or stand two minutes,
yet walk imagining a dialogue
between the devil and myself,
not knowing which is which or worse,
saying,
as one would instinctively say Hail Mary,
I wish I could die.

("Home," Robert Lowell)

What is counted for or against the styles of Ashbery or Lowell or Schuyler, their tediums or brilliancies or innovative flights, will be secondary to the notion of freedom that their examples can represent to later poets. The historical agony of feeling that there is an authentic and inauthentic mode of being, one pointing to the future, the other stuck in the past, loses its grip when you abandon the notion of some grand, historically mandated scheme. Likewise for the notion that there is a historically favored form pitted against an outworn mode. But it's a rare soul who can do without feeling that one's art isn't going to be ratified by the future: I suspect that even the most enlightened among us still hold to the myth of the future as the place where we'll be accepted and understood, if only as a useful goad for us to keep on writing—but why should we imagine that our formal preoccupations should be enshrined or elevated to the heights of a universal poetics? And besides, no matter how exclusionary our aesthetic structures are, or how fiercely we espouse our ideas about what art should be, the poems we write are something other than those structures, they may even repudiate those structures: they exist beyond us and our intentions.

10

The year is 2050, or 3050, it doesn't really matter since you died a long time back . . . but through some weird hookup between your brain and a video chip, you get to watch, even in death, the end of the movie: human beings are being replaced by beings like Milton's angels; they don't need reason or logic, they miraculously intuit. They assume whatever shapes they want, male, female, male/female. When they fuck, their spiritual substances—for that is what they are, etherealized substance, spiritualized matter—completely intermingle like vapor passing into vapor. But of course their chosen mode of fucking is the autoerotic: why involve others and their messy bodies, why not be your own self-sufficient world? Yet their sensory equipment is so far superior to yours that the smallest metabolic function of their least angelic cell is to you as if you were being born or dying or having an orgasm. You speculate that these angel replacements will develop their own language for the culture of the body, but it won't be the body as you understand it, not the aging body locked into time. Eternity has given up on the productions of time, and for you, as for others who believe in time, time is running out.

Meanwhile, these beings vaunted obedience to God—well, not God, but their obedience to the principle of Timelessness, with a capital "T"—for them, knowing nothing of a world of contingency or death, obedience is a simple choice that always makes them rejoice in having chosen to play their harps and hymn the magnificence of a world immune to time, their obedience *is* the poetry, the art, the music they make . . .

Still, you begin to wonder: Isn't all this hymning and harping intolerable? If you weren't already dead, you'd resurrect impulse, you'd find a way to keep time going. And yet you can't help but wonder if time itself is on a loop, going in a circle, endlessly cycling and recycling the same old tired dualisms: freedom vs. bondage, form vs. formlessness.

Well, you always were a skeptic: skeptical about the notion that the structures of consciousness are identical with the structures of art; skeptical that transcendence and immanence could ever be meaningfully separated; skeptical that anyone would want to be known as having been "ahead of their time," since time in the present was always so fleeting, ungraspable. Maybe now that you're dead, you can learn to live without any of the old antinomies. But still, you resist being assimilated into those angel beings' soupy hymns and shimmering strings. What else is this Timelessness you instinctively recoil from, but the embodiment of your fear that history may be at an end, that the time of today will no longer flow into the time of tomorrow? Like Montale, you love the age in which you were born because you, too, wanted "to live in the stream rather than to vegetate in the marsh of an age without time."

Well, if you weren't dead, all this might truly disturb you, this condition of timeless freedom that looks like slavish obedience. But how would you conduct your revolt, what manifestoes would you write? You, who lived inside time, how could you even approach the mentality of those strange new beings, let alone find words that would tempt them to defect and enter the old world of process and decay? These beings that are replacing you and your kind, they don't see life in terms of rules, all the dualisms have collapsed, justice and injustice, good and evil, are merely interchangeable insignia, as these new beings themselves are interchangeable, porously passing into each other. What need do they have for rules? Besides, your brand of the avant-garde would eulogize the stupidly physical nature of earthlings, would resist the angelic temptation to wipe out all distinctions between the world of mental action and the world of objective forms. You reflect on all the pleasure and happiness, as well as the torments, that came from observing boundaries between self and world, from agreeing on the game's rules, however much a cheater you found yourself out to be. You chafed at the rules, but the rules inspired and quickened you: you measured your little freedoms in terms of your infractions and refusals.

But since you *are* dead, and since the movie really seems to be almost over, why shouldn't you throw off death and join these angel beings whose obedience annuls the passage of time? Why not collapse all boundaries between you and them, why shouldn't the movie keep on playing through all eternity? But once history has ended, reached its Hegelian apotheosis, then colors, lights, sounds, textures of every conceivable variety, all the action and motion of a living world will cease. And since you aren't yet an angel, since the movie is still running at twenty-four frames a second, and you have enough residual consciousness left, even in death, to feel your blood coagulating in your veins, your skin growing cold, you know that your body is still part of time, that Timelessness is nothing but a theory your flesh refutes.

11

I was wrong about the movie, I mean, about it's being a movie: even as I write this, my change into one of the new angelic orders has been taking place right before your eyes. Will its completion be hidden from me? Will these last moments of transformation be painful, will my face shine with light, and will my skull feel like it's splitting open, the way that ancient Roman gossip, Suetonius, describes Caligula's transformation into a god? And once I've reached my new state, will there be any looking back? And for you who have not yet transformed, how will I look to you? Will I have become something monstrous in your eyes? And without knowledge of my prior state, how will I know what I've lost or gained in my retreat from the quiddity of the world?

Danto, Arthur C. *After the End of Art: Contemporary Art and the Pale of History.* Princeton, N.J.: Princeton University Press, 1997.

Mayakovsky, Vladimir. *The Bedbug and Selected Poetry.* Max Hayward and George Reavey, tr. Patricia Blake, ed. Meridian Books: The World Publishing Company, Cleveland and New York, 1960.

Part III

Against the Text
"Poetry Makes Nothing Happen"

~

A young man goes on a journey to find word about his father. He visits one of his father's old friends who fought with his father in a war that ended twenty years ago. Many of the combatants have gotten home safe, but there are still some who are MIA: the case with the young man's father. His father's friend begins to spin yarns about his own homecoming, tales of hardship, of near starvation, of killing thirst, of winds that won't blow. And just when his suffering is at its worst, at the point where death is imminent for him and his crew, out of the deeps of the sea comes a sea nymph to help him. The intervention of the supernatural, the credulity with which the young man listens to the story, the hope that his own father's fate may also be blessed by such a turn of events, gives the story in the young man's ears the force of a prophetic dream.

Now, let's suppose that the young man goes on a journey only because he is a character in a story: he knows that he's a character, and he knows how the story will turn out: there will be blood and mayhem and death at the end, and he will be one of the agents behind this slaughter. But it's only a story and he's tempted to become a shoe salesman instead, to tell off the author and step into the reality of smelly feet and bunions and bad wages, and on his day off to go to petting zoos and talk dirty to the animals, and to get himself arrested and appear on *Animal Planet* and become a kind of celebrity with his own animal show in which he goes around the world collecting anecdotes about bizarre sexual behavior among dolphins and whales and seals and the other poster children of the animal kingdom.

His show becomes an instant hit and is soon playing all over the world, even on the satellite dish in the enchanted grotto on the uncharted isle where his father is being held captive by the most hospitable of jailers and lamenting the thinness of his life of myth. And one evening, after making love with Calypso, Odysseus happens to see Telemachus transformed into a celebrity—his son, talking in a salacious way about the mating habits of polar bears. He and Calypso are both so horrified by the spectacle of Personality, that Calypso agrees at once to let Odysseus go home to Ithaca and get Telemachus back to the business of serving in the myth of retribution and vengeance.

And so Odysseus and Telemachus are standing in the hall near the end of the slaughter, when Phemios the singer, putting down his lyre, rushes up to Odysseus and pleads for his life, saying that he sang under compulsion: and Telemachus looks at his father, and sees how photogenic he is: and as the singer pleads with them, saying that he can sing like a god, you can hear down in the underworld the souls of Agamemnon and Achilles talking over old times. And then the souls of the dead suitors come winging down like bats, confessing their guilt to the cameras that are placed everywhere in Hades. And Telemachus steps forward and begins to tell the studio audience all about it, just why the killing had to take place according to the myth, and how his father is blameless, and how, he Telemachus, will never go back to broadcasting, but is satisfied with the lines he's been given to speak by blind, old Homer.

Too Much of the Air: Tomas Tranströmer

~

My first glimpse of Tomas Tranströmer was many years ago in Provincetown, Massachusetts, as he ducked his head under the metal lip of a twelve-seater plane's exit door, then stepped hesitantly down the stairs to firm ground. He seemed a little shaken, his long face blanched, his features reminding me, when I think of it now, of the circus horse in a late Bonnard painting: gentle, wary, potentially sad. "I don't mind large planes or middle-sized planes [his English was slightly gutteral, his intonations lilting in a mild brogue], but small planes—you feel too much of the air under you." That remark, direct, plainspoken, but also flirting with the metaphysical, has seemed over the years a keyhole into his work: a void; a sense of hovering above that void; the nerves registering each tremor with precision; the mind fighting back the body's accelerating fear.

The reception of his poems thirty years ago is now part of American literary history: serviceably and widely translated from the Swedish, they were talked about by many of his English-speaking admirers in terms of "deep image." It's hard to recall how passionate poets were about this notion, which fuzzily suggested that poetry could state absolute truths if only the images poets evoked welled up from deep enough sources uncontaminated by history and the follies of reason. Such an idea's devotion to poetry as an autonomous category, unbeholden to social uses of speech, still holds a deep appeal, a linguistic Eden of primal power. But it ignores what poetry most wants to do—or at least the poetry that I most want to read—which is to confront the reader with a world of private thoughts and feelings as contingent as the sudden anxiety a passenger might feel in his journey over the abyss while registering each bump and dip as an utterly objective, historically determined shock.

Much contemporary poetry feels a little mannerist, extreme rhetoric pretending to be bumps and dips, or willed obscurity masquerading as the abyss. Naïve or simplistic as its premises might be, at least "deep image" expressed a powerful yearning for a state of conviction that didn't flatten out, on close reading, into a studied set of stylistic maneuvers—as if style were anything less than the quality of perception. In the 1970s Tranströmer's poems were treated as proof and example of the vaguely Jungian tenets of Deep Image, and soon became subsumed by the style of the day—a surrealism that smacked of automatic writing, whose imagery was drawn from elemental antinomies: light/dark, stone/water, fire/ice.

The foreign poet who is currently being inoculated with American aesthetic concerns is Paul Celan—he seems to give license to a different kind of automatic writing, the sort you would expect from poets bred up on John Ashbery, but lacking his humor and lexical range, combined with high-sounding abstractions, a sort of mystical mummery of "difficult" ideas. Yet Celan's "style," fetishisized by many of his American champions because of its linguistic aporias and disjunctions, is really a by-product of his intense struggle to register interior experience with absolute objectivity. Ashbery's invitations to language to help create interior experience couldn't be more different. That Celan and Ashbery can be spoken of in the same breath shows just how historically unnuanced this current mix and match of styles is.

Deep Image has had its day, though its ahistorical premises have been taken up in this new method's assumption that style is merely a manipulable function, easily disconnected from the individual poet's personal and historical circumstances. That Tranströmer's poems have outlived the aesthetic program that first made them popular is not only an indication of their enduring quality, but also seems an ironic comment on our current intellectual climate, in which criticism seems more interested in issuing directives to artists than in addressing itself to the actual experience of individual works of art. Given the proscriptive nature of criticism's tone, it's not surprising that the line between art and criticism has blurred. But if poets (and poets are also critics) are to continue in their traditional imaginative role of envisioning the spaces that their poems then fill, they need to be especially wary of treating their art as if it were merely a set of linguistic codes handed down to them by the operations of criticism.

Our current technicians' understanding of poetry as language system is symptomatic of a largely unvoiced anxiety about the capacity of art to adequately register the shocks of contemporary experience—what Baudelaire in the nineteenth century recorded in his poems as the decay of tradition under assault from the processes of mass urbanization and technological advance. Those processes have only accelerated in our century, making it wholly understandable why Deep Imagists sought to counter that anxiety by locating "truth" outside our daily experience of mass society. And our current interest in Celan as filtered through Ashbery is also invested in preserving a sense of vital inwardness that isn't so desensitized that it can barely register shock.

The problem with both Deep Image and our current technicians' willful sleight of hand is their ahistorical relationship to their models: to do anything but mop up surface mannerisms of another writer (and this is especially the case with distinctive stylists like Ashbery, Celan, and Tranströmer) requires a keen knowledge of how the structures of poetry and the structures of consciousness differ. To hear the traditional formal elements in Ashbery, a reader needs an ear educated in the history of English literature to know when the poet is resorting to deliberate parody or pastiche.

Otherwise, the self-generating quality of his language degenerates (as is often the case with his imitators) into license for mental flux, flux that tries to redeem itself by adopting a tone of high seriousness characteristic of Celan.

Similarly, Deep Image as a doctrine of composition gave countenance to poets to indulge in a different species of mental flux, one conditioned by the mythology of an Edenic return to language as a sacral instrument. This mythology ignored one of the prime concerns of Tranströmer's poetry: in order to record the shocks of contemporary life, the poet must be willing to enter into history, to conjure it not merely as chronological sequence, but as unique texture and feel, what Walter Benjamin called "aura." Deep Image, however, was committed to locating itself in a world of prehistory, as if the mind were a direct conduit to the eternal collective unconscious, and the time-bound structures of poetry were only a hindrance to the reception of archetypes.

The true marker of Tranströmer's poetry is not Deep Image's desire for unmediated process or the current fascination with stylistic bricolage, process "liberated" from its historical origins. His intention isn't to suppress or outmaneuver the shocks of experience for the sake of primal purity or a portentous, knowing tone, but to make the poem a place where these shocks can occur. The eerie coolness and detachment of his poems are a summons to these shocks that constantly forbode imminent catastrophe. The catastrophe hinted at is the intrusion of irrational forces—natural, historical, psychological—into moments of shock that seem on the verge of erupting into visionary transcendence that would compensate the poet for being at the mercy of these same forces.

Yet this potentially consoling vision is always short-circuited into a direct confrontation with these forces: the vision becomes the moment of this confrontation, while the possibility of transcendence is deferred until the next trial. In his poem "Grief Gondola No. 2," an homage to Liszt's piano pieces by the same name, "the green cold of the ocean" that "presses upward through the palazzo floor" transforms later in the poem to "the deep that loves to invade humanity without showing its own face." Both of these visionary moments, which start off by registering the shock of artistic creation, unpredictably veer off into the irrational world of the poet's own dreams that develop in ways beyond his control, or the control of the structures of art.

This moment of vertigo, of the sense of the nonhuman void revealing itself beneath the invisible but human face of the deep, is one of the triumphs of Tranströmer's poetry. His sensitivity to the deep as the source of human creativity in response to the timelessness of the void suggests how alert his imagination is, always poised on the brink of revelation, but infinitely patient, careful to let these otherworldly revelations take place on their own terms. "The still, sad music of humanity" that resonates from the deep, and the intimation of the void underneath that music, can't be counterfeited by a blind trust in unconscious processes or by appropriating other poets' hard-won intuitions, as if those intuitions could be reproduced at will, regardless of their historical and personal contingencies.

By contrast, Tranströmer's poems imagine the spaces that the deep then inhabits, like groundwater gushing up into a newly dug well. And those spaces are anything but ahistorical. In fact, history itself is the main force that occasions his encounters with the deep. In "Vermeer" as in "The Forgotten Captain" the poet confronts the rising of the deep as it announces its own arrival in historically defined circumstances, a seventeenth-century alehouse in the former case, a World War II convoy patrolling the North Atlantic in the latter. Tranströmer's sense of the continuity between history and our private fates sets up what Baudelaire called *"correspondance"* in which "the lyrical stirrings of the soul, the wave motions of dreaming, the shocks of consciousness" vibrate with and against the specific social conditions we are born into. Tranströmer's poems are acoustically perfect chambers in which all of these contradictory vibrations can be heard without straining. In "Streets in Shanghai" the intoxication of the crowd resonates against darker notes: "We look almost happy out in the sun, while we bleed to death from wounds we know nothing about."

This inclusive, paradoxical habit of vision contributes to what I find most appealing in Tranströmer's work (and perhaps most damaging to our current period style). You can see this rare quality hinted at in the title of his short prose memoir included in *For the Living and the Dead,* "Memories Look at Me." Baudelaire's lines "L'homme y passe à travers des fôrets de symboles/Qui l'observent avec des regards familiers" ("Human beings wander through forests of symbols/Which look back at them with a knowing stare") suggest the reciprocity between the forests of symbols that we make of memory through the means of art, and the actual lived events that will have been our lives. Tranströmer's sense that memories have eyes that look at us from their own vantage point independent of our attempts at remembering insists on the objective quality of the past while acknowledging the contingent nature of memory. All is not at the mercy of language sieved through the ceaseless processes of mental flux; nor is language necessarily an enemy of recollected emotions objectively recorded through poetic form.

Tranströmer's comprehensive understanding of how the forests of symbols establishes deeply personal correspondences to our imaginative lives argues quietly against certain premises of poststructuralist language theory. In terms of personally experienced emotion, there is nothing arbitrary or politically coercive about inherited poetic structures that challenge us to greater coherence in the face of our own fear and confusion before the menacing paradoxes Tranströmer proposes at the end of "Streets in Shanghai" or in "Island Life, 1860": "This moment's stain that flows out for eternity/ this moment's wound that bleeds in for eternity." The poet's recognition of two kinds of time and their interrelationship through the stain and the wound demonstrate how individual fates impinge on categories like "eternity." The poet's notation of the date signals his respect for the manmade, historically situated forests of symbols that buffer us from the void, but also resonate with its unsettling influences.

Tranströmer's work constructs spaces that allow us to penetrate to that void, but without denying the contingent nature of the poem's historical moment. By this quiet way of confronting the void in which "the deep-sea cold" rises into our being, he makes his poems hospitable to the abyss while still acknowledging the vertiginous feel of too much emptiness underneath us. At the ending of "Vermeer" he takes this dynamic between the void and private subjectivity a step further:

> The airy sky has taken its place leaning against the wall.
> It is like a prayer to what is empty.
> And what is empty turns its face to us
> and whispers:
> "I am not empty, I am open."

Objectively voiced, this simultaneous denial and affirmation points beyond itself with unsentimental cool to a realm where the void itself hints at the correspondences between us and it, an invitation almost to inhabit that openness. Perhaps what we most need to learn from Tranströmer's poetry is the grave tact of his making, his wary refusal to march into that void accompanied by linguistic flourishes and salvoes, while allowing the tenderness of this moment between us and that instant of openness to resonate and expand.

Raleigh's Ride

~

Walsinghame

As you came from the holy land
    Of Walsinghame,
Met you not with my true love
    By the way, as you came?

"How shall I know your true love,
    That have met many one
As I went to the holy land,
    That have come, that have gone?"

"She is neither white nor brown,
    But as the heavens fair,
There is none hath a form so divine
    In the earth or the air."

"Such an one did I meet, good Sir,
    Such an angelic face,
Who like a queen, like a nymph did appear
    By her gait, by her grace."

"She hath left me here all alone,
All alone as unknown,
Who sometimes did me lead with herself,
And me loved as her own."

"What's the cause that she leaves you alone
And a new way doth take,
Who loved you once as her own
And her joy did you make?"

"I have loved her all my youth,
But now old as you see,
Love likes not the falling fruit
From the withered tree.

"Know that Love is a careless child,
And forgets promise past;
He is blind, he is deaf when he list
And in faith never fast.

"His desire is a dureless content
And a trustless joy;
He is won with a world of despair
And is lost with a toy.

"Of womenkind such indeed is the love
Or the word love abused,
Under which many childish desires
And conceits are excused.

But true love is a durable fire
In the mind ever burning;
Never sick, never old, never dead,
From itself never turning."

—attributed to Sir Walter Raleigh

Raleigh the saturnine skeptic, whose South American voyages of plunder and exploration would earn him the nickname, "Butcher of Guiana," resists the balladeer of "Walsinghame," his Neoplatonic, thoroughly heartbroken lament. What tentative consolation the final stanza offers, the "durable fire" of true love echoing painfully off "dureless content" two stanzas back. Even the flame of love "In the mind ever burning;/ Never sick, never old, never dead,/ From itself never turning", hints at a fiery ether of self-contained isolation. Forever unreachable by the hard give-and-take of human affection, this love's timeless immunity to sickness, age, and death sorrowfully underscores the human limits that the triumphant stoicism almost overturns. Yet the voice's poise and supernatural calm as it reaches for the casual, unemphatic feminine rhyme hovers above the quiet anguish like the quaver of an overtone.

Perfectly achieved, effortless, above all *spoken,* this naturalness of diction recalls Yvor Winters's statement about poetry "which is perhaps the hardest to compose and the last to be recognized . . . a poetry . . . not striking or original in rhetorical procedure . . . but which permits itself originality . . . only in the most restrained and refined of subtleties in diction and in cadence, but which by virtue of those subtleties inspires its universals with their full value as experience." By universals, Winters means something like the poem's general truths, though these truths are realized in us only because of the poet's complex intonations. And though the speakers in this poem clearly never strain after Browningesque "personality," nevertheless the skeletal narrative supplies the aura of individual circumstance. The disillusioned universals in the last four stanzas possess not only philosophical detachment, but a hard edge of personal rancor. When the speaker lapses into the cliché of the fickle mistress in the penultimate stanza ("Of womenkind such indeed is the love"), his self-pity is undercut by the next line's tough-minded recovery of perspective ("Or the word love abused")—though without totally relinquishing the sense of personal injury that keeps the final stanza rooted in the complexity of our conflicting feelings toward others. The speaker's display of temperament has the effect of keeping the final stanza from seeming like easy eloquence: beneath the masterful sublimity lurks the troubled reminder of our darker impulses.

Less than Neoplatonic cool also marks the speaker when earlier in the poem, in what seems like a highly conventional gesture, he says of his mistress "There is none hath a form so divine/ In the earth or the air." Since Chaucer, carnal obsession on a pilgrimage is a commonplace; but the other pilgrim's enraptured acquiescence to the lover's obsession by claiming "Such an one did I meet, good Sir,/ Such an angelic face,/ Who like a queen, like a nymph did appear/ By her gait, by her grace" effectively collapses the sacred and the sexual. Neither speaker seems worried about, or even cognizant of, this conflation of a pilgrimage to a shrine dedicated to the Virgin Mary with the lover's quest to find news of his mistress. But the eager, self-conscious, smutty zest with which a religious poet like John Donne would have treated such a paradox is alien to the poem's grave, utterly transparent style. Perhaps this simplicity of address coupled with a lack of Christian self-consciousness explains in part the poem's great attraction to a contemporary reader: The pilgrim/lover speaks to our half-ashamed, half-conscious fears of abandonment, of waning sexual attractiveness, and of a consolation not dependent on a changeable, sectarian God but located, "ever burning," in the alchemical fastness of the mind.

Here I'm driven to ask how many champions of rhetorical ingenuity can begin to match the subtleties of the poem's formal resources? Of course, even at their most convoluted, Sidney and Donne, like Raleigh, are emotionally all there. Verbal contortion, verbal transparency, either mode can be a lifeline or blind doodling. And yet rhetorical pyrotechnics, especially in our own period, can dull our responses to quieter frequencies—though for me, the poetic texture of "Walsinghame" is almost overwhelmingly complex: the songlike quality of call and response between the lover and the other pilgrim that creates a charged dialectic between past joy and present pain; the syntactical parallelisms that drive home the speaker's moral judgments with irrevocable finality ("He is blind, he is deaf when he list . . ."); the many instances of repetition, in which echolalia creates a haunted, obsessive sense of sorrow ("She hath left me here all alone,/ All alone as unknown . . .") while tonal shifts in pivotal phrases grow progressively more ironic, more heartbroken ("Met you not with my true love . . ." "How shall I know your true love . . ." "But true love is a durable fire . . ."); the frequent loosening of ballad meter to accommodate the colloquial diction and to keep the rhymes from becoming overly insistent, both features that appeal to contemporary ears ("What's the cause that she leaves you alone/ And a new way doth take,/ Who loved you once as her own/ And her joy did you make?"); all these subtleties help bring home what Winters called "the truth of a truism." At the same time, the poem's unself-conscious indifference to either Christian guilt or consolation, its secular frankness about the fading of sexual vitality, makes "Walsinghame" a quietly radical love poem.

In how many other poems in English does a male speaker acknowledge "Love likes not the fallen fruit/ From the withered tree"? Even his moment of mysogynistic bitterness ("Of womenkind such indeed is the love") opens up to a less partial, if no less saturnine vision of lovers' relations. The jilted lover's sour grapes, his attempt at philosophical detachment, the dispassionate calm with which the rest of the stanza chastens his loss of cool—these complexities both embrace and ward off the final stanza's bleak grandeur.

In this quatrain, the self-constancy of the fire, "from itself never turning," stands quietly, but fiercely indifferent to Mary's intercession or Christ's bounty. Still, it's tempting to envision Raleigh riding a horse in the shade of tall chestnut trees that grow together on either side of the muddy or dusty path trod by pilgrims on their way to the shrine. Unself-consciously carnal, skeptic that he was, what would Raleigh have seen in the madonna's wooden face? But, of course, the shrine was destroyed fourteen years before Raleigh was born. Perhaps the poet who wrote this poem was a phantom, the collective voice of anonymous balladeers, which my version of Raleigh overhears as his horse clops along between hedgerows nervous with insect rant and hum.

Meanwhile, the historical Raleigh, who, in exchange for his freedom from thirteen years of imprisonment in the Tower, had promised to enrich James's bankrupt England, was beheaded on October 29, 1618, for his failure to bring back nonexistent gold from Guiana (the lines that begin "Even such is time" were found at Westminster after his execution). But as my phantom poet rides through fields and woods, the words, whether composed by "Raleigh" or the singers of the hedgerows, continue to ripen with the force of philosophical revelation: Our three ineluctable negatives—sickness, age, death—drive the lover past complaint to the heights of speech.

Frank Bidart's Voice

Who among our contemporaries writes better than Frank Bidart?—though "writes" feels wrong. His poems don't seem so much written as spoken, and not so much spoken as dreamed—the way voices are dreamed. His philosophical obsession with, and revolt against, the "givens" of existence—gender, mortality, our biological instincts—are so subtly vocalized that it's hard to resist his poems' unsettling intimacy.

The weird, oneiric, inward gesture of Eliot murmuring in *The Waste Land,* "I think we are in rats' alley/Where the dead men lost their bones"—is also Bidart's when he imagines: "slow bodies like automatons begin again to move down//into the earth beneath the houses in which they/live bearing the bodies they desired and killed . . ." The unruffled quality of Bidart's voice, lulling, cool, clashes with the horror movie awfulness of what he is evoking. Homicidal zombies seem like votaries in a ritual trance. Our tabloid fascination with the serial killer meets the ancient cult atmosphere of Dionysus or Cybele. Western civilization's scholar, Weegee-like student of the *noir*-ish edge, Bidart's charmed, dialectical voice pendulum-swings through its disparate materials.

Bidart is attracted to sources in which high metaphysical speculation collides with messiness and torment: Lear, say, storming on the heath. If he uses one of Ludwig Binswanger's case histories, the poet grafts his voice to the voice of a suicidal anorexic, Ellen West. If Nijinsky, the visionary madman of Nijinsky's diary. If

St. Augustine, the libidinal, Oedipal son of *The Confessions* sublimating incestuous impulses into visionary ardor. Meditative grandeur that seems to soar above human chances is rebroadcast, in Bidart's voicings, as a deeply private, tormented prayer—and then let down into animal extremes: "First, I was there, where unheard/ harmonies create the harmonies//we hear—//then I was a dog, sniffing/your crotch." Sides of the same coin, perhaps. The poet revolts against his spiritual sources and drags them in the mire—only to humanize them. Baudelaire's angel, whose halo has been knocked into the mud of a Parisian boulevard, and who revels in the city's soiled nature, is one glimpse into Bidart's divided nature. Another is the purity, and almost heroic conviction, of these lines: "WHETHER YOU LOVE WHAT YOU LOVE//OR LIVE IN DIVIDED CEASELESS/REVOLT AGAINST IT//WHAT YOU LOVE IS YOUR FATE."

The odd rightness of Bidart's career has to do with the fidelity of his intentions sustained over many years. Fidelity to what, though?

My first meeting with Bidart's poetry came a few years after *Golden State* appeared. At that time my head was full of John Crowe Ransom and Allen Tate—the civility of the former, the savage rhetoric of the latter, baffled and delighted me. But *Golden State* was in an altogether different linguistic key: I remember being astonished that Bidart could speak of driving on a freeway cloverleaf, the radio turned up to blasting, in terms of religious ecstasy—a sensation utterly new to me in poetry, especially since I'd also spent my adolescence in Southern California driving on freeways and felt more of a dead-time, meditative drone than transcendence. The authenticity and strangeness of Bidart's sensibility, which felt things close to the bone, seemingly rawly personal but balanced at every point by a supple, analytical mind, troubled and elated me: How did Bidart pull it off? I could see how Tate did it, and to a certain extent, Ransom. But the plainness of Bidart's writing, its immunity to imagistic panache . . . and at the same time the subtlety of his music in an idiom that seemed indifferent to the "norms" of "good writing" as exemplified by Tate and Ransom—I was enthralled, and overwhelmed by its apparent newness.

I floundered about with *Golden State* until I came across a copy of Montale's "Xenia," the Italian poet's level-voiced, ironic, sorrowing farewell to his dead wife: "They say that mine/is a poetry of non-belonging./But if it was yours, it was someone's . . ." Montale's intimacy of address and his yearning philosophical intelligence suddenly showed me the way into Bidart's world. The two poets' plainspokenness, and their lack of traditional poetic ornament, seemed a rebuke, in Bidart's words, "to the lies/of mere neat poetry."

Stylistic mavericks can be tedious, their effects hardening into self-caricature. In contrast, Bidart's stylistic disaffections are underwritten by philosophical ones. All of Bidart's work, but especially his first two books, *Golden State* and *Book of the Body,* reveals (just as Montale does in "Xenia") a world of enlightened but disenchanted spirit. In both books, Bidart's troubled relationship to his parents grounds his philosophical questioning. The poet discovers that his desire to reconcile the past in order to live more fully in all his faculties in the present, as attractive as it sounds!—is also a way of annihilating the past. The rebelliousness of Bidart's intelligence, much like Montale's, endorses the notion that "the past in maiming us,/makes us." The "mountain of FEELING," if it is to survive as anything but glib transcendence, must remain "un-mappable."

But can it? Once a poem gets written, the mountain begins to flatten out, the map takes over, the mountain grows more and more remote. The thrust and slash of peaks across the sky is reduced to the mapmaker's inks. As an artist striving after intelligibility and order, Bidart has "the illusion that his poems . . . had cruelly replaced his past, that finally they were all he knew of it."

Perhaps this illusion explains why the poet keeps going over the same material, often transformed through personas: his parents' marriage, their divorce, their separate lives and deaths, his overriding need for union with his mother: "THERE WAS NO PLACE IN NATURE WE COULD MEET." His attraction to emptying the past by replacing it with "poetry" is counteracted by his imagination's drive to revive the past by using poetry as a spell to summon the dead back to life. For Bidart, poetry is a lifeline, not a tombstone, an opportunity to transform the past into something less partial or blinkered. Hopeless ambition, noble, doomed . . . to imagine that we can make the lives of the dead sweeter, more suited to their capacities for happiness . . . and less theirs, less real, more on the poet's terms.

But the irreducibility of Feeling, its weird particulars that we thread our way through and that weave the texture of our experience—all this Bidart captures, not by rendering it imagistically, but by distilling it into the peculiar, personal qualities of his poetic voice.

More than most poets, Bidart's voice has signature qualities that his prosody (adapted from Pound's gossiping, helter-skelter, heartbreaking *Cantos*), punctuation, and careful scoring of his syntax make expressive on the page. How immediate and physically there in the mind's ear is the voice of the speaker in a Bidart poem. The sound of sense, in Frost's phrase, is absolutely overwhelming. The typographical explosion of Bidart's middle period, his hectoring capitals and menacing italics in *The Sacrifice,* especially, and his devotion to punctuation to express precise vocal tones, reveals his need to keep the "mountain of FEELING" in sight by using his voice as a theater to dramatize the balked, involuted shiftings of his speakers' emotions.

On a deeper, almost atavistic level, Bidart's voice is the medium of his dead parents . . . and of himself as the child who watched his "parents'/blighted lives blighted in the service of Venus." The consequences for the child produced by such blight underlies his interest in mediumship. In order to readjust the imbalance of power between child and parents, he undertakes to resurrect their voices through his: the medium isn't simply the receiver and transmitter of the deads' frequencies. He jams the airwaves with his own interference pattern, introducing his attraction to philosophical meditation in order to bolster his case that "The brown clapboard house,/in spite of its fine pioneer tradition,/because of the absence of the knowledge in its/lines of other architecture [. . .]/reminds me of my parents."

Lack of knowledge about the world, about the possibilities for other ways to live—his parents' forward-faring, damaged, and damaging generation. That "the brown clapboard house" and the insufficiency of its "pioneer tradition" remind him of his parents isn't delivered as an indictment, but comes across as the pose of speculative calm. Reason, order, the dream that art and culture can lift us beyond the past, are all condensed in the yearning one senses underneath the rational poise of the speaker's voice. But a son's need to climb intellectually and emotionally above the ruin and vital thrashing of his parents' lives is also a gesture of defiance. Bidart's philosophical distance is an expression of this and of his attempt to redress the helplessness of the child still looking for a lifeline out of Venus's irrational blight. No wonder the poet takes ideas to heart in all their heady, high-altitude promise.

Both the vessel of his parents' lives and the adjudicator of their failings, Bidart takes ideas more seriously than most poets. This needs some explanation: ideas in themselves mean little to Bidart. He connects them to modes of conduct, to human vicissitude—to the wilderness of his parents' marriage, say, or to his own compulsions, limitations, and complex ways of feeling. (Bidart would amend the William Carlos Williams dictum, "No ideas but in things," to "No ideas but in human actions.") Ignorance of ideas about other ways to live limited—cruelly, in the poet's estimation—his parents' lives . . . and Bidart's own life unfolds in the shadow of such knowledge. So ideas, their potentials and poverty, their glamorous aura of transformation and change, pulsate at the heart of his poetic dramas.

His poems always embody ideas enlisted into dramatic action. The action is often tragic, disturbingly unnoble, doomed to repetition, as if all we learn from our disasters is how to repeat them in subtler, more ingenious ways. On the other hand, grace that comes with understanding exists side by side with the cold-comfort bleakness of many of Bidart's momentary resting places:

Man needs a metaphysics;
he cannot have one.

Or

—Hell came when I saw
MYSELF . . .
and couldn't stand

what I see . . ."

Or

. . . she had failed because her fate, like
all fates, was partial.

Isolated from the dramas that frame them, these conclusions seem radically disaffected. But in the vital weave of story, they motivate significant action—the kind of action that reveals the essential shape and consequence of a life. And because Bidart is a narrative poet, ideas must always be acted on, acted through, by the speakers of his poems.

Bound to the ideas that shaped their fates and incorporated, through his mediumship, onto the page, Bidart's speakers have a hallucinatory vividness—they are as physically present as the dead who, in dreams, reach out and touch us. His desire to give their voices weight on the page meshes with his desire to recall the dead to life—and not simply as spirits or memories, but as flesh, flesh aroused by other flesh:

> *on such a night,*
>
> *at such an hour*
>
> . . . grace is the dream, half-
> dream, half-
>
> light, when you appear and do not answer the question
>
> that I have asked you, but courteously
> ask (because you are dead) if you can briefly
>
> borrow, inhabit my body.
>
> When I look I can see my body
> away from me, sleeping.
>
> I say *Yes.* Then you enter it
>
> like a shudder as if eager again to know
> what it is to move within arms and legs.

I'm being only a little bit fanciful when I suggest that Bidart literally wants to bring the dead back to life: the poet's use of punctuation, typography, and white space to weight and point the movement of the voice through the materials of the poem is, in fact, a conjuring of spirits, a way of giving substance and dimensionality to the word-ghosts speaking from the void flatness of the page. Try eliminating throughout his work the capitals, the italics, the elaborate punctuation, the downward stagger of the syntax breaking across the lines—and the voices materialized on the page grow wispy, thin.

What I'm driving at is the underlying motivation of Bidart's formal eccentricities. His need to question the dead, in order to reconcile those things that another side of the poet realizes are forever irreconcilable, has driven him to extreme measures. But not so extreme when you understand the gravity of his desire to re-animate the dead and see reflected in their actions the blighted, or partial, or disturbing truths that shaped their fates.

To bring the dead back, the poet becomes the vessel "[. . .] of the dead, the voice erased/by death now, for a time, unerased." The voices of the dead echoing inside his voice, his imagination haunted by memories of their estrangement and pain, how deeply the poet dreams of reunion, renewal, forgiveness! And if he seems to blame himself for dreaming such dreams, to see something falsely ameliorating in his desire for reconcilement, this only intensifies his yearning. A latter-day Tantalus in the pit, he reaches upward for fulfillments out of reach—and discovers "CORRIDORS within WALLS,//(the disenthralling, necessary, dreamed structure/beneath the structure we see.)"

At this point, one wants to flinch—and point to other gestures. They exist, especially in his most recent book, *Desire.* Taking up his old *cri de coeur* to his mother, "THERE WAS NO PLACE IN NATURE WE COULD MEET," the poet quarries out of Ovid's *Metamorphoses* a momentary meeting place. Using Myrrha's incestuous relations with her father as a mythic analogue to desire attained at any price, Bidart dispenses with much of the more self-conscious *coloratura* of his middle period. The long title poem is more like other poems—conventions of dramatic lyric are honored, though complicated by the eerie cool, and heartbroken fluency, of the poet's voice mourning both his mother, and his own lover's death. The lover and mother shadow and complicate each other, just as they shadow and complicate the figures of Myrrha and her father. The liminal nature of identity in the poem underscores the polymorphous energies of desire—at least until those energies narrow to the consummation of father and daughter. This union ultimately results in Myrrha's transformation into a tree, not human, not dead, but Nature without consciousness of guilt. Yet the trace of the incestuous relation still exists in the form of myrhh—aphrodisiac, embalmer's oil, insistent of sex—and the birth of Adonis, avenger on Venus of his mother's blighted life.

This many-edged whirl of conflicting associations crystallizes into a dream vision: The dead lover returns to take possession of the poet's body, and the poet, gratefully it seems, submits: "I thought, *I know that he will return it.*//I trusted in that none/ earlier, none other." In the beautiful litany that follows these lines, the sense of grace achieved, of ecstatic union in Nature's despite, is one of the most compelling vocal moments of Bidart's career:

> I tasted a sweet taste, I found nothing sweeter.
> Taste.
> My pleasant fragrance has stripped itself to stink.
> Taste.
> The lust of the sweetness that is bitter I taste.
> Taste.
> Custom both sweet and bitter is
> the intercourse of this flesh.
> Taste.
> The milk that is in all trees,
> the sweet water that is beneath.
> Taste.
> The knife of cutting is the book of mysteries.
> Taste.
> Bitterness sweetness, eat that you may eat.
> Taste.
> I tasted a sweet taste, I found nothing sweeter.

Taste.
These herbs were gathered at full noon, which was night.
Taste.

The poet's voice is all stark simplicity, eccentric but unforced, "disenthralling"—that is, freely moving, free to circulate among extremes, free to submit (or not) to the "necessary, dreamed structure," harbinger of an ultimate reality, that has been the object of the poet's desire and loathing for the past thirty years.

There is nothing cheaply happy in this dreamed moment of union. Bidart's ambivalence about reconciliation with the past colors this meeting of the dead and the living. Only in grief and loss does the meeting take place; only in dream, and only after death, does the poet allow the dead lover to take full possession of his body. The precondition for union is obliteration. What underlying adjustment to the relations of the dead to the living is Bidart's voice enacting, if not the fearsome, partial, contingent nature of union with time-bound, flesh-bound bodies?

Of the poet himself in the flesh, I have my many versions, formed, year in, year out, over the past twenty-five years—disharmonious ones, all equally pushing to the forefront, none definitive, all definitive of a moment: the poet walking with head bowed, hands folded behind his back, something parochial and clerical in his bearing. Or sitting surrounded by a jungle of books and videotapes, his mail in the sink—and in the oven. Or at a reading, listening intently to another poet, his face concentrated, measuring, gauging . . . or reading his own work, his absorption into the poem's emotion registering on his face, now blank, now grimacing, now musingly calm, while an aura of distance and transport surrounds his tall, slightly stooped figure.

Perhaps he is never more himself than in casual, but intense, conversation, searching for the appropriate word to name some shortcoming or felicity or paradox in a poem that he has just read. His hands move to his forehead and form a sort of hood for his eyes, while two vertical furrows crease the middle of his brow. He looks at you, through you, abstracted. You can sense him testing what he feels against the words scanning through his mind, trying to make the feeling and the thought align with the word. There is a pause, a slight suspension of gravity in the room. At such moments, in my mind's eye, he seems to float a little below the horizon line, drawn down by his effort at concentration, interrogating what it is he actually feels. And when he speaks, haltingly, then more fluently, qualifying further and further, striving for precision, I can sense his brute confidence in the primacy of emotion, of art *as* emotion, in his voice's weight and drag.

Hers Truly:
A Note on Elizabeth Bishop's Letters

~

Frank Bidart tells the story that near the end of Elizabeth Bishop's life she was thumbing through a volume of essays on contemporary poetry: Robert Lowell, John Berryman, Sylvia Plath, Randall Jarrell . . . but nothing on Bishop. Closing the book, she said quietly, "It's like being buried alive."

How would Bishop regard her posthumous fame? When she died in 1979, she was clearly in Lowell's shadow, though their names seemed indissolubly linked, the result of their lifelong friendship. But in the decades since her death, her reputation has boomed: she has made it into the classrooms; general readers have discovered her; critics routinely tout her modesty, her reticence, her aversion to self-display. And in contrast to Lowell's genius for disturbing self-portraiture, her poetic persona seems almost aristocratically genteel.

But the image that emerges from her letters is much less varnished. An obsessive letter writer, Bishop poured much of her creative life into her correspondence. She can be as fascinatingly gossipy as Madame de Sévigné, as profound as Rilke though without the *fin de siècle* soupiness, and as brilliant and affectionate a chronicler of domestic goings on, and of people's flaws and foibles, as Chekhov. Of course her letters reveal her own vulnerabilities and frailties. And in the selection of her letters, *One Art: Elizabeth Bishop Letters,* the untouchable poise of her poetic persona gives way to subtle self-contradiction. Her modesty seems as much shyness as a moral stance. Her reticence was in part a desire to keep hidden her shame over her drinking bouts and depressions. Her distaste for self-dramatization seems a defense against her attraction to personalities more edgy than her own.

But Bishop's letters do much more than feed a fan's voyeuristic hunger for "details." Mapped in this selection of over 500 letters—drawn from more than 3,000—is the day-to-day terrain of a poet who sidestepped Yeats's dichotomy of choosing perfection either of the life or of the art. She accomplished this by recognizing the continuities between her talent for improvising an eventful daily life and the often painful subjects that she treated with such precise cool. Her choice to live in Key West, and then in Brazil, before moving to Boston to teach at Harvard in the last decade of her life, was as valuable to her as Frost's fifteen years dalliance with farming.

In a letter to Marianne Moore in 1943, she describes waterspouts in Key West: ". . . I've been living in almost complete solitude. I don't really mind so much. . . . I was sure I'd described waterspouts to you long ago . . . you can see the water or mist or whatever it is going up inside in puffs and clouds, very fast, just like smoke up a chimney . . ." This moment, right down to the understated admission of loneliness, resurfaces more than thirty years later in this passage from "Crusoe in England": "Glass chimneys, flexible, attenuated,/ sacerdotal beings of glass . . . I watched/ the water spiral up in them like smoke./ Beautiful, yes, but not much company." Equally remarkable in both the letter and poem is Bishop's mastery of tone—the letter's plainer, more relaxed style as appropriate to its occasion as the poem's self-consciously artful "sacerdotal beings of glass."

I don't want to overemphasize the letters as a quarry or testing ground for her work. While the interplay between her letters and poems exemplifies what Lowell meant by "one life, one writing," Bishop is as much interested in describing a calf being born or her latest trip down the Amazon as she is in talking about literature. And yet the scope of these letters goes beyond what they reveal about her poetry or her virtuosity in rendering her daily experience. Taken together, the letters represent not only an unofficial autobiography, but evoke an American artistic and social milieu that has all but vanished.

From our current cultural perspective, a striking feature of that milieu was the unself-conscious alliance between genteel wealth and artistic bohemianism. After a difficult childhood (her father died when she was eight months old; she never again saw her mother after she entered an asylum when Bishop was five), for most of her adult life a modest legacy from her father supplemented by grants and fellowships left her free to devote her time to literature, travel, and, of course, letter writing. This romantic image of Bishop as a sort of quasi-aristocrat in pursuit of "aesthetic impressions"—it is surprising how many of her admirers promulgate this view—accounts for part of her mystique since her death. But the letters tell a more complicated story, one tainted on occasion by minor snobberies and the inveterate traveler's tendency to reduce "the locals" to local color.

But snobbery in a letter is different from snobbery in real life. The letters demonstrate that in her actual dealings with people she was unfailingly democratic—if to be democratic means always to strive to be genuinely courteous and empathize with other people's troubles and failings. Today, her good manners might be derided as mere gentility: but in a letter to Marianne Moore, her "political values" are aptly expressed by this exasperated comment: "I am utterly disgusted with 'social-conscious' conversation—by people who always seem to be completely unconscious of their surroundings, other people's personalities, etc."

This sensitivity to others shows up in how carefully she pitches her voice to the ear of her correspondent. Her letters to Moore are always decorous, mirroring back Moore's own tone of quaint, fond formality. To Lowell, she is more unbuttoned; but in speaking of his work, she is routinely self-deferential, even when arguing that he should disguise or cut some painful moment of autobiographical candor. But perhaps the letters to Loren McIver and Frani Muser are the most frank, the most vulnerable, the most revelatory of her fundamental nature. Her self-doubts about her art, especially her lack of productivity; her domestic sorrows; her lifelong struggle with asthma that rendered her at times a semi-invalid; and, of course, her chronic confusion about her own alcoholism appear with unself-pitying frankness, her self-condemnations leavened by some detail of landscape or a moment of gently self-deprecating humor. And when speaking of her poetry—especially to other poets—her habitual modesty seems absolutely genuine. Always her own harshest critic, she cultivated a refreshingly workman-like attitude toward her vocation (she often mentions having "sold" a piece of writing)—and seems entirely free of artistic posturing or of making the kind of drippy vatic pronouncements that soup up other poets' letters.

Throughout her career her modesty and stringency never relaxed, and in keeping with that tough-mindedness, I won't pretend that her letters equal her poetry and prose, despite how lively and deeply pleasurable they are to read. But I can't imagine any biographer doing more justice to her life and social world than she herself has already done. What mars most autobiography is self-consciousness: but Bishop's spontaneous, daily devotion to her friends as expressed through these letters inadvertently reveals, casual layer by layer, her failings, her sorrows, her unique nobleness of mind.

At the End of Our Good Day: Randall Jarrell

~

I first read Randall Jarrell's poems in the back of a Baltimore bookstore when, as a college student, I'd just begun to try to write poetry. His publisher had also released a collected volume of Elizabeth Bishop's. Both books were wildly out of alphabetical order, but shelved, weirdly enough, side by side. Some poetry reader who knew a great deal more than I did must have been browsing and then, distracted or in a hurry, left them that way.

I'd heard of Lowell, but not Jarrell or Bishop. Now that all three are dead, one name conjures up another with almost familial insistence. During their lifetimes the lion's share of notice went to Lowell, though his breakdowns, his marital resolutions and irresolutions attracted as much attention as his work. If from time to time Jarrell and Bishop smashed their lives to pieces (in Jarrell's case, according to William Pritchard's biography, the turmoil seems mainly to have been internal), they lived away from the magnifying-glass scrutiny of literary gossip, Bishop's Brazil, Jarrell's Greensboro fantastically far from Lowell's Boston and New York. Bishop's drinking, Jarrell's breakdown and putative suicide at fifty—in a letter written when he was thirty-three, he describes himself as leading "an odd, independent, unsocial life remarkably unlike other people's lives, the life of someone whose principal work-and-amusement is writing and reading and thinking about things."

Lowell's "one life, one writing"; his "words meathooked from the living steer"; his late ungainsayable *ars poetica,* "Yet why not say what happened?"—all this depended on something having happened. In one of Jarrell's last poems, "The Player Piano," his perennial alter ego, an older woman, says, "If only, somehow, I had learned to live!" And in a letter written after his breakdown and a month before his death: "I've always wanted to change, but not to change into what you become when you're mentally ill."

At some point, most poets' lives go dead on them—to paraphrase Lowell, they reflect, moralize, imagine: Some single faculty keeps on moving and fanning the air, but the whole-man has stopped. Of course Lowell's illness kept him from the "immunity to soil, entanglements and rebellion" which he praised, envied, and quietly censured in Jarrell: Wasn't his old friend a little above it all? Bishop's unhappiness, valor, and humor—how often her critics have commented on the sheen of her poems' scoured surfaces! And yet something heartbroken stares back from her stoical, self-contained gaze, a terror like Jarrell's snow-leopard, "the heart of heartlessness." But Jarrell's beautifully flashing, amazingly flexible armor of European culture so useful to his criticism, his Freud, the Brothers Grimm, Proust, Chekhov, Rilke—did he live perhaps a little vicariously? Did he feel this in his forties, until at fifty, something in him rebelled?

When Jarrell thinks discursively in his poems (dramatic monologues generally in women's voices like "Next Day" or "The Woman at the Washington Zoo"), he feels and talks like a woman who feels and talks like Jarrell. When he acts (his Rilke translations, war poems, and fairy-tale fables), he is a child with an adult's intelligence searching for Mother and Father. In all his poems—and surely in his last best book, *The Lost World*—his sexual identity is strangely indeterminate, an intellectualized, tormented, half-joking androgeny.

In his dramatic monologues Jarrell's female speakers are thinly disguised versions of himself: What woman—or man but Randall

Jarrell—quotes, while shopping in the supermarket, William James: "... Wisdom, said William James,// Is learning what to overlook"? But this woman-as-Jarrell also haunts his criticism: his provocative essay on Frost's "Home Burial," in which an estranged husband and wife try to mend the breach caused by the death of their newborn child, is strangely severe on the husband. In taking the woman's part in this poem, Jarrell tends to see the man as slow, dull-witted, even physically and sexually brutal.

Frost isn't nearly so efficient in placing blame: even if the man is what Jarrell paints him, the reader still feels as much pity as scorn. Jarrell's sense of his own superiority as a critic chills his feeling for the husband's inarticulate, hurt, woefully desperate attempt to make contact with his wife:

> "My words are nearly always an offense.
> I don't know how to speak of anything
> So as to please you. But I might be taught,
> I should suppose. I can't say I see how.
> A man must partly give up being a man
> With womenfolk. We could have some arrangement
> By which I'd bind myself to keep hands off
> Anything special you're a-mind to name.
> Though I don't like such things 'twixt those that love.
> Two that don't love can't live together without them.
> But two that do can't live together with them."

Jarrell is right to condemn the man's sensitivity as "a willing, hopeful form of insensitivity," but his ear misses the pitying, awkward grandeur of the man's speech. In describing the husband's proverb about those who do and do not love as a "partially truthful but elephantine aphorism that lumbers through a queerly stressed line a foot too long," he scores a point, but misses the sad, terrible heart of Frost's poem.

And yet he gains far more than he loses by using "Home Burial" as a template for his own internal contradictions. His essay has the power and conviction of spiritual autobiography, his breathlessness tracking the woman's psychological fluctuations in a mixture of Freud, stylistic analysis, and such imaginative empathy that Jarrell and the woman almost merge. The man is of the world, all body and will. The woman is a force of the imagination doomed to inhabit the world of body and will. There is no reconciling these two: Frost's poem also says this, but not in the sorrowing, partial way Jarrell sees it. Frost is harder, more matter-of-fact, inclined even to shrug a little at this man and woman. While Frost made it a point to discriminate between art and life, for Jarrell the two knit seamlessly together, revealing just how literary a sensibility he possessed.

That Jarrell could live so deeply in books made him a superb critic—did it help or harm him as a poet? The physical world, the world of bodies that criticism glances at but never seems to see, even as a poet, this was not his subject! And yet his empathy for Whitman, Williams, Frost, Lowell—didn't his enthusiasm betray a longing for an entrance into the violent, reckless, exuberantly physical realm his criticism made for each of them? In prose he loved Kipling, Tolstoy, Chekhov, the Turgenev of the hunting sketches. And though his powers of description did justice to the physical world, description was not, as it was for these others, revelation. Revelation was dialectics, his endless recourse to "And yet . . ."

The war poems—they are less dialectical than anything he ever wrote, as close as he comes to entering a purely physical world. Here time does not balloon into the once-upon-a-time timelessness of the fairy-tale fables or the lyrical eternal present of his Rilke translations. Time in Jarrell's war is a moment just before death in a fighter, a bomber, a parachute; or the moment when the sleeping soldier dreams his escape from the barracks and is back home, a child among women who take care of him; or the moment when a guard starts to sing "Sam Hall" and the prisoners he's guarding stop picking up trash and grin. Single dramatic moments that blossom into consciousness as testaments to "scenes of war," but also root down into the unconscious as ogre-soldier children playing the adult game of war: "In bombers we named for girls, we burned/ The cities we had learned about in school—"

The hurt of the war is real to Jarrell, but perhaps embodies another, more personal hurt. In a letter quoted in William Pritchard's biography, Jarrell speaks of his parents' divorce: "I've lived all over, and always been separated from at least half of a very small family, and been alone as children ever are." A lost child's search for Mother or Father—the clear, homely simplicity of Jarrell's loneliness lies at the heart of the war poems. His search for origins figures as a source of hidden power for some of his most objective, most intensely personal writing.

This loneliness haunts the lost bomber-pilot children who search for the Mother-Carrier strafed and torpedoed into flames. They find instead the ghostly Father incarnated in the weapons themselves. (Jarrell's equation in "Home Burial" of male sexuality with will, and of will with the murderous force that shapes soldiers, underlies this connection.) The tracers wriggle like sperm and the fighters appear "like the apparition, death," in the great glass dome of the bomber's gun-turret. Jarrell displaces death onto machines; or he sees it as the unconsciousness of sleep; or as an abstraction synonymous with the authority of the State. Death never comes to Jarrell's soldiers with the brute, bitter finality displayed in Wilfred Owen's poem, "Asleep":

> Sleep took him by the brow and laid him back.
> And in the happy no-time of his sleeping,
> Death took him by the heart. There was a quaking
> Of the aborted life within him leaping . . .
> Then chest and sleepy arms once more fell slack.

In Jarrell, nothing so physically—or sexually—graphic; he reserves that for the deaths of the planes themselves: Male orgasm as destruction underlies this imagery: "The red wriggling tracers [. . .]/ Hunt out the one end they have being for,/ Are metamorphosed into one pure smear/ Of flame, and die/ In the maniacal convulsive spin/ Of the raider with a wing snapped off, the plane/ Trailing its flaming kite's-tail to the wave." As befits a mechanized war, the dead pilot inside vanishes into the details of the plane's destruction.

Even when Jarrell envisions the death of a pilot, instead of really dying with quaking and convulsions like Owen's sleeping soldier, the pilot has a moment of recognition—and then *doesn't* die: "[. . .] the pilot,/ Drugged in a blanket [. . .]/ Knows, knows at last; he yawns the chattering yawn/ Of effort and anguish, of hurt hating helplessness—/ Yawns sobbingly, his head falls back, he sleeps." Jarrell's sobbing pilot could be a child crying himself to sleep: having suffered the global tantrum of the war, he realizes the full anguish of his own helplessness. And while he comes face to face with oblivion, his war seems another order of experience from the war of Owen's soldier, the "aborted life within him leaping." At least the pilot's war includes moments, terrible though they may be, of self-recognition. In Owen's war, his soldiers—with the cruelest, most irremediable irony—often simply die.

In *The Lost World,* Jarrell's search for origins finds an ending both happy and unhappy: his grandparents, the Mama and Pop of his childhood poems. But his adult journey backward to childhood is counterbalanced by the book's other concern: woman.

But a Jarrell Woman, not the highly individuated women in Lowell's or Bishop's work. In Jarrell, women often serve as opportunities for charming, self-ironic commentary on men's unreal expectations of them: that they verge on stereotype can make his wit seem labored. At times one wonders how a man who taught most of his life in a women's college, married twice, his second marriage making him the stepfather of two daughters, could be, in these poems, so blasé and predictable. And yet Jarrell's use of a female persona is almost always interesting: Why this access to feeling denied him in his own voice?

In part, when Jarrell writes about women in his own persona, the supercilious tones of the critic keep intruding—he becomes chatty and loses the immediacy and power of direct presentation. But more to the point is the source of Jarrell's defensiveness: in his essay on "Home Burial," Jarrell conflates the husband's sexuality with the spade that he used to dig his own child's grave. For a Freudian like Jarrell, the connection must seem obvious. But Jarrell's animus, ostensibly from the wife's point of view, about her husband's "tool," makes one wonder: "Her next words, 'and still your spade kept lifting,' gives the man's tool a dead, mechanical life of its own; it keeps on and on, crudely, remorselessly, neither guided or halted by spirit." And yet the grave needs to be dug. Shouldn't it be enough to do the shoveling of your own child's grave without worrying if the spade is guided or halted by spirit? The man can't afford to pay someone else. For a progressive liberal like Jarrell, he takes an awfully dim view of this hard-pressed farmer's sweat and labor.

Perhaps Jarrell's superior rambling, his torturous, half-joking elaborations of male and female stereotypes, masked his anxiety about his own sexual nature. In these lines from "Woman," his edginess about the physical nature of sexual love makes his wit seem a little forced, even prudish: "When, like Disraeli, I murmur/ That you are more like a mistress than a wife,/ More like an angel than a mistress; when, like Satan,/ I hiss in your ear some vile suggestion,/ Some delectable abomination,/ You smile at me indulgently: 'Men, men!'" This exchange between husband and wife makes sexual desire seem like a game of talking dirty—though in this case the dirty talker is an extremely literary one who says "vile" and "delectable" instead of something more direct. (This is Lowell: "We stand to leave,/ your breasts touch my chest;/ under our clothes, our bodies/ are but as bodies are.") And instead of hissing back, the wife—at once playmate, mistress, mother—only murmurs indulgently to this stagy Disraeli-Satan, recognizing the childish element of make-believe in the whole setup.

But Jarrell isn't always so evasive. "The Bronze David of Donatello" powerfully explores the homoerotic side of Jarrell's essentially undifferentiated sexual nature. In the poem Jarrell sees the statue as a metaphor of sexual foreplay and conquest. Jarrell identifies himself with both lover and beloved, with the sexually ambiguous, weirdly virginal, weirdly whorish boy David (whose "rib-case, navel, nipples are the features/ Of a face that holds us like the whore Medusa's—/ Of a face that, like the genitals, is sexless"); and with the adult-ogre's severed head on which the boy's foot rests. Goliath, who "snores a little in satisfaction," seems as much the boy's lover as his foe, his helmet's wing "[. . .] like a swan's wing up inside the leg," reaching "[. . .] almost, to the rounded/ Small childish buttocks." If victory is sexual victory, Goliath is as much a conqueror as David.

But such frankness is rare in his poems about women (as opposed to when he speaks in a woman's voice). In the best light, perhaps Jarrell used stereotypes intending to explode them. As it is, they do too much work, emotional and aesthetic, in these poems—and preserve him from delving into the ambiguities of "our bodies/ are but as bodies are."

In Jarrell's dramatic monologues, his irony falls away, he becomes grave, direct, open. In "Next Day," one of his finest poems, his female persona talks about her own sexual desires as a middle-aged wife and mother: "[. . .] Now that I'm old, my wish/ Is womanish:/ That the boy putting groceries in my car// See me. It bewilders me he doesn't see me." No jokiness or smirking in this avowal. And even when Jarrell resorts to his old standby "vile" to describe sexual fantasy ("And, holding their flesh within my flesh, their vile// Imaginings within my imagining,/ I too have taken/ The chance of life."), the irony is plangent, sadly in keeping with this Everywoman. Having attended the funeral of her friend the day before, she realizes that aging and death are as terrifyingly specific as her "[. . .] friend's cold made-up face, granite among its flowers."

In "Next Day" the body, in consonance with Jarrell's own ambiguous sexual nature, is a prison-house of shifting, almost meaningless identities: "No one has anything, I'm anybody,/ I stand beside my grave/ Confused with my life, that is commonplace and solitary." The only escape from this bleak conclusion is in a mythic world before time and identity. In "The House in the Wood," one of Jarrell's best fairy-tale fables, "[. . .] what was before the world/ And will be after, holds me to its black// Breasts and rocks me: the oven is cold, the cage is empty,/ [. . .] the witch and her child sleep." Jarrell conjures this limbo in the unsettling terms of Hansel and Gretel: What will the witch-mother do to the child if ever she should wake?

In another, though no less troubled escape, Jarrell sets against the world of time his own mythical childhood. In "The Lost World" he never directly mentions his real mother and father, the sexual, time-bound beings that produced him. His own persona as a boy, his idealized grandparents, Mama and Pop (already too old to be sexual, at least in the poem), float in the ether of his precarious Eden. That Jarrell wrote "The Lost World" in his last troubled years explains in part his desire for an imaginative haven. But his impulse to examine the forces—sexuality and death—that make the child father to the man keeps disrupting his idyll. The poem's achievement lies in how skillfully Jarrell plays his grown-up persona off his child persona to re-create the aura of his own lost innocence.

In some of the most memorable writing of his career, he describes Mama, who "[. . .] looks with righteous love/ At all of us, her spare face half a girl's," as she enters a chicken coop and, by wringing a chicken's neck, unwittingly initiates her grandson into the world of time. As the chicken lunges and reels in circles, the boy watches Mama standing "[. . .] like a nun/ In the center of each awful anguished ring." The disparity between Mama and her action is too much for the boy to fathom—he leaves this to the grown-up Jarrell, who sees Mama "Standing like Judith, with the hen's head in her hand." Judith—the seductress and murderess of Holofernes.

By now the polarity between nun and Judith should be familiar, already figured in Woman as playmate, wife, mother, mistress. But what keeps Mama from becoming a straw woman is the objective manner in which Jarrell records her actions ("She enters a chicken coop[. . .]/ [. . .] She chooses one,/ Comes out, and wrings its neck."); and the care Jarrell takes to keep his grown-up self from intruding on the boy's terrified reactions:

> The thudding and scrambling go on, go on—then they fade,
> I open my eyes, it's over . . . Could such a thing
> Happen to anything? It could to a rabbit, I'm afraid;
> It could to—
> "Mama, you won't kill Reddy ever,
> You won't ever, will you?" The farm woman tries to persuade
> The little boy, her grandson, that she'd never
> Kill the boy's rabbit, never even think of it.
> He would like to believe her . . . And whenever
> I see her, there in that dark infinite,
> Standing like Judith, with the hen's head in her hand,
> I explain it away, in vain—a hypocrite,
> Like all who love.

With great fluidity and compression Jarrell registers the stages of the boy's mounting panic; then he shifts into third person in which he presents with skillful understatement both the boy's and Mama's conflicting viewpoints; and then he finishes the passage in his own adult voice by ruefully acknowledging that love is innocent only if we can explain away the contradictions in those we love.

These superbly handled dramatic modulations carry through

to the poem's conclusion several lines later, in which Jarrell manages to regain some equanimity through the figure of Pop. Pop as surrogate father, even the All-Father, foils the mad scientist in the boy's magazine. He reassures the child that the mad scientist couldn't really destroy the world: "'[. . .] No, that's just play,/ Just make-believe,' he says. The sky is gray,/ We sit there, at the end of our good day." Of course Jarrell's use of "there" instead of "here" shows just how far the grown-up poet is from the boy. And the historical irony of the mad scientist's make-believe isn't lost on Jarrell, who mentions Armageddon in other poems.

Pop's failure to protect the child from the male provenance of war, Mama's unwitting collusion in introducing the child to death and the hypocrisies of love—these ironies hedge considerably the optimism of the poem's last line. But if the sky is gray for the grown-up poet, his skill in weighting the couplet in favor of "our good day" forges not only an emblem of reconciled opposites, but expresses his adult solicitude for his own child-self: the grown-up Jarrell knows just how provisional is any reconcilation with the past. He decently keeps to himself his own adult doubts in the interest of the child's momentary happiness.

In imagining what Jarrell will mean to the future, I think back to my own experience in that Baltimore bookstore. He seemed nearer to me than either Bishop or Lowell, whose technique and presence in their poems seemed unapproachably accomplished. Jarrell was baggier, his prosody a little haphazard, his childhood, just as mine was, still close about him. Pop the welder and my own father, who first worked for the railroad, then ran a drive-in theater, were far more likely to have met than my father and Commander Lowell; or my grandparents and Bishop's grandparents, who seemed otherworldly rustic, almost fairy-tale people. But it wasn't only class that made me at home in Jarrell's work. His Great Books sensibility was inviting to a novice because of its idealism: Jarrell believed in greatness and made one aware of the gravity of calling oneself a poet.

Each generation finds a mirror in another. The kind of poem that Jarrell, that Bishop and Lowell wrote, seemed to me then an untapped resource. The generation of Beats and Deep Image poets, some of them taught by Lowell and Berryman, broke from their teachers with radical finality, their poetry, when I was a student, "the new" I wrestled with—but only halfheartedly. It was Jarrell, Lowell, and Bishop who really sustained my interest, who kept alive for my generation a New Critical bias in reading and writing. But of course my choices were sloppier than I've made them out; galaxies of poets spun in my head without my being quite certain of the how and why. Jarrell stood apart—no poet so accomplished seemed at the same time so helpless or so accepting of his own helplessness. His belief in poetry as the work of a daemon fueled my raw belief in my own inner voices. Young poets will always favor Jarrell for his generous and painful conviction that the imagination is continually in a state of becoming, that nothing in poetry or in life is ever finished or perfectible.

To Go Nowhere: Derek Walcott

~

Derek Walcott is a poet of many ambitions. He's written the big long poem, such as *Omeros,* in which he tries to make slavery, imperialism, and the daily life of the West Indies among fishermen and barmaids align like magnetic filings to the force field of Homer. He's written dramatic monologues in which his face keeps showing through the mask. The speaker of "The Schooner Flight" in *The Star Apple Kingdom,* one of his best poems, and best books, is Walcott's altogether more robust and sexy version of Prufrock. He's also written sequences of lyric meditations, as in *Midsummer,* a book that tracks the flux of consciousness through the dark wood of middle age. His book, *The Bounty,* takes a cue from *Midsummer:* these poems are also lyric meditations and weave a loose net to trap the sights and sounds and smells of daily life in the West Indies. But the book isn't satisfied with sensory repletion. Perhaps because Walcott is in his sixties, he seems hungry for some form of visionary experience that will counterbalance the stark fact of death. What better and more problematic place to look than the Garden of Eden?

The bounty of Eden's tropical landscape isn't the only set of associations the book's title conjures. H.M.S. Bounty, the famed ship of Captain Bligh, automatically calls up the rebellious energies of its crew. And then there is the unbounteous Captain Bligh himself, whom Walcott portrays as "the God-captain [. . .] cast adrift/by a mutinous Christian." So Fletcher Christian, the name of the officer who raised the ship against Bligh, makes a cameo appearance in this volume as fallen Adam. And H.M.S. Bounty's mission, to bring the manna of breadfruit back from the South Seas to England's colonial holdings in the West Indies, indicates the historical worm in the paradisal apple. Walcott's bred-in-the-bone knowledge of the Caribbean's colonial past has made him deeply skeptical of the myth of Eden.

But in his poetry Walcott still yearns toward a place of timeless natural beauty and spiritual communion. For the satisfaction of such desires, the poet looks to literary convention. An elysium in the western seas that resembles the Caribbean's tropical bounty has been part of European literary tradition at least since the fabled island of Antilia (from which we derive Antilles) began to show up on Renaissance charts and maps. The oldest suggested etymology (1455) fancifully connects Antilia with the Platonic Atlantis, another visionary utopia located on an island. Of course, this Caribbean version of Eden is from the perspective of its Dutch, French, Spanish, Portugese, and English colonizers. Walcott has inherited this myth through them, and through the main line of Western literary tradition (Homer, Dante, Shakespeare) that he's transformed with such virtuosity to suit his own local historical conditions. But despite his affection for this tradition, he still looks askance at the myth enshrined by many of that tradition's finest writers. For Walcott, the bounty of Eden is shadowed by the face of "the white God [. . .] Captain Bligh."

But to have said this is to imply, a little too portentously, that Walcott's relationship to this myth is more or less tortured. In fact, the myth holds great appeal for the poet, especially now that his antennae are attuned to "presences" and "seraphic radiance" that make "(don't interrupt!), mortals rub their skeptical eyes." In this line, part of the book's title poem, the poet's half-humorous interjection disarms the skeptic reader's resistance to such otherworldly phenomena. Walcott knows that these seraphs and presences are also literary projections. But having obliquely signalled his own doubts about visionary experience, Walcott has written a book shot through with otherwordly glimmerings.

One of the ways Walcott makes these visionary perceptions of Eden palatable in *The Bounty* is through his faith in metaphor. From this vantage, Baudelaire and Rimbaud figure in this volume as minor tutelary spirits. Both French poets added to the tradition of Eden as a paradisal elsewhere. Rimbaud looked toward French holdings in Africa, Baudelaire looked west to Martinique. But for both poets, the tropics become an idealized place of mind. The soul went untainted by daily realities, the pursuit of sensual pleasure and transcendence were one: humankind was freed from corrupting social forms. In their versions of tropical paradise, the Word was still pure; its power to create metaphor embodied the divine—the gods weren't mere figures of speech.

To put it another way, one could say that Rimbaud and Baudelaire, as well as Walcott, tend to use metaphor with almost sacral conviction. Compare this attitude with many contemporary poets' stance toward metaphor as only another device for testing the capablities of language itself. The desire to make a home truth show clear through the use of metaphor has given way to a fascination with the processes of association. The valences of metaphor flatten out into poetic *jeux de mots* that are often highly entertaining, novel, and amiably irreverent toward "the big statement." But for Rimbaud, metaphor promised no less than an alchemical transformation of the world. For Baudelaire, it intimated access to a forest of symbols replete with mystical meanings.

Perhaps because he has such affection for Western literary tradition, Walcott has resisted the notion that poetry is a strictly verbal universe. For all their rhetorical muscle, the poems in *The Bounty* don't give in to the temptation to allow the currents of language to follow their own autonomous drift. They constantly struggle to embody the myriad shining surfaces of the world—and, for that matter, of intimations of worlds beyond the world. In these lines from section four of the title poem, metaphor isn't simply another technical device for exploring the range and possibilities of language:

> "Across white feathery grave-grass the shadow of the soul
> passes, the canvas cracks open on the cross-trees of the
>   *Bounty,*
> and the Trades lift the shrouds of the resurrected sail.
>
> All move in their passage to the same mother-country,
> the dirt-clawing weasel, the blank owl or sunning seal."

Here, the voyage of the *Bounty* parallels the soul's passage from this life to the mother-country of death. (This quotation comes from a revised version of an original set of galleys. In the original version, there was no period after "[. . .] resurrected sail." The lines once read: "[. . .] the resurrected sail//and all move in their passage. [. . .]" The addition of the period in this later version seems to me to have interrupted the once powerful sweep of the compound sentence across the stanza break. In the earlier version, the motion of this sentence beautifully enacted the movement of the boat as it gained momentum.) The metaphor of the soul's shadow swelling into the great wind that refreshes the ship of death's sails has become a springboard for visionary experience—it isn't simply a technical device, or a more or less virtuosic example of stylistic sleight of hand.

Walcott is like Rimbaud in that he believes in language as a magical rite, and not merely as a manipulable code. And he shares Baudelaire's craving for, but deep skepticism of, spiritual transcendence and its worldy forms. But Walcott was born in twentieth-century St. Lucia, not nineteenth-century Paris. Rimbaud and Baudelaire's poetic notions of tropical paradises must now compete with the Tourist Board's package-deal weekends. What for the Frenchmen was an otherworldly escape from bourgeois Paris is home-ground for Walcott—home in all its complexity, the dearness and dirt of day-to-day life. Part of that life, as I mentioned earlier, is the colonial legacy, for good and ill, of Europe.

In "Manet in Martinique," Walcott describes the interior of a house furnished like a nineteenth-century salon:

> I felt an immeasurable sadness for the ship's sails,
> for the stagnant silence of objects, the mute past they carry,
> for the glimpse of Fort-de-France harbour through latttices,
> *"Notre âme est un trois-mâts cherchant son Icarie"*—
> Baudelaire on the wandering soul. This was in the false
>   métropole
> of Martinique. A fan stirred one of Maupassant's tales.
> Where was the spirit of the house? Some cliché with kohl-
> lined eyes, lips like Manet's bougainvillea petals.
> I sensed the salon, windows closed, was trying to recall
> all it could of Paris; . . .

In the first line, the speaker's sadness results from a simultaneous rootlessness and desire for home. This "false métropole" engenders in the poet the feeling of exile in his own homeland. The mute past of objects that evoke Paris corresponds to Walcott's sense of identification with Baudelaire's line about the wandering soul searching out Icaria. But Icaria, an ideal republic in a fable by the nineteenth-century French Communist, Etienne Cabet, feels a little dusty in this deserted salon. The soul's visionary quest for Eden has boiled down to a hunt for a bloodless political abstraction. Walcott's empathy with the cultural markers of this scene is tempered by his suspicion that the spirit of the house is a cliché. Yet he doesn't disdain that spirit. In a moment of fellow feeling, he pities it for its own sense of exile.

In poem *"1"* in the second section of *The Bounty,* he shows with mordant wit that he, too, is capable of being seduced by cliché. In the vague manner of a casual tourist, he describes his visit to a coastal town in France: "[. . .] it is near Dinard,/a town with hyphens,

I believe in Normandy/or Brittany, and the tide went far out and the barred/sand was immense. I was inhabiting a postcard." To a local, Normandy isn't Brittany, and daily life isn't tinted like a postcard: but if Baudelaire and Rimbaud imagine the Caribbean as Eden, why shouldn't Walcott be prone to similar idealizations? Of course the difference between the Frenchmen and the St. Lucian is that he is highly conscious of his own tendency toward idealization. Walcott lives in a world of postcolonial consequence. His self-irony possesses the perspective of historical hindsight.

The second half of the poem intensifies this irony by describing the poet's musings on a watercolor he painted of this same beach. As the poet meditates on how the reputed timelessness of art estranges us from the processes of life and inevitable decay, the poem develops into an ironic lamentation on Walcott's sense of his own mortality:

> Why write this now? I did a good watercolour
> and it stands there on the wall. . . .
> . . . .
> Now, so many deaths, nothing short of a massacre
> for the wild scythe blindly flailing flowers and grass,
> and the stone seaside city of graves expends its acre
> and the only art left is the preparation of grace.
> So, for my *Hic Jacet,* my own epitaph, "Here lies"—
> write, "This place is good to die in." It really was.

The final line affirms that home, rather than the abstract world of the watercolor, is the place of choice to die in. (This is another instance in which Walcott revised the original galleys. The final line of the above quotation used to read: "say, this place is good to die in. It really is." For me, the lofty formality of the rewritten line tends to flatten out the original line's attractive combination of self-irony, intimacy, and grief into a somewhat more conventional tone of elegy.) The elliptical *double entendre,* "It really was," ironically suggests that home, because it really was there for us to touch and smell, is the *only* place where living and dying or "the preparation of grace" can physically occur. (Again, the change from "is" to "was" vitiates this irony.) Of course to achieve grace we must give up the world our senses bring us—so much for the consolations of a painted Paradise and the imagination's powers in the face of mortality.

But despite Walcott's skeptical relation to the notion that art can redeem us, his visionary impulses aren't invalidated by his knowledge that "Between the vision of the Tourist Board and the true/Paradise lies the desert where Isaiah's elations/force a rose from the sand." As a figure for Walcott's own visionary yearning, his choice of Isaiah—the eloquent, saturnine poet/prophet—melds the poet's skepticsim of, and enthusiasm for, the transcendent potential of art. The desert of humdrum existence is counterbalanced by the rose of poetic reality that springs from the quotidian sand.

This transformation is dynamic, rapture devolving into skepticism. In the title poem of the volume, a superb elegy for the poet's mother in which she becomes a muse of history, and of Walcott's private anguish about his ambivalent relation to home and memory, he castigates his own rhetorical gift: "[. . .] pardon me,/ [. . .] / as I watch these lines grow and the art of poetry harden me//into sorrow as measured as this, to draw the veiled figure/of Mamma entering the standard elegiac." Art estranges even as it memorializes. The mental suffering that pervades this book "[. . .] Because memory is less/than the place which it cherishes," and because of a "[. . .] life of incredible errors," is kept in perspective by Walcott's determination to avoid the "standard elegiac" of self-pitying autobiography. His elegy for his mother is as much an elegy for the intellectual legacy of colonialism that helped form, and deform, his motherland, as it is an expression of personal grief.

Walcott is equally wary of self-pitying sentimentality when he looks beyond the borders of St. Lucia. In poem "*10*" in the second section, he admits that his susceptibility to a dark view of history may simply be another version of the "standard elegiac." The poet may be so gloomy not principally because of genocide or imperialist oppression or what have you, but because he's spooked by his own shadow. In other words, historical suffering becomes an objective correlative for private pain:

> A dark fear of my lengthened shadow, to that I admit,
> for this crab to write "Europe" is to see that crouching child
> by a dirty canal in Rimbaud, chimneys, and butterflies, old
>   bridges
> and the dark smudges of resignation around the coal eyes
> of children who all look like Kafka. Treblinka and Auschwitz
> passing downriver with the smoke of industrial barges

The metamorphosis of Rimbaud's streetwise kid into the children of the holocaust presaged by Kafka reveals the end of the line of Rimbaud's hope to transform Europe into a sensual paradise. And yet the fact that Walcott feels obliged to put Europe in quotes shows just how skeptical he is of history's abstractions—not to say art's abstractions, which reduce individual children to Kafkaesque types. On the other hand, the progression from dirty canals to Treblinka and Auschwitz is interrupted by the apposition of chimneys and butterflies. The ashes that will pour from the crematorium smokestacks are the imagistic reverse of the butterflies. For all Walcott's keen awareness of history as butchery, and of his suspicion that a dark view of things is only the result of a psychic toothache, his skeptic's eye still sees the natural world as an emblem of renewal.

His faith in nature often grants the poet moments of genuine consolation, even transcendence. However, the absolute demands that Rimbaud made on art to transform reality (at least before his disillusionment with poetry and his participation in the most brutal activities of French colonialism—running guns and trading slaves in Abyssinia) give way in Walcott's poetry to a more canny—and humane—*via media*. In "37," the volume's final poem, the poet recognizes that "[. . .] the right light, this pewter shine on the water," isn't dependent on "the carnage of clouds" or on "self-igniting truth and oracular rains," but on "[. . .] these shallows as gentle as the voice of your daughter,/while the gods fade like thunder in the rattling mountains." By renouncing "the carnage of clouds" for the more contemplative "pewter shine on the water," Walcott is opting for the peace that passeth understanding over Moses and the burning bush.

But how much of a real comedown is his renunciation? There is, after all, something less than awe-inspiring in the rattle of those mountains. They almost seem like a flimsy stage set above which the special-effects people are doing their best to make the gods seem imposing. Of course, I'm overstating a little—Walcott does identify the gods with the primal thunder. But in using an adjective like "rattling," the poet seems to hint that there are other forms of transcendence than being struck by lightning. The thirst of a Rimbaud for sublimity in realms beyond what "really is" is transformed in Walcott's poetry to a desire to connect with such a basic human emotion as finding pleasure in your daughter's voice.

I ought to say that "37," for all its celebration of the ties of earthly, filial love, is an unabashedly lofty self-exhortation. The poet adopts the persona of Oedipus on his way to his apotheosis at Colonus—Walcott hasn't renounced sublimity altogether. But for Walcott, the violent aspects of visionary transport are too close to the irrational destructive energies, both human and divine, that have caused Oedipus to murder his father, marry his mother, and to be cast out by his own people. Walcott knows that the hapless Oedipus has paid a terrifying price for his visionary confrontation with the gods. This explains why, earlier in the poem, Walcott exhorts his alter ego, "learn, wanderer, to go nowhere like the stones [. . .]"; and several lines later to "Sit on your plinth in the last light of Colonus,/let your knuckled toes root deep in their own soil."

Yet the prospect of the visionary exile at last come to rest in his own homeland remains provisional. To go nowhere like the stones is to admit that Rimbaud was right about poetry's ability to lead us from this world into a paradisal state of being. There is nowhere on *terra firma* where you will find Eden, or the taciturn white city of the dead (mentioned later in the poem), except in the mind's realm of vision. And even if Oedipus's tortured spirit succeeds in taking root, even if he discovers peace and fulfillment in the gentle shallows of his daughter's kindness, this moment of grace is set in relief against intolerable, former suffering:

> go where the repetition of the breakers grows easier
> to bear, no father to kill, no citizens to convince,
> and no longer force your memory to understand
> whether the dead elect their own government
> under the jurisdiction of the sea-almonds;
> certain provisions of conduct seal them to a silence
> none dare break, and one noun made them transparent,
> where they live beyond the conjugations of tense
> in their own white city. How easily they disown us,
> and everything else here that undermines our toil.

The city of the dead is its own self-enclosed community sworn to a silence none dare break, no matter the visionary designs that poetry may have on them, even if those designs include a final reckoning with Oedipus's own tormented memories. And yet the poet retains his faith in language: it is, after all, a noun that renders the dead transparent. Despite their oath of silence, despite the ease with which they disown the suffering that the living must undergo, the dead are still projections of "the conjugations of tense," and of the love, guilt, and sorrow of their survivors.

In Rough Waters: Seamus Heaney's *Government of the Tongue*

~

"The trouble with criticism," as Robert Lowell once remarked, "is that it makes points." Fueled by Seamus Heaney's rich and strange inner life, *The Goverment of the Tongue* transcends this judgment. These essays, composed with a seemingly casual vigor over the course of almost ten years, mesh and wheel with the authority of obsession. They make an informal *ars poetica,* one designed to propel the poet into a more broadly imagined artistic future. But most important of all, writing of this caliber signals an effort at self-transformation, a longing for the authority and self-sufficiency of what Yeats called the finished man among his enemies.

Heaney's concern to square art with life makes the book a welcome throwback to the essayists of the eighteenth and nineteenth centuries. Like Hazlitt or Lamb, Heaney places insightful personal reminiscence alongside literary analysis. The effect is a kind of darting, rolled-sleeve alertness that lets you feel the force of Heaney's emotional and intellectual life. In comparison, most contemporary "methodologies" and "theorizings" have their veins bulging in their foreheads. By straining so hard, they tend to miss why people actually read poetry, much less write it. But Heaney's essays on Patrick Kavanagh, Robert Lowell, and Sylvia Plath are as good as his own best poems.

The demon behind this book also drives Heaney's poetry: in the "hair-raising bigotries" and "repetitive intolerance" of Northern

Ireland's public life, Heaney has "no mettle for the angry role." And this *via negativa* feels slack-shouldered to the poet, especially when the "lucent syrops" of literary tradition can sweeten the facts of violent random death. Given Yeats's sad conclusion, via Patrick Pearse, "that in every generation/ must Ireland's blood be shed," it's small wonder if Heaney sometimes feels at odds with the tolerances and subtleties of art. And yet this lack of mettle isn't a shrug of despair or indifference, or a nervous twitch from his Catholic upbringing. In "Station Island," Heaney's most complex response to both the public and private dimensions of Ulster's troubles, the poet contrives edgy, purgatorial meetings with the dead spirits of fosterers and alter-selves. One of them—the unappeased spirit of his murdered cousin—blames Heaney, almost as much as the sectarian death-dealers, for the current state of affairs in Northern Ireland. Of course, Heaney makes the spirit speak—but his cousin's accusation, that Heaney "confused evasion and artistic tact," is pitched in such a skillfully dramatic way that the charge seems almost autonomous, welling up from deep in Heaney's historical consciousness.

His is not the only sleep troubled by such moral tossing and turning. His removal to the south of Ireland, which in some minds constituted a spiritual betrayal of his Ulster roots, gave rise not only to his "friends/Beautiful prismatic counselling," but to "the anvil brains of some who hate me." Such fiercly polarized response indicates that Heaney's "responsible *tristia*" (the moral unease sparked by perpetual political crisis) is in part tribal, a whisper in the ear of friend and enemy alike. This lends his cousin's indictment the eerie force of personal and cultural revelation. There is nothing slyly self-exculpating in Heaney's ventriloquism, nothing of the breastbeating self-regard of the penitent who takes a too-conscious pleasure in confession.

But the dynamics of violence force roles on people. In this sense, the fact that Heaney has "no mettle for the angry role" suggests more a lack of talent or temperament for gunplay and slogans than an outright refusal to embrace such a role. To inhabit such ethically uncertain ground is precisely Heaney's artistic mission. And while he declines to be the bard of Unionism or the IRA, he's acutely aware of the role's attractions and of the pressures that create it. Department-store sabotage, the half-joking conjunction of mass killings and soccer scores—given such a macabre moral landscape, how tempting to adopt the settled vantage of sectarian politics, especially when they promise release from Heaney's own self-recrimination. And yet the collision between Heaney's humane good nature and the violent provocations of Ireland's political and literary life sets off the ethical reverberations and discriminations that make him such a credible poet. The "mettle" of Heaney's politics is not to let himself be co-opted by extremists on any side.

Unfortunately, Heaney's almost reckless courage in taking such a stance is largely lost on American readers. This isn't simply because Ireland's history is politically complex. Rather, we seem to feel most at home with Heaney's depictions of the rural otherworld of the small family farm. Perhaps we superimpose on Heaney's poems a sentimentalized version of our own troubled, horse-and-plow past because we need to see in Heaney a writer who hasn't broken his compact with nature. But what gives ballast to his Millet-like evocations is his exacting moral intelligence, as accustomed to haws and rosehips as to halters and strappados.

This moral intelligence is at its most polemical in his essay about the impact of Eastern European poetry on writers in the West. Heaney castigates the United States and England for failing to respond in ample enough artistic terms to the barbwire history of Eastern Europe. For Heaney, these "tragically tested lives" are a more reliable spiritual gauge of the post-Auschwitz world than "our own recent history of consumerist freedom and eerie nuclear security . . ." In the work of Zbigniew Herbert and other Eastern bloc poets, Heaney hears a note at once "elegiac for and posthumous to the European civilization which produced it," a note which "we who . . . have our being in English" have neglected.

But Heaney's "we" seems more a grammatical and social courtesy than a confession. For one thing, his historical consciousness, bred in explosive Ulster, is on a par with his sensibility to the East:

> Mandelstam and other poets from Eastern bloc countries are often invoked . . . [O]ne of the challenges they face is to survive amphibiously, in the realm of "the times" and the realm of their moral and artistic self-respect, a challenge immediately recognizable to anyone who has lived with the awful and demeaning facts of Northern Ireland's history over the last couple of decades.

Bombings and rosary beads, woodkerns and army barracks, sectarian funeral trains and the slippery course of married love—in his poems these seesaw back and forth, threatening and confirming, Thanatos got up as an Orangeman, Eros bent over, searching for a plunge-line nightdress. The concerns of Heaney's own poetry gainsay his brilliantly realized argument that the historical nerve of English is broken and the Grail of poetry has moved East. Cross-cultural influences work both ways. Isn't it just as likely that a Polish poet, musing over the moral heft of Heaney's English, might feel chastised and quickened? Why, this poet could wonder, does Polish poetry seem so straitened, so pale, so unable to address field, flag, and family in tones like these?

Heaney's concern that life in the West has undermined English as a poetic medium also surfaces in his zeal to square the life lived with the poem written. He naturally gravitates toward poets like Mandelstam and Herbert because they seem models of right poetic and worldly conduct. But this predilection limits the range of Heaney's investigations. What is the relation, say, between Celine's fascism or Yeats's advocacy of eugenics and the psychic drives that set the artistic engine running? I also think of *Beta* in Czeslaw Milosz's *The Captive Mind:* sobering, exhilarating, finally terrifying, Milosz's essay analyzes how *Beta's* psychic mechanisms, knocked out of synch by historical circumstances, never again regained their delicate timing. However, when Heaney does examine lives that, once driven on the rocks, finally broke apart, he can be brilliant. His corrective view of Sylvia Plath's poetic development is extraordinarily insightful:

> The "being" of this poetry . . . is constantly being pressed with meanings that sprang upon it the moment Sylvia Plath died by her own hand. Even an image like the dead crab, strayed headstrongly beyond his fellows, is retrospectively canvassed to serve the plot of suicide's progress. I would prefer to read the crab image as I believe the poem wants us to read it: as a relic that saved face, a talisman which helped the protagonist to face the bald-faced sun, an earnest of art's positively salubrious resistance to the shambling pull of the death wish.

While Heaney prefers to see in Plath's poems the manifestation of a strong life-surge, he is perfectly aware of her darker instincts.

Heaney is not only concerned that literature keep faith with reality, specifically that of "occupation, holocaust, concentration camps, and the whole apparatus of totalitarianism": he is equally concerned that the artist, tested by reality, keep faith with his own vocation. In Heaney's view, Wilfred Owen and Yeats represent opposing poles, or paths, of poetic conduct. Owen, an officer in World War I, performed what most Englishmen thought of as their unquestionable patriotic duty in order to question whether it was duty at all. A natural conscientious objector, he deplored leading his men to death, but contravened the claims of personal conscience in order to awaken a more general conscience. Owen "earned the right to his lines by going up the line," thus paying for his tenancy in the palace of art by ransoming his life to historical circumstance. Yeats, on the other hand, held such faith in art's authority to confer meaning that he overbore history, making history his subject: if he had to suffer, it was better to create the world in which he suffered.

The artist's relation to the fulcrum of history is only one aspect of earning the right to poetic speech. This is as much a matter of language as a balancing act between conscience and imagination. Not surprisingly, in his essay on Auden, Heaney regrets Auden's "final complaisant incorporation" into a social and literary establishment that the youthful Auden spurned. Early Auden is an affront to the expectation that language massage, rather than ruffle, our sense of everyday experience. Of course Heaney reads in early Auden foreknowledge of the shocks of World War II and the checkpoints and machine-gun posts of the postwar period. But deeper than this is his regret that the language of later Auden no longer chafes and hassles but settles down almost exclusively to the work of making us feel at home. Heaney points out that this is understandable when you consider that one impulse of poetry is legitimately directed toward the "rational project of settling mankind into a cosmic security." But in relation to his own poetic course and poetry's potential both to keep faith with its own expressive concerns and to bear witness to postwar reality, Heaney would prefer the right to impudence, to raise hackles, if by doing so poetry could "keep on coming into a fuller life."

It shouldn't be surprising that a sensibility like Heaney's, formed in the polarized mlieu of Paisley and the Pope, Pearse and the "eructation of Orange drums," should associate access to this "fuller life" with moral and experiential extremes. In light of this, Heaney's disinclination for the angry role seems paradoxical, until one considers that the radicalism of Heaney's stance is to advocate humanist truths over political ones. However, the conflict between the two makes it necessary for Heaney constantly to reevaluate the terrain of his own moral commitments. No wonder Heaney admires Mandelstam's certainty that humanism's claims transcended those of Soviet hegemony. But Northern Ireland is not a totalitarian regime: its political and moral aspirations are far more murky. This makes a final reckoning (which, in any case, may only be a trick of historical hindsight) impossible. In "The Disappearing Island," Heaney expresses how this uncertainty, alleviated only by extreme measures, can become a prerequisite for "vision":

> Once we had gathered driftwood, made a hearth
> And hung our cauldron like a firmament,
> The island broke beneath us like a wave.
>
> The land sustaining us seemed to hold firm
> Only when we embraced it *in extremis.*
> All I believe that happened there was vision.

In the offhand doubleness, at once dismissive and affirming, of the final line, Heaney refuses to privilege the imagination's work of vision over that of establishing a domestic norm. Nevertheless, that Heaney is drawn to Wilfred Owen, Robert Lowell, and Sylvia Plath shows how strongly he identifies with sensibilities pushed to the wall. This reveals the darker, inherently less social side of the desire (which he expresses in his fine essay on Patrick Kavanagh) to write a poetry which is "not a reactive response to some stimulus in the world out there" but "is a spurt of abundance from a source within" and which "spills over to irrigate the world beyond the self." While the process of spilling over legitimizes "the spurt of abundance" welling up in the self, nevertheless it is the self's primacy that Heaney emphasizes. He recognizes the self's responsibility to enliven the world out there, but is wary of harnessing his imaginative powers to conventional social and spiritual expectations.

Lowell's violence, Plath's overbearing intensity, Owen's almost suicidal courage—these may be signs of psychic morbidity, but they are also vital signs.

What Heaney is searching for is the kind of *via media* proposed by Zbigniew Herbert:

> You understand I had words in abundance to express my rebellion and protest. I might have written something of this sort: "O you cursed, damned people, so and sos, you kill innocent people, wait and a just punishment will fall on you." I didn't say this because I wanted to bestow a broader dimension on the specific, individual, experienced situation, or rather, to show its deeper, general human perspectives.

This "general human perspective"—what Yeats called the ability to hold reality and justice in a single thought—has always been one of Heaney's poetic gifts. What is new and what Heaney instinctively admires is the equitable, slyly humorous way in which Herbert ducks the angry role, without elaborate explanation or self-justification. Herbert's attainment of this inner freedom, in which he knows "what we have learned in modern times and must never forget even though we need hardly dwell upon it," is precisely the liberation that Heaney seeks.

The poetic terms of this freedom are complex. Ideally, Heaney would like lyric impulse to constitute radical witness:

> Mandelstam died because he could not suppress his urge to sing in his own way. It so happened that he had no anti-Communist sentiments to voice, but nevertheless, because he would not change his tune as the Kremlin required, he represented a threat to the power of the tyrant and had to go. He therefore stands for the efficacy of song itself."

While I agree with Heaney's ideal, as a reader unaccustomed to totalitarian pressure or sectarian threats, my sense of poetic witness has more to do with acknowledging darker drives in one's society and self than with the high-relief moral choices of confronting tyrannical power. If there had been no Stalin to press heroic meanings on Mandelstam's poems (in the same way Plath's suicide pressed meanings on hers), one might see in the isolation that the Voronezh notebooks relentlessly celebrate the psychic equivalent of a death wish. For a conscience as finely strung as Heaney's, this may be a matter of course and not a matter for comment. Still, the unpredictable nature of art's "chemical suddenness" may have as much to do with destructive psychic drives as constructive ones. Ultimately I'm convinced, along with Heaney, that Mandelstam's poems align themselves with the latter. But I also want to honor those artistic instincts like Plath's that chronicle the dirty work that goes on in the human psyche.

Another point of difficulty arises from the historical hindsight that colors Mandelstam's poems and life. Other poets—Akhmatova comes to mind—managed to survive Stalin, their integrity intact. I'm aware that in the chaos and paranoia of the 1930s purges, thousands upon thousands died who never put pen to paper. I'm not implying that Mandelstam might have saved himself by being more malleable or keeping a lower profile. Rather, in a situation where people perished regardless of their political loyalties, caught up almost at whim in the grinding wheels Stalin set in motion to consolidate his power, the randomness of Mandelstam's fate—as much as its singularity—needs to be borne in mind. To lose sight of this is to view Mandelstam from the promontory of a fulfilled poetic destiny, as a sort of martyr of the imagination nailed by history to the cross of his own poems. Heaney avoids this, careful in his use of Mandelstam's biography to keep his eye on what is "human" in the "general human perspective." Still, Heaney's use of Mandelstam as an emblem inadvertently abets this pull toward abstraction, so I want to underscore the provisional nature of Mandelstam's freedom. Even after he regained his poetic voice—he spent five years in silence, struggling to free himself from the Stalinist imperative to write poetry, "National in form, Socialist in content"—his life continued to be a muddle of fear, despair and hope. The most pointed example of this is his last letter:

> I got five years for counterrevolutionary activity by decree of the Special Tribunal. The transport left Butyrki Prison in Moscow on the 9th of September and we arrived on the 12th of October. I'm in very poor health, utterly exhausted, emaciated, and almost beyond recognition. I don't know if there's any sense in sending clothes, food, and money, but try just the same. I'm freezing without proper clothes.
>
> *—letter to his brother Alexander Emilievich, October 1938*

If we lose sight of the cost of Mandelstam's inner freedom, we are too easily reassured of his spiritual victory over oppression. Worse, we lose sight of Mandelstam the man, desperately concerned with clothes, food, and money. Who can know if Mandelstam, afraid to eat food given him by his jailers, didn't at times regret having failed to be more in tune with Stalin's new artistic criteria? I don't mean to devalue Mandelstam's struggle, only to suggest the difficulty of trying to rivet the flux of an isolated, outcast human soul.

Heaney's fortitude in aspiring to a life that will be the assured sponsor of poetry's authenticity, as well as his faithfulness to creation's "free biological play," are reassuringly reckless. Like Mandelstam, Heaney plays for high stakes: what other contemporary writer, stirring up such rough waters, could navigate so truthfully and spiritedly while at the same time giving so much pleasure? The vitality of Heaney's prose in itself grants passage over crosscurrents of moral and intellectual difficulty. If Heaney is right in thinking that a poetic future depends on "the gravity and purity of the mind's appetites and applications between moments of inspiration," then *The Government of the Tongue* is a nervy, formidable and welcome omen.

Postscript:

The omen was fulfilled, both in the eyes of the world and in the judgments of most poets throughout the world, when Heaney won the Nobel Prize in 1995. Since then, sectarian violence has died down in Ireland as the result of an uneasy but more or less stable peace; Russia has become a more or less oligarchic state; and the United States has suffered what could be called extremist sectarian violence in the form of the destruction of the World Trade Towers. When I wrote that as a reader I was unaccustomed to totalitarian pressure or sectarian threats, this was before 9/11, the current Bush administration's security policies, and the wars launched in Afghanistan and Iraq. The bellicose stance of current U.S. foreign policy toward the Muslim world almost guarantees further terrorist violence on American shores. We may well be entering a time when the note of posthumous elegy for European civilization that Heaney hears in Herbert and other former Eastern bloc poets will find an ironic counterpart in the headlines of terrorist actions still to be committed. In any case, it would seem that "our own recent history of consumerist freedom and eerie nuclear security . . ." came to a symbolic and literal end on 9/11. The current Bush administration seems to be the primary elegist for that freedom and security. The strange fact of living in a country that claims to be a superpower, yet is obsessed with internal security, that wants to promote democracy but does so by embracing a doctrine of pre-emptive war, makes the ironic stance that Heaney praises in Herbert's work a promising mode to deal with such contradiction.

On an even darker note, when torture in Abu Ghraib prison came to light, and when civil liberties are suspended for people who are suspected of terrorist activities, so that they basically disappear into our prison system, then the forces Heaney associated with totalitarian regimes seem well on their way to undermining how we in the West view our freedoms. Obviously, the United States has not descended to the level of the old Soviet Union and its prime symbol, the Lubyanka prison. But the slow creep toward totalitarianism is unmistakable. Given these circumstances, I think that Heaney's intuitions about "the gravity and purity of the mind's appetites and applications between moments of inspiration" are all the more prescient. How artists conduct themselves not only has grave consequences for their art, and for what Herbert called "the deeper, general human perspective." That conduct will also determine whether letters like Mandelstam's last one will continue to be written as matter-of-fact, inadvertent indictments of our time.

Visitations and Seductions: Thom Gunn

~

My last year of college, on a spring night in Baltimore, I heard Thom Gunn read to an edgy auditorium: most were enthralled, though some expressed skepticism about "the talking dog," Gunn's animal alter ego in his poem "Yoko." The intelligent sweetness and rigor of that poem—that anyone could so forthrightly speak from a dog's viewpoint about the world's richness of smells, excrement an opportunity for nose and brain to speculate on "[. . .] how what is rich and fierce when excreted/ becomes weathered and mild/ but always interesting"—offended several of my acquaintance with its unabashed sophistication: formal precision in diction was not how a dog ought to speak.

I confess that I, too, was bewildered by Gunn's poems—they displayed singular nerve, but also had the aplomb of traditional formal achievement: his motorcyclists were as much courtiers as motorcyclists, secular reincarnations of Fulke Greville, adepts of philosophical speculation and metaphysics: "My human will cannot submit/ To nature, though brought out of it." Yet in a poem like "The Goddess" Gunn understood the sexual desire of a soldier looking for a pick-up—although the soldier's hunger for "a woman, any woman/ her dress tight across her ass/ as bark in moonlight" was only another instance of Proserpina's springtime imperative to the earth to bud and bloom.

I had never heard poetry like this before: intellect conceded nothing to emotion, and because of that resistance, both seemed stronger. The nascent poets of my own generation were squeamish about the place of intellect in poetry. In part this was defensive, the beginner's anxiety about not knowing enough, of having nothing to lean on—not even talent, merely the promise of talent. But it was also a muzzy kind of aesthetic class warfare: intuiting our shortcomings but unable to stare them full in the face, most of my fellow poets viewed "The Tradition" with prickly animus, since it was clearly built on formal premises that demanded a virtuosity none of us possessed, or could imagine possessing. But Gunn's virtuosity was as much due to "The Tradition" as to his openness to "other" traditions sanctioned by poets we'd barely heard of or were just getting to know: early Williams, Pound, Bunting; Creeley, Duncan, the Ginsberg of "Howl," "Wales Visitation," "Kaddish"; Mina Loy as opposed to H. D.

It's a commonplace to call Gunn a hybrid, but not so easy to identify the oppositions that mark his poems: postwar London wariness/ late 1960s San Franciscan tolerance; rhymed verse/ intractable subject matter; free verse/ scrupulously cool autobiography; the realm of the senses and sexual adventure/ understatement and casual reserve. But there are other, more fundamental, paradoxes: Samuel Johnson cautioning Boswell that he needn't experience evil in order to know, and therefore shun it, is counsel that Gunn would agree with in theory. Yet Boswell surely has the last word in Gunn's romance with experience, which elevates the idea of risk to a central moral quandary: In "In Time of Plague" the poet considers whether or not to share a needle with two "fiercely attractive men," asking himself, "am I a fool,/ and they direct and right, properly/ testing themselves against risk,/ as a human must, and does,/ or are they the fools, their alert faces/ mere death's heads lighted glamorously?" Risk is also synonymous with Eros in "New York," in which the poet likens lovemaking to his partner's dangerous, but exhilarating, occupation as a high-rise construction worker; in "The Idea of Trust" it becomes the marker by which trust is measured, since it implies a willingness to chance betrayal.

And in "The Man with Night Sweats," risk and trust counterbalance one another: "I grew as I explored/ The body I could trust/ Even while I adored/ The risk that made robust."

But antinomies eventually frustrate—the greatness of Gunn's poems inheres in how his moral intelligence constantly dramatizes to itself the rests and holds of its discoveries: the processes of his mind in motion achieve a hallucinatory vividness so intensely personal that Gunn seems a far more intimate writer than poets more forthrightly autobiographical. A loose analogue is the effect of St. Augustine's *Confessions* that insists self-revelation discipline itself to transcendent forms. Gunn is clearly not a Christian so the forms he intuits and serves are more like what Eve discovers after she eats the apple in Milton's *Paradise Lost:* knowledge, then experience. And I would add to these, in addition to risk and trust, change, friendship (sexual and Platonic), limits of judgment and of personal identity.

When I survey my list of Gunn's abiding themes, I'm a little surprised to note that friendship has taken the place of love. And yet Gunn's sense of eros (especially in *Moly, Jack Straw's Castle, The Passages of Joy, The Man with Night Sweats,* and *Boss Cupid*), has little to do with exclusive possession of his partners, evincing more the qualities one expects from friendship: empathy with scrupulous limits; a wary delight in what your friend can and cannot give; a tolerance for other people's claims on your friend's attentions.

This detached attachment finds expression in a poem like "Sweet Things" in *The Passages of Joy.* Humorous, unburdened by possessiveness, the poem portrays its speaker's anticipation of a chance sexual encounter by celebrating his prospective partner: "How handsome he is in/ his lust and energy, in his/ fine display of impulse." These lines typify a bohemian ethic of pleasure that reflects how deeply and seriously Gunn took the cultural upheavals of the 1960s and which has become central to his work since he wrote this passage in "Touch": "[. . .] the place [. . .] seeps/ from our touch in/ continuous creation, dark/ enclosing cocoon round/

ourselves alone, dark/ wide realm where we/ walk with everyone." The possibility of orgiastic union is wonderfully unsettling in a writer whose poetic roots are in part so traditional. Heterosexual mores, and the tropes they often generate, are frequently so conditioned by monogamy that poems like "Sweet Things" or "Touch" come to seem like quiet, but radical, revisions of love poetry in English.

But it's a little dreary to frame Gunn's work in terms so abruptly abstract, a too calculating and narrow assessment: how to speak about poems that have gained such a central place in imagination that they often seem like the voices of one's own most private and valued reveries?

The Man with Night Sweats is so rooted in particulars that it seems almost patronizing to refer to it as a book about AIDS. The great elegies in the concluding section record individual lives and deaths, each sufferer achieving an irreducible identity. In these poems Gunn's style—spare, lucid, unfussily formal—is marvelously equipped to render details of lives; make character judgments; intuit the emotional complexity of personalities corroding under ferocious onslaughts of physical debility and change. But Gunn never intrudes on these lives by pushing himself into the foreground—he never appropriates his subjects' sufferings for stylistic bravura.

The poet's compassionate restraint in portraying the processes of dying and grief accounts for the coolness of tone characteristic of these elegies. Empathy, Gunn seems to imply, is severely bounded by the limits of personal identity and can take us only so far in understanding other people's emotions. And yet his choice to honor these limits and downplay his subjects gives the reader greater access to such highly charged material.

This paradox informs a poem like "Lament," in which Gunn so skillfully dramatizes the story of a friend's hospitalization and death that the intimacy we feel toward this young man almost equals the poet's own. Nevertheless, Gunn's formality in diction and technique (he uses run-on couplets) puts the reader on official notice that certain traditional standards of decorum will be maintained. Once the first few couplets have established this understanding between reader and writer, the balance between decorum and intimacy helps make the poem a place of communion—though only if we stretch ourselves through the discipline of contemplating the young man's hope, the final workings of his pain.

Perhaps it's time to repatriate the notion of love, friendship being too partial a term to express the magnitude of selflessness that Gunn's *Collected Poems* communicates to a reader. Yet how reticent Gunn is in casting his persona as a lover, his overt love poems developing such highly specified contexts that they resist the critic's interest in flashy generalization. Not surprisingly, "The Hug," "The Differences," "Philemon and Baucis," and "Odysseus to Hermes" (all from *The Man with Night Sweats*) mainly focus on the actions of others: the speaker becomes so absorbed in the significance of those actions that sometimes the poems seem on the verge of bypassing the speaker entirely.

And yet the speaker's self-abnegation has its rewards, though to perceive these depends on giving oneself over to experience as opposed to trying to master it. In "The Differences" Gunn remembers a time ". . . When casually distinct we shared the most/ And lay upon a bed of clarity/ In luminous half-sleep where the will was lost." The lovers "share the most" by maintaining their separate identities, not by merging; and yet their simultaneous separateness and communion aren't accomplished by acts of will, but by the grace conferred on them by clarity.

In keeping with this unwilled, unsettled selflessness is Gunn's notion of love as constant process, "invented in the continuous revelation." The content of that revelation is expressed in "Odysseus to Hermes" as the ability "to find again that knack/ of opening my settled features,/ creased on themselves,/ to the astonishing kiss and gift/ of the wily god to the wily man." To keep open to the spontaneous visitations and seductions of the cunning Hermes—

inventor of the lyre, god of crossroads, of thieves, luck, wealth, and fertility, conductor of souls to Hades—requires what Gunn's poems show him peculiarly fit for: the ability to give up the self to change in others, to change in oneself and in the world. In that sense, for all Gunn's reticence in putting himself forward as a lover, his devotedly impersonal attachments make him one of the great love poets in English.

Exit Interview with Myself as a Ghost (G)

~

I: Why didn't you tell me that you have a twin brother?

G: Do I? I don't remember having a twin brother.

I: Well, you do. His name is Tim. An identical twin brother, I might add.

G: Tim, how interesting, now that you remind me, I do remember.

I: That's the key to everything. All your views on the self are simply a function of your having a twin brother. That's why you're so interested in being more than one person at the same time.

G: No, I'm interested in being myself, only I don't have the capacity anymore, I lose track so easily.

I: Look, I have something I want to tell you.

G: Let me guess, your brain tumor is making you aphasic, and every word you say is really another word? In other words, when you say, *Look I have something I want to tell you*, what you're really saying is, *I don't know who I am please help me.*

I: No. Yes.

G: Precisely my point.

I: I'm so confused. And my brain tumor is making me more so.

G: Confusion, yes, I remember confusion, I sometimes get nostalgic for confusion.

I: What, you mean death doesn't allow you to be confused?

G: No, there's no confusion, or rather, the category of confusion means to me what madness means to the sane: "sane enough to be executed."

I: You mean it's a relative condition?

G: Yes, relative, though only from your point of view, here eveything moves too freely one thing into another for a concept like confusion to make sense.

I: I wish I had a twin. It's lonely to have a brain tumor and not have a twin.

G: Do you like "Knock Knock" jokes?

I: Not particularly.

G: Knock Knock.

I: Oh for God's sake.

G: Knock Knock.

I: Look, I'm really not interested.

G: Knock Knock.

I: All right, all right: Who's there?

G: Shakespeare.

I: Shakespeare who?

G: Shakespeare who wrote *Hamlet,* don't you know that the first line of *Hamlet* is "Who's there?"

I: Is that a rhetorical question?

G: Tell me about this twin you'd like to have.

I: I don't know what to say except he or she wouldn't say "Who's there?"; they'd know who was there.

G: I remember talking to my twin once, and having the weird sensation that someone had tapped into our phone line and was not only overhearing what we were saying, but was actually using us like ventriloquists' dummies to say through us what it wanted us to say to each other, and it wasn't an unpleasant experience, exactly: it had about it such domestic familiarity, as if who I was and who my twin was were fused in the mind of whoever was listening: our mother, I suppose, as if we were still in the womb, but the sensation passed, it was like in Bishop's poem, "In the Waiting Room," the sheer strangeness of being an "I" took hold again, and then faded out into the details of the day, but it made me so happy, it was like what Marianne Faithful said about heroin, she said it with such sadness in her voice, that it was a way to be happy, and that it worked, for a while.

TOM SLEIGH's books include *After One, Waking, The Chain, The Dreamhouse, Far Side of the Earth, Bula Matari/Smasher of Rocks,* and a translation of Euripides' *Herakles.* He has won the Shelley Prize from the Poetry Society of America, an Academy of Arts and Letters Award in Literature, an Individual Writer's Award from the Lila Wallace Fund, and grants from the Guggenheim Foundation and the National Endowment for the Arts. He teaches in the MFA Program at Hunter College and lives in Brooklyn.

Interview with a Ghost has been typeset in Minion Pro, a typeface designed by Robert Slimbach and issued by Adobe in 1989.

Book design by Wendy Holdman. Composition at Prism Publishing Center. Manufactured by Sheridan Books on acid-free paper.